SWIMMERS AMONG THE TREES

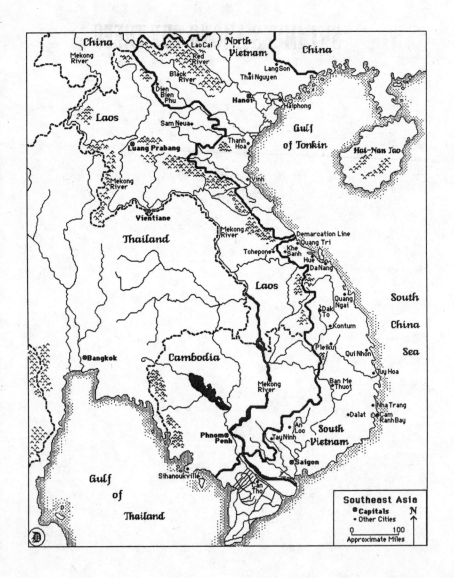

China

Mekong River

Lao Cai

North Vietnam

China

Red River

Black River

Lang Son

Thai Nguyen

Dien Bien Phu

Hanoi

Haiphong

Sam Neua

Laos

Thanh Hoa

Gulf of Tonkin

Luang Prabang

Hai-Nan Tao

Mekong River

Vinh

Vientiane

Mekong River

Demarcation Line

Thailand

Tchepone

Khe Sanh

Quang Tri

Hue

DaNang

Laos

Quang Ngai

Dak To

South

Kontum

China

Bangkok

Pleiku

Qui Nhon

Sea

Cambodia

Tuy Hoa

Ban Me Thuot

Mekong River

Nha Trang

An Loc

Dalat

Cam Ranh Bay

Phnom Penh

Tay Ninh

South Vietnam

Saigon

Sihanoukville

Gulf

of

Thailand

Can Tho

Southeast Asia
● Capitals
• Other Cities
N

0   100
Approximate Miles

SWIMMERS AMONG THE TREES

SEALs in the Vietnam War

JOEL M. HUTCHINS

★

PRESIDIO

Published by Presidio Press
505 B San Marin Drive, Suite 300
Novato, CA 94945-1340

ISBN 0-89141-439-8

All photos courtesy U.S. Navy except where noted.
Printed in the United States of America

CONTENTS

FOREWORD

During the course of the Vietnam War, United States Navy Special Warfare Groups—SEALs and Boat Support Units—were given an abundance of opportunities to exhibit their diversified skills. In keeping with the fact that these were naval units, a great deal of their activities concentrated on coastal and riverine operations, much of the latter being focused on the areas in and around the Mekong Delta. But as the war progressed, so did the scope of the Special Warfare Groups' operations. This was especially true of the utilization of SEAL detachments.

Initially, many SEAL activities dealt with the concentrated efforts of the National Liberation Front (NLF) forces, operating freely throughout the Mekong Delta as well as in the Rung Sat Special Zone (RSSZ) just south of Saigon. Both areas provided the NLF with perfect havens for their forces. Hundreds, or more accurately thousands, of Vietcong (the military arm of the NLF) were known to have been based in both areas. Their units were widely dispersed throughout those regions in well-fortified encampments, taking full advantage of the idiosyncracies of the topography to conceal their presence from most of the Allied forces' routine aerial and surface reconnaissance efforts. Where firm ground permitted, some encampments augmented their fortifications with bunkers and tunnel complexes.

The Vietcong (VC) concentrated mainly on controlling one or two neighboring small sections of terrain at a time. To accomplish this task, they would kidnap and assassinate residents of rural villages and perform other acts of terrorism, to keep the local populace under their control. After a time, they would gradually merge the small sections they controlled into slightly larger spheres of influence. They were relentless and extremely patient in their efforts, viewing the war as a very large, very dry forest, in which their units would act as hundreds of tiny, hot embers. Any one ember, of course, could be easily extinguished. But since there were so many embers in so many different locations simultaneously, the possibility of one or more of them erupting into a wide wall of flame was ever present.

From the standpoint of a head-to-head confrontation, the U.S. and other Allied forces should easily have held the upper hand in dealing with their communist adversaries. Allied troops far outnumbered the VC forces and had a tremendous edge in firepower, logistics, and the ability to deploy troops into widely separated areas of operation using fast, heavily armed helicopters. But the Allied troops had been trained primarily in a decidedly conventional approach to warfare. Unfortunately for these troops, much of the war was being fought in areas where extreme mobility and stealth were key. Most areas were covered by dense jungles, steamy, mucky swamps, or both. And nowhere in all of South Vietnam was such terrain in greater abundance than the Mekong Delta and the Rung Sat Special Zone.

For the average Vietcong, who went into the field carrying only his individual weapon, perhaps a hundred rounds of ammo, and enough water to last him a day, such terrain was difficult but not impossible. However, the technologically advanced U.S. grunt, often carrying as much as eighty pounds of gear, found such terrain a complete nightmare. The VC knew this was the case, having had prior experience against conventional forces during the French occupation of their country. That experience had proven to them that, when dealing with technologically superior adversaries, guerrilla tactics are the great equalizer.

By 1966, things had gotten so bad in both the Mekong Delta and the Rung Sat Special Zone that the South Vietnamese government was conceding large sections of some provinces to the VC rather than continuing to send their troops into situations in which they would surely be ambushed and their ranks decimated. It was imperative that someone go into those areas, find the VC units, and eliminate them. If the VC were allowed to consolidate their spheres of influence and increase their troop strength, they could soon pose a significant threat to the security of the rest of the Delta, the RSSZ, and eventually even to Saigon itself. Such a possibility was unacceptable.

The decision to deploy SEAL detachments into the Delta and the RSSZ was a logical one. They were profoundly skilled in covert reconnaissance and intelligence operations and in the art of guerrilla/counterguerrilla warfare. And although it took the detachments a few months to get comfortable with the surroundings and to become familiar with how the VC conducted their operations, they soon got the hang of things. Initially, SEAL ambush/recon teams located the enemy and then dispatched him. When possible, prisoners were taken, although capture was not then considered a primary objective. However, as SEAL operations intensified, the standard operating procedure regarding contact with the enemy was modified. Capture became the preferable approach because the opportunity to debrief a live prisoner greatly enhanced the possibility of increasing the existing intelligence database.

As SEAL operations became increasingly more successful, so did the overall scope of their activities. SEAL personnel soon were being tapped for duty with the Studies and Observations Group (also known as the Special Operations Group, or simply as the SOG), an arm of the Central Intelligence Agency (CIA). SOG operations were designed to gather intelligence relative not only to efforts of communist forces in South Vietnam but also to the burgeoning communist efforts in Cambodia, Laos, and Thailand. By late 1967, SOG operations had become almost the only role of a large contingent of SEALs in Vietnam.

As the war pressed on, SEAL successes against communist forces throughout Southeast Asia continued. The SEALs proved themselves to be a highly efficient response to the Vietcong's guerrilla tactics. In the following chapters we will examine the SEAL mission during the Vietnam war, with special attention to the years 1966 to 1969. By examining many examples of SEAL operations conducted during that time frame, it is hoped that the reader will gain some insight into how such operations were actually carried out. It is also hoped that such examples will provide some understanding as to how the SEALs, an organization that began in 1962, had by 1969 become the foremost counterinsurgency force in existence.

1 EARLY DAYS IN THE RUNG SAT

At a little past 6:00 A.M. on a dreary, rainy morning in early August 1966, an oil tanker glided slowly along the Nha Be River en route to Saigon. The area through which the channel coursed was known as the Rung Sat (a loose translation of the Vietnamese is "where the trees live in salt-water"), a somewhat dismal four-hundred-square mile expanse of mangrove swamps and mudflats. Approximately fourteen miles south of the port of Saigon the channel begins to take a series of lazy, snaky turns. The going was tricky along that particular stretch of water because the channel bottom, although sufficiently deep for large vessels to move safely along in midstream, was otherwise extremely shallow. If a ship ran aground in such areas, the channel would be completely blocked until the grounded vessel could be extricated. In the interim, no other river traffic could pass to or from Saigon.

As the tanker slowly eased its way through the first section of snaky turns, eight Vietcong were waiting for the vessel's approach just a few hundred yards ahead. The Vietcong made up a "sapper" team, whose purpose was to either sink the tanker in midchannel or force it to run aground along the channel's left or right shoreline. In order to achieve their purpose, the members of the sapper team had deployed a command detonated mine directly in the tanker's path. And to ensure their potential for success they also had brought along a 75mm recoilless rifle and a 60mm mortar. Whether or not the mine did its job, the recoilless rifle and the mortar would be used to inflict maximum damage on the grounded vessel, making it more difficult for other Allied vessels to tow the disabled tanker out of the channel.

When the tanker had moved to within two-hundred meters of the proposed ambush site, the sapper team's position suddenly came under intense automatic weapons fire. The heavy fusillade lasted less than ten seconds but resulted in five of the sappers being killed outright; the other three sappers sustained wounds of varying degree. Before the three wounded VC could understand what had happened, four men with decidedly western features, their faces streaked in splashes of green and black, pounced on them, securing them and their weapons even before the smoke and echoes of gunfire had cleared. Although the survivors had no way of knowing it at the time, they had just had the dubious distinction of being counted among SEAL Team One's earliest victims.

The first SEALs had arrived in Vietnam in 1962. They were deployed initially to Danang as members of Mobile Training Teams (MTTs). Each team consisted of seven to ten men whose primary mission was to act as advisers to South Vietnam's Coastal Warfare Force personnel. Both SEAL Team One and SEAL Team Two personnel staffed those early MTTs. They quickly went about training the Coastal Warfare Force seamen in advanced methods of land and sea navigational techniques, maritime interdiction operations, and the most advantageous use of small arms and heavy automatic weapons.

The first nonadvisory, fully combat-oriented SEAL detachment to arrive in country was SEAL Team One's Detachment GOLF, which consisted of one platoon. (SEAL platoons usually consisted of two or three officers and twelve enlisted men, as opposed to the more usual forty- to forty-five- man platoons found in conventional force units.) The detachment was immediately deployed to Nha Be, just southeast of Saigon in Gia Dinh Province, on the northwest periphery of the RSSZ. Detachment GOLF immediately set about developing intelligence regarding the RSSZ's resident VC units, their troop strength, and the location of bunkers, fortified encampments, food and weapons caches, et cetera. The development of such intelligence was of vital importance because the RSSZ was by far the largest area in South Vietnam where the VC were very nearly in control. Its close proximity to Saigon made it imperative that the area be neutralized as quickly and completely as possible.

Throughout most of the Vietnam War, Saigon found itself in a position very similar to that of ancient Rome. During the reign of Julius Caesar, when the Roman Empire comprised most of what was then the known world, it was said that "all roads lead to Rome." As the seat of government and economic power, Rome attracted those who wished to take advantage of that power as well as those who wished to usurp it. If one wanted to topple the Roman Empire, one would have to ultimately take Rome itself. That was true of Saigon as well at the height of the Vietnam conflict. Although local government in South Vietnam existed on the hamlet, village, and province levels, Saigon was the seat of the central government. It was also the hub of the nation's economy and the central nervous system of its military structure. Accordingly, Saigon was the obvious goal of the communist effort.

The strategic importance of Saigon was most dramatically evidenced in the III and IV Corps Tactical Zones (CTZ), both in close proximity to the capital. The economy of these two zones depended more heavily on Saigon than did the economies of the I and II CTZs. In any event, every road and river route in the III and IV CTZs lead ultimately to Saigon.

The fact that all rivers led to Saigon makes it easier to understand the primary reason that the Mekong Delta and Rung Sat Special Zone were of such immense strategic importance to both sides during the Vietnam conflict. In these regions there were many more rivers and navigable channels than there were usable surface roads, making waterways the easiest and most efficient routes for commercial, excursional, and military travel.

The economic structures within the Delta and the RSSZ included fishing, produce farming, timber harvesting (for lumber and charcoal production), silk processing, and rice farming. More than half of the Mekong Delta's silt-rich land area was and is dedicated to cultivation, especially rice production. The resultant crop has consistently been of such mammoth proportions that the Delta has often been referred to as the "rice basket" of Southeast Asia.

Although the purchase and sale of all these goods and foodstuffs occurred at the village and hamlet levels, most items were reserved for transport to the teeming markets of Saigon. There they would fetch the highest possible prices. It was also through the Saigon markets that such items would eventually raise the interest of international buyers.

The same was true of the goods coming from the rubber plantations northwest of Saigon, tea from the provinces to the north, and the carved seashells, lacquerware, and other craft goods from many other locations surrounding the capital. Not only was there a great market for all goods that could find their way to Saigon, but the capital city was also the main import and export center for all of the South. In effect, it was not only the doorway to the world but also the door through which the world's goods would enter South Vietnam.

The bulk of Saigon's import and export trade was almost totally dependent on maritime shipping. Although many items found their way into the city via Highway 1, Route 4, and a few other well-traveled surface arteries, the vast majority of trade goods arrived by boat or ship. It was the odd item, indeed, that did not arrive in the city on one of the many channels or canals branching off the vast Mekong River. And it was an even odder item that, when exported, did not leave the city by ship, sailing slowly down the Saigon River toward the South China Sea and then along one of the hundreds of shipping lanes en route to its destination in some faraway city in Europe, the United States, Africa, or other parts of Asia.

Basically, that was the way in which essential commerce has always been practiced in the Delta and the RSSZ. Such commercial trade practices were extremely lucrative, an abundantly sweet business. But as with delicacies, the sweet commercial endeavors drew flies. In the Delta and the RSSZ the flies came in the form of pirates, brigands, and antigovernment insurgents.

For many centuries, pirates had operated in the waters off the coast of Vietnam, as well as ranging far inland on the hundreds of rivers and canals that flowed to the sea. Even though Saigon came to be the capital of South Vietnam only during the regime of President Ngo Dinh Diem (1956–63), it has always been the country's economic hub. As a result, pirates and bandits of every stripe have been drawn to the waters in and around the mouths of the Saigon, Vam Co Dong, Vam Co Tay, and Mekong Rivers, waiting to pounce on any vulnerable merchant vessel or sampan passing through the area.

These same pirates also came to use the Rung Sat as their main base of operations due to its absolutely ideal terrain. Because the Saigon, Nha Be, Dong Nai, Long Tau, and lesser tributaries snaked tortuously through the entire region, pursuit of a pirate vessel seeking refuge there could be quite dangerous. Once the pirate vessel made it into the labyrinthine waterways, the pursuer faced the prospect of suddenly becoming the hunted instead of the hunter. If the pirate vessel could lure its pursuer into following closely behind, other pirates on shore would wait upstream at one of the narrow bends in the channel. Just as the hapless pursuer passed the narrow area, the pirates on shore would pull a log boom across the channel behind it. At that same moment the pirate ship would turn about to bear down on the now-trapped hunter.

What started as just a number of small pirates' camps liberally sprinkled throughout the four-hundred-plus square miles of the Forest of Assassins (as the RSSZ had come to be called) soon evolved into several rather large villages. And even though other endeavors slowly supplanted piracy as the region's main commercial enterprise, piracy has persisted, to the present time on a limited basis. In a way, piracy has remained a sort of cottage industry for certain inhabitants of the Rung Sat.

Many other outlaws shared the pirates' appreciation of the Rung Sat. Thieves, murderers, revolutionaries, even social outcasts went scurrying into the densely vegetated, boggy region, seeking sanctuary from the police, militia, or angry, freshly fleeced merchants. Pursuit was far too perilous to maintain for long, due to the treacherous terrain and the unlimited opportunities for ambush that it offered.

Peaceful peasants continued to make up the greatest portion of the region's population, however. The main commercial enterprises remained the cultivation and harvesting of rice, fruits, and vegetables, the harvesting of wood for charcoal production, and the taking of shrimp and fish from the area's streams and rivers. But despite the fact that such peaceful peasant villages far outnumbered the outlaw strongholds, there was never any doubt that the outlaws ran the show in the RSSZ.

During the French occupation of Vietnam, the Vietminh used the Rung Sat as a safe area and its main base of operations for launching attacks in the Saigon, Delta, and Camau Peninsula regions. French military units venturing into the area in search of insurgents quickly determined that such forays were foolhardy. Moving against the Vietminh in the RSSZ took too high a toll in material and personnel to warrant continuing such operations. So when the Vietminh forces retreated into the safety of the Rung Sat, the French forces would quickly break off pursuit.

During the early fifties, U.S. military advisers made their initial appearance in what was still French colonial Vietnam. Their primary role was to provide instruction in the proper utilization of U.S. weaponry, which had been sent in support of the French efforts to stem the communist threat in

Southeast Asia. By July 1954, the French had experienced their humiliat-
ing defeat at Dien Bien Phu; the Geneva Accords had been signed, divid-
ing the country into North and South Vietnam at the seventeenth parallel;
and the U.S. advisers were beginning to get a taste of the frustrations that
the French and others had experienced in trying to deal with the communist presence in the Rung Sat Special Zone. A greater appreciation of
those frustrations came in 1956, when the last French trooper left South
Vietnam.

And so, by 1962, when the first SEAL MTTs arrived in country as
advisers to the Coastal Warfare Force, the U.S. role in South Vietnam had
gradually evolved from a rather limited advisory capacity into one of far
greater scope. One of the primary roles of the Coastal Warfare Force was
to intercept or otherwise disrupt communist efforts at resupplying their
forces by sea. The vessels available to the Coastal Force for performing
this vital task consisted solely of junks. For that reason, the unit was more
commonly referred to as the Junk Force and the indigenous personnel
attached to it as Junk Force commandos. The commandos were definitely
among the most committed men in the South's armed forces, and many
stories abound regarding their famous sat cong (Vietnamese for "kill communists") tattoos. In fact, some commandos went so far as to add a tat-
tooed dotted line, running along the throat area from collarbone to
collarbone (as in "cut along the dotted line"), giving an added indication
that they had no fear of dying at the hands of the enemy.

The MTTs also devoted much of their time to training another group of
equally dedicated South Vietnamese defenders known as the Lien Doi
Nguoi Nhai (the name literally translates to mean "team of underwater
fighters"). Much time and effort was expended in the training of the
LDNN, or Vietnamese SEALs, as they were also known. Some of the
aspects of that training included guerrilla/counterguerrilla operations,
clandestine insertion/extraction techniques, operation and maintenance of
conventional and unconventional weaponry, advanced land and underwater demolition techniques, and utilization of scuba and rebreather gear.

Over the next several years, the overall role of U.S. forces in South
Vietnam went through some rather significant changes. What had begun
as a strictly advisory role gradually evolved, by 1965, into a full combat
posture. By December of that year, nearly 185,000 U.S. military personnel were in country, and the total number of American dead had exceeded
six hundred. By that time the "advisers" had fully evolved into bona fide

combatants, no longer restricted to only taking hostile forces under fire as the last means of self-defense. Now, the former advisers were not only able to accompany South Vietnamese forces into the field, they were also planning and executing their own operations and campaigns against the communist forces.

When the efforts of the VC began to intensify significantly in the Mekong Delta and the RSSZ, understandable fears for the ongoing integrity of Saigon's defenses heightened. Communist forces in the RSSZ had grown from a few hundred in 1964 to several thousand by 1966. These men definitely felt that they were in full control of the area. In fact, that confidence so emboldened them that they had not only taken to routinely mining the Saigon, Nha Be, Long Tau, and Dong Nai Rivers but had also begun to take merchant vessels under fire, using mortars, rocket launchers, and recoilless rifles. Vietcong tax collectors operated openly throughout the entire RSSZ, and indigenous villages were routinely used as rest areas and resupply stations.

Even during the time of the French occupation, communist forces in the South had been receiving the vast majority of their supplies from coastal infiltration operations. Freighters from communist countries, or countries sympathetic to the communist insurgents, would wait well away from the coastline to rendezvous with communist junks or speedboats. Supplies were transferred to those smaller vessels, which then headed straight for the rivers of the Mekong Delta, RSSZ, or any of the hundreds of other areas where rivers emptied into the South China Sea, all along the more than one thousand miles of South Vietnam's coastline.

In March 1965, a joint operation, (code-named Operation Market Time) involving the U.S. Navy, South Vietnamese Navy, and U.S. Coast Guard set about intercepting and shutting down the communist seaborne supply lines. This group was designated as Task Force 115, the Coastal Surveillance Force. It consisted of motorized junks, Inshore Fast Patrol Craft (PCFs, also known as Swift boats), Fast Patrol Boats (PTFs, of the Nasty and Osprey class), P-3 Orion and P-5 Marlin aircraft, and eighty-foot or larger cutters. Although originally under the command and control of the Seventh Fleet, in August 1965 Rear Adm. Norvell Ward was named Chief of Naval Advisory Group, Vietnam, and overall commander of Market Time operations.

Seaborne infiltration routes, which had long been the main communist supply pipeline, by December 1966 were reduced to a mere trickle, requiring the VC and the North Vietnamese Army (NVA) to rely more heavily on the ever-evolving Ho Chi Minh Trail and the Truong Son Corridor (communist supply trails within South Vietnam that paralleled the Ho Chi Minh Trail). The effectiveness of Operation Market Time had also been significantly enhanced by a second U.S. Navy project, begun in December 1965 under the code name Operation Game Warden. In April 1966 Rear Admiral Ward would also become Commander of Naval Forces, Vietnam, and take responsibility for both Market Time and Game Warden operations. Navy Task Force 116 was given responsibility for conducting the operation and quickly caused a tremendous drop in communist efforts to bring supplies and reinforcements into the Mekong Delta, RSSZ, and other riverine areas. So successful was this operation, in 1967 Task Force 117 was organized and given the specific task of interdicting VC and NVA supply efforts in the Mekong Delta and RSSZ areas of operation.

Because the coastal infiltration routes had been of such tremendous logistical importance to the communist forces operating in the Mekong Delta and RSSZ, it should come as no surprise that the VC were highly motivated toward protecting their shipments. For that reason, the stopping and boarding of suspicious vessels, at sea or along the region's many rivers and canals, frequently proved to be high-risk operations. In far too many cases, the crew of a communist junk would take a quickly closing, intercepting vessel under fire with recoilless rifles, rockets, or heavy automatic weapons. Or the suspect vessel might heave to and allow the intercepting vessel to come almost alongside before taking it under fire. And then there were the more fanatical VC crews who, having determined that escape was futile, would wait until being boarded before blowing themselves, their own vessel, and the intercepting craft out of the water.

Most of the vessels that were stopped proved to be innocent fishermen, who may have been a bit perturbed by the situation but wisely cooperated with the inconvenient intrusions. But even so, each situation was approached as cautiously as possible. Upon establishing radio contact with a suspect vessel, its crew was advised that any failure to comply with boarding instructions would result in the immediate sinking of their craft. If a vessel's crew was either slow in replying by radio or otherwise exhibited some reluctance toward being stopped and boarded, the vessel's bow and deck would be immediately raked with automatic weapons fire, or a round from a deck piece would be fired across its bow. The object was to make sure that the suspect vessel and its crew, whether friendly or not, would be completely aware that the intercepting craft was fully in charge of the situation. Although such tactics may sound harsh, they actually served to make boarding operations much safer for all involved.

Beginning in March and April 1966, Detachment GOLF sent a few surveillance teams, consisting of four to seven men each, into the heart of the RSSZ in support of Operation Jackstay. Jackstay was a joint amphibious operation that also involved elements of one of the 5th Marine Division's Regimental Landing Teams (RLTs), as well as a few landing craft from Task Force 116. While the bulk of the RLT moved against already known VC positions near Can Gio and Dong Hoa, the SEAL squads and several equally small teams of Marines from the RLT's Force Recon Company moved as quickly and quietly as possible into the very heart of the RSSZ, establishing surveillance points to monitor VC activity over a wide area.

During the course of Operation Jackstay, the SEAL and Force Recon units observed a lot of movement along the extensive network of rivers and streams throughout the RSSZ. They also uncovered many well-camouflaged VC fortifications, rice caches, sampans, sweet-water wells, bunkers, and a portion of a small tunnel complex. Within the first twenty-four hours of the operation, the SEALs and Marine recon squads recorded several confirmed VC KIAs (killed in action). More importantly, the intelligence developed by Detachment GOLF SEALs during Operation Jackstay greatly enhanced the effectiveness of the operations they would conduct in the RSSZ throughout the remainder of the SEAL presence in the Vietnam War.

Late in the evening of the first day of Operation Jackstay, a SEAL recon team set up an observation post near a small stream a few miles west of Can Gio in the southern RSSZ. The team did not have to wait long; within a half hour of getting into position, four Vietnamese came strolling down a path a few meters east of their position. The lead man was lighting the way with a carbide lamp, and its faint light was just enough for the SEALs to see that at least three of the men were carrying AK-47s. That bit of information made the team's job much easier, because they did not have to wonder whether or not the men were VC or just innocent local villagers. Peaceful civilians did not carry AK-47s.

The four men moved quickly toward the near bank of the stream, only a few meters from the observation post, and immediately busied themselves with removing a pile of palm fronds and other similar foliage from a well-hidden sampan. Then the men slipped into the small vessel, pushed away from the bank, and began to move rapidly downstream away from the SEAL position. Although the SEALs had wanted to take the four men prisoner, the fact that they were moving away so quickly left no other option but to take the vessel under immediate fire, which resulted in all four VC being killed outright. The SEALs quickly secured the sampan and searched it, hoping that it might contain supplies or perhaps some documents. Unfortunately, the sampan contained no such items, but the team did have four dead VC to their credit, along with three AK-47s, the sampan, a little less than a hundred rounds of ammunition, and a couple of crude handmade grenades. Not bad at all for less than an hour's work.

During those early days and weeks of Operation Jackstay, SEAL recon teams had a great deal of contact with the Rung Sat's indigenous personnel. In some cases a small group of VC might be moving along a narrow path or through some dense undergrowth when they were suddenly pounced on by several SEALs who seemed to literally explode from the foliage on all sides. Or a few local fishermen might be slowly poling their sampan along one of the narrow, shallow streams when anywhere from four to seven SEALs would seem to rise up from the mud along the stream bank. In the case of the VC, they would be taken prisoner, if possible, or quickly dispatched with automatic weapons fire. The civilians, on the other hand, would be stopped, searched, and interrogated. Once the SEALs were satisfied that the civilians were not VC, they would be sent on their way, perhaps a little shaken by their experience but glad that it was over.

Regardless of whether the individuals being detained were VC or merely simple, peaceful peasants, all of the inhabitants of the Rung Sat were thoroughly shaken by the SEALs and their actions. For one thing, South Vietnamese forces only rarely ventured into the RSSZ in search of local VC units. And when they went in, they didn't go far. But the SEALs were obviously westerners. Historically, westerners had made even fewer forays into the Rung Sat because whenever they did, they always seemed to flounder around in the muddy, densely vegetated terrain. Yet these newly arrived westerners called SEALs not only seemed to be able to maneuver easily through the area, they ranged far and wide, penetrating deeply into its very heart. It began to seem to some locals that the SEALs were better adapted to life in the area than the usual inhabitants were.

By the end of 1966, Detachment GOLF had proven that SEALs would be, without doubt, the best response to the guerrilla activities of the VC in the RSSZ. As of December 31, they had accounted for nearly one hundred VC KIAs (confirmed and probables combined) and destroyed scores of hootches, bunkers, sampans, and freshwater wells. They had also burned or captured more than twenty thousand tons of rice and other foodstuffs. By no means had the SEALs of Detachment GOLF taken over control of the RSSZ. But they had made it clear that control was something that the resident VC could no longer take for granted.

One small example of just how well those early operations proved to be was the discovery of a fairly sizable rice cache in the southern part of the Rung Sat. A recon team had set up their observation post along the west bank of a small stream that branched off the Vam Sat River a few kilometers north of the village of Xom Ly Trung. The area was two miles west of an abandoned French fort on the edge of a vast stretch of mangrove swamp. Only a few minutes after setting up, the team noticed a large amount of sampan traffic going to and from an area of thick palms some fifty meters to the east of their position. The situation obviously warranted investigation, so the three-man team slowly moved to within ten meters of the suspicious area.

Once in that new position they were easily able to observe a small cluster of hootches, heavily camouflaged against aerial observation. During the ensuing twenty-four hours, the team patiently watched as sampan after sampan beached along the stream's edge, just south of the encampment, and the occupants unloaded sacks of rice and, from time to time, boxes of ammunition, which were then stowed in the hootches. This data was radioed in. A little after dark on the following evening, a Heavy SEAL Support Craft (HSSC) eased into the far end of the stream, blocking it off so that no sampans could retreat. Eight SEALs scampered ashore from the craft and joined their three comrades just east of the VC encampment.

After deploying themselves along two sides of the camp's perimeter, they moved in quickly, totally surprising the five VC who were in the camp at that time. Fortunately, the VC did not resist and no shots were fired. That meant that the SEALs had five prisoners, along with more than a ton of rice, several automatic weapons, and several hundred rounds of ammunition.

2 BECOMING GUERRILLAS

The reason for the SEALs' early operational successes during Operation Jackstay came as a direct result of the training they had received during Basic Underwater Demolition/SEAL or BUD/S, the basic training regimen that all prospective SEAL candidates must complete. It is a three-phase, twenty-six-week-long-course conducted at the Naval Special Warfare Center (Naval Amphibious Base) in Coronado, California. The program derives much of its format from the old Underwater Demolition Team (UDT) training program, a logical extension since UDTs contributed extensively to the origin of the SEALs. The physical training associated with the BUD/S indoctrination course has been widely accepted as being one of the most demanding regimens ever devised.

Physical conditioning is an integral part of all three phases of BUD/S, but in Phase One it is very nearly the primary focus. Then, each class of candidates is immediately plunged into one of the most basic elements of SEAL life—teamwork! Everything is done as a unit. The achievement of each individual becomes the achievement of the team. When an individual fails, the team fails. It does not take long for the class to learn that a certain degree of group failure is programmed into the training.

From the first day in the program, a graduated yet relentless program of sit-ups, push-ups, rope climbs, and as much running as a young, well-conditioned heart could ever desire quickly educates each man to the fact that his preconceived limits were far below what he was truly capable of tolerating. But just as he is adjusting to his newfound limits, those limits are then expanded as the class is introduced to two new training elements known as log and boat drills. This transition marks the point when many candidates first begin to seriously question the logic of their ambition.

Log Physical Training is the more proper name for log drills. But no matter what terminology is used, the logs, each of which weighs in the neighborhood of two to three hundred pounds, soon become the subject of recurring nightmares for Phase One candidates. Each candidate is assigned to a six- or seven-man crew, and each crew is assigned to a log. The crews then begin to perform various exercises while holding, lifting, pushing, carrying, or dragging the heavy wooden objects. To break up the monotony of doing calisthenics with the logs, the crews race each other, their heavy wooden burdens perched on their shoulders. Covering several miles during such races is typical.

The crews work similarly with one of their more standard pieces of equipment, the Inflatable Boat System (IBS). Each IBS consists of the inflatable boat itself along with paddles, a carbon dioxide inflation cylinder, hand pump, repair kit, and a few other ancillary items. Each fully rigged IBS weighs close to three hundred pounds and is the responsibility of the particular crew assigned to it. The crew carries its boat wherever possible and keeps it clean and in good repair at all times. As was the case with the logs, the crews perform various tasks and calisthenics with their IBSs, as well as race other crews, either while carrying their boat high above their heads, or paddling out through the breakers into open water and then back to shore again.

Physical conditioning during BUD/S is further enhanced by an intensive regimen of running (during training, candidates literally run everywhere) and swimming. Anyone who knows anything about conditioning understands the excellent stamina-building benefits associated with running. The same is true of swimming. During the initial phase of training, candidates spend endless hours swimming or just lying in the always-frigid surf pounding the sandy Coronado strand.

Aside from the benefits associated with the daily swims, the year-round temperature of the surf (a constant chilly fifty-five degrees Farhenheit) also helps the students understand that wars do not usually take place under the most advantageous conditions. By keeping in mind the buddy principle, which is stressed often throughout BUD/S, the students quickly learn to cuddle up to or even lie on top of one another to avoid hypothermia. Such cooperation was quite effective in dealing with the cold, windy nights encountered by those who had to lie for hours, or even days, in a recon position at the height of the monsoon season in the Mekong Delta or Rung Sat Special Zone.

Perhaps the most important part of Phase One comes during week four, when Hell Week begins. Hell Week invariably kicks off in the middle of the night, just when a sleeper's body has managed to completely relax and his dreams have become most vivid. It is at that moment that the world outside the students' barracks suddenly erupts with sounds of small-arms fire and exploding simulator charges. At that same time, instructors rouse the still-groggy students, advising them that the exercise has begun and that they must move out to begin escaping and evading a mythical pursuing aggressor force.

For the next six days the students are kept on the move, running through the loose sand along the beach, flopping down into the surf, or crawling through flooded "demo" pits that are chest deep with foul-smelling mud while half-pound TNT charges roar all around them. Then it's on to boat drills, surf swims, back to the beach for more running, and later, perhaps, a friendly race along the dunes while humping their beloved logs or IBSs. Over the course of those six days the students manage to squeeze in a total of only three to four hours of sleep. During this week of pain and exhaustion many students will push themselves to go on despite stress fractures, muscle strains, sprained ankles or knees, dislocations, fractured fingers, or lacerations of varying severity. But it is during Hell Week that the greatest amount of attrition among the various BUD/S classes occurs.

Then, as quickly as it had begun, Hell Week abruptly ends. At that moment a tremendous sense of relief comes over each student like a warm wave over a tropical shore. The long hours of lying in the cold surf, of trying to wolf down food while sitting or kneeling in mud up to the armpits, and dragging a rubber boat up onto the beach for the zillionth time seem far-off, foggy memories in the students' exhausted minds. But at the same time they are also aware of other things as well. Each man has proven to himself that he can contribute valuably to the group's success and that he is a true team player. More importantly, he has also learned that he can surmount any obstacle if he puts his mind to it, and that he will fail only if he chooses not to succeed.

After Hell Week, the final three weeks of Phase One, as well as all of Phases Two and Three, seem almost relaxing by comparison. Even so, there still remains much to learn and accomplish during the remainder of BUD/S, such as basic ambush techniques, land navigation, intelligence gathering and debriefing, survival, first aid, sentry neutralization, prisoner handling, small-arms familiarization, demolition handling and disposal, scuba and closed-circuit breathing systems, reconnaissance fundamentals, weapons maintenance, and guerrilla tactics. After satisfactorily completing the remainder of BUD/S, the students go on to jump school, before being assigned to a SEAL team on a six-month probationary basis. Upon completion of the probationary period, if the "probie" has been judged to be SEAL qualified, he receives his permanent assignment to a team.

The foregoing brief synopsis of BUD/S is not intended to provide an in-depth understanding of the training regimen. Rather, it is offered to give some insight into how well prepared each SEAL was, both physically and mentally, to deal with the harsh conditions encountered in the Rung Sat. Hopefully, it will also illustrate the way in which the men were prepared to assimilate all of the factors needed for them not only to deal with a hostile guerrilla force such as the VC, but more importantly to function as an efficient guerrilla force. As the old saying goes, "To catch a thief, send a thief." If SEALs had to neutralize a hostile guerrilla force, they had to counter with an equally efficient guerrilla force. The SEALs knew that if they were to become efficient guerrillas, they would have to master the most important and potent weapon in the guerrilla's arsenal—the ambush.

Those SEALs who were being prepared for duty in the Republic of South Vietnam were taken back through techniques they'd already mastered: land navigation, weapons proficiency and field maintenance, air strike and artillery adjustment procedures, and, of course, SERE training (Survival, Evasion, Resistance, and Escape). But it was the training in ambush techniques that would later serve the SEALs well during their years in Vietnam and especially in the RSSZ. The VC had developed ambush tactics to the level of an art form, using them to nullify the superiority in firepower enjoyed by the Allied forces. Now the VC would begin to experience the art of ambush from the other end of the muzzle. With each day, week, and month spent in Vietnam, SEALs added refinements and smoothed out wrinkles, until the ambush became one of the main weapons in their ever-expanding arsenal.

Every now and then, I like to think back to those whimsical, carefree days of my adolescent years, especially Saturday mornings. Saturday mornings were special because that was the time when your parents would give you a couple of bucks and send you off to the special matinee at the neighborhood movie theater. It would usually start at about 10:00 A.M. and typically included two full-length features, three or four serials, and quite often as many as a hundred cartoons. At least one of the main features and two or more of the serials always turned out to be a cowboy movie, the main stars usually being Lash LaRue, or Roy Rogers. It always seemed that at some point during a cowboy flick someone would be ambushed by a "dirty, filthy dry gulcher" or a "dad gum, rotten bushwhacker!" Regardless of the phraseology used, ambushers were always looked on as being low-life bastards who played the game unfairly. Even today, most people seem to view the ambush as some form of strictly cowardly act.

Nothing could be farther from the truth.

For the most part, guerrilla forces literally live or die based on their ability to successfully employ ambush tactics against much larger opposing forces. Such was certainly the case for the VC, who were not only outnumbered by ARVN troops but were outgunned as well. And let's not forget that the VC insurgents were also opposed by U.S. units (as well as by the military units of other foreign allies of the South Vietnamese government), who had a vast array of sophisticated weapons, an excellent means of logistical and medical support, and highly efficient naval and air capabilities. A guerrilla force would have to be insane or stupid to try to go up against such vastly superior opposing forces head to head. As we all know, the VC were neither insane nor stupid. In fact, they were both logical and astute in their response to the situation.

One thing they realized was that some of the Allied troops' advantages (almost unlimited supplies and ammunition) could actually be turned to the VC's own advantage. They watched the U.S. grunts (as basic infantrymen were fondly called) and quickly noticed that they wasted a lot of energy in their day-to-day activities. For example, their patrols seemed to act as though they had huge rubber bands attached to their rucksacks. On a Tuesday morning a company might be airmobiled into a zone where the VC presence had been reported to be significant. Once the enemy had either been neutralized or had withdrawn, the grunt company would return to its base camp, only to repeat the procedure again, perhaps somewhere else, a day or two later. As the VC watched the grunts go through that monotonous ritual day after day, week after week, they noted that the tedium made the Americans less and less alert.

To compound matters, each grunt had to hump eighty pounds of equipment and personal items into the field in his cumbersome ruck. Try to imagine how laborious it would be to hike five to six miles along a well-paved, level roadway with eighty pounds of gear strapped to your back. And while you're at it, imagine covering that same distance in one-hundred-degree heat and stifling humidity while trying to move through dense underbrush, up steep inclines, or through ankle-deep mud. The average civilian would try such a crazy task for only a mile or so before dropping his ruck and throwing in the towel. The average grunt humped many times that far every day he spent in the field.

By conventional standards, the grunt's burden was understandable. Whenever he set out from his base camp in search of the enemy, he could be gone for several days or weeks. Since he and his unit would range through terrain miles from the unit's base perimeter, he had to take into the field whatever he felt he would need for the duration of the operation, such as two or three changes of socks, three to five days' worth of rations, foot powder, insect repellent, towels, a poncho and/or poncho liner, five or six fragmentation grenades, salt tablets, Halzone tablets (for water purification), several battle dressings, six to eight quarts of drinking water, one or two smoke grenades, and one or two Claymore mines.

In addition to those items, he also carried his weapon along with five to six hundred rounds of ammunition. Each man also carried an extra two hundred rounds of ammunition for his squad's M60 machine gun and an extra battery for the unit's field radio. We can't forget that the field uniform he wore wouldn't be complete without his steel helmet and heavy, cumbersome flak jacket. With such a burden, is it any wonder that U.S. infantrymen referred to themselves as grunts?

In stark contrast to these heavy loads, the VC infantrymen went into the field in a far simpler fashion. Since they operated almost exclusively in their own backyard, there was no need for them to carry large quantities of ammunition and other types of gear. All each VC needed was his weapon, at most one to two hundred rounds of ammunition, a couple of fragmentation grenades, a sleeping hammock, and a two- to five-quart flexible water bag. The typical food ration often consisted of a gummy mound of rice, approximately the size and shape of a softball, wrapped in a cloth and slung from his belt. If more gear was required for a specific operation, it was usually carried in a lightweight ruck, about the same size as a small backpack. But no matter what items the VC found necessary to carry into the field, the main emphasis remained the same. Each member of the unit had to retain as much speed and mobility as possible.

Because the VC and NVA were indigenous forces, they knew that the terrain and the climate could be used to drain the energy from an enemy who did not understand the necessity of working in harmony with the environment. The VC and NVA were guerrillas and understood that traveling light allowed them to cover wide stretches of terrain quickly, without compromising their stamina. As guerrillas they knew that an extra grenade or an extra hundred rounds of ammunition were most often just extra weight in their scheme of hit-and-run tactics. Even if they really thought that such extra items might be of benefit, they still kept them to an absolute minimum.

Large-scale, sustained engagements were infrequently employed by communist forces, and if so very judiciously. They preferred to hit quickly and then withdraw. Such tactics were far less taxing on their manpower and material. It also allowed them to employ the "energy drain" strategy against their heavily burdened U.S. adversaries. The strategy was of great importance to the VC's tactics because it not only sapped the Americans' physical strength but also began to gradually erode their confidence and ability to maintain concentration under fire. That last part was of extreme importance to the VC. A typical example of just how the VC put that strategy into play follows.

Let us assume that a U.S. infantry platoon is sweeping through a difficult section of thick, hilly terrain. It's late in the morning, the temperature is already well above ninety degrees, and the humidity is about 85 percent. As the grunts move carefully along a narrow trail, a small group of VC suddenly fires on them from an area of dense cover just ahead. The grunts return the fire and prepare to assault the VC position, but before they can get under way the VC withdraw, being careful to leave an easily identifiable trail. After luring the heavily burdened grunts into following the trail into a section of gummy marsh, the VC disperse, this time making sure that they have covered their tracks thoroughly.

The Americans slog around the marsh for some time searching for signs of the VC ambushers but find nothing except fatigue and frustration. The VC open up on the tired grunts again and quickly withdraw. This time they again leave a highly visible trail intended to lead their tired, panting, lumbering pursuers into an area in which several crude booby traps have been set. The booby traps are small because their intended purpose is to wound a victim, not to kill him. An alert individual might have a good chance of spotting the hazard before triggering it. But by now the grunts are tired, frustrated, and angry. Too intent on catching sight of his tormentor, an exhausted grunt snags a trip wire. The booby trap explodes and the wounded man screams out in pain. Two or three of his buddies rush to his aid, triggering one or two more booby traps in the process.

Meanwhile, the lurking VC add to the pandemonium by once again bringing the exhausted and confused platoon under fire. After inflicting another casualty or two, the guerrillas withdraw.

In some cases the VC might leave the area, being content to have wounded a few members of the U.S. platoon and to have put a little doubt into the minds of the rest as to just how much sense it really makes to be so far from home. But in other cases the VC might pretend to withdraw, out of sight in the trees, waiting for the platoon to call in a chopper to extract the wounded. Then, when the chopper touches down, the VC takes it out with a rocket-propelled grenade. In such circumstances, air support seems a little less potent and grunts in the field feel more vulnerable than superior.

In no way do I intend for the preceding example to imply that our Army and Marine Corps infantrymen in Vietnam were inept. Quite the contrary; they were, for the most part, members of the best-trained and best-disciplined armed force ever to take the field. Their training, however, was intended primarily to prepare them to deal with conventional engagements, and so it did little to allow them to respond to guerrilla tactics. To compound matters, the terrain found in Vietnam, as well as throughout most of Southeast Asia, provided one of the best areas for waging unconventional warfare.

The specialized training offered not only in BUD/S but also after a SEAL had been assigned to one of the teams was slanted primarily toward the guerrilla approach to warfare. Initially, SEALs were to be used as counterguerrillas or counterinsurgency specialists. But let's not get hung up on semantics. No matter how you want to look at it, you cannot be a counterguerrilla if you don't know how the guerrilla thinks and how he puts his tactics into play. Once you understand that, you see the beauty and logic of that tactical approach and also the fact that only a similar set of tactics can adequately counter it. You also appreciate that many of these tactics rely on the guerrilla's willingness and ability to ply his trade sometimes in the most inhospitable terrain.

One area of South Vietnam where the foregoing was quickly proven to be true was the Rung Sat. The resident VC forces seemed to draw strength from the mangrove stands, the bamboo groves, and the thick, sometimes double canopied forests of banyan, cajeput, *sao,* gum, and other types of evergreen and hardwood trees that carpeted, blanketed, and tightly embraced the undulating waterways and oozing, silt-rich mud of the Rung Sat. And it was out of that morass, that melange of timber, water, grass, and ooze, that Charlie—the VC—would suddenly erupt, to rip out the throat of an adversary who had been momentarily distracted by the sudden appearance of a python, krait, or cobra. The snake was only a distraction; Charlie was the real danger.

Some of the techniques necessary to make an ambush successful are stealth, surprise, speed, and a high volume of deadly fire, delivered as rapidly as possible, without compromising accuracy. Getting to and from the ambush site as quickly and quietly as possible, without leaving any signs of the ambush team's exact strength or size, is of great importance, as it brings added psychological impact to the operation. After all, the object of the ambush is not only to kill or maim the enemy but also to impress on him that he cannot afford to feel secure anywhere, not even at home. Therefore, it is essential that the ambush team have a great capacity for mobility, not only en route to the ambush site but in withdrawing from it as well.

The VC fully appreciated the benefits of mobility within the RSSZ. They and their predecessors in the Rung Sat (Vietminh, pirates) had long relied on the rapid deployment opportunities made possible by the RSSZ's diverse network of rivers, canals, and streams. From time to time they would send a platoon or company-sized force into a hamlet or village in one part of the area at dawn, ostensibly to resupply or draft "volunteers." They would then withdraw and turn up in another village by late morning, many miles away from the first, long before a runner from the first village could arrive to warn the second village of that same day's earlier intrusion.

That capacity for rapid troop deployment served them even better when responding to raids into the RSSZ by ARVN troops or other Allied forces. No matter how large the opposing force, the VC could put platoons, companies, or even battalions into the field in response within minutes. More importantly, they could redeploy, resupply, and reinforce their units much more rapidly and efficiently than their enemies could. Should their adversary begin to achieve an advantage, the VC units could quickly withdraw, leaving no trail for the pursuer to follow. For them, the waterways were roads and trails, with sampans, junks, and pirogues (dugout canoes) serving as their troop transports.

Convoy routes, highways, and trail systems heavily used by enemy forces were the settings in which ambushes most frequently occurred, which is only logical for several reasons. First of all, there was a high probability of a sizable enemy presence. And if the route passing through the kill zone happened to be a major supply route, the successful ambush resulted not only in the enemy's loss of personnel but in his loss of material as well. Further, it delivered a telling psychological blow, preventing the enemy from feeling secure in the use of his own transportation network and causing him to devote greater energy to logistical problems than to tactical ones.

Soon after Operation Game Warden got under way, it became evident that small, highly mobile guerrilla-type units would be needed if the full scope of the operation's desired effect was to be realized. Shutting off the enemy's seaborne supplies was only the first step and could not succeed in totally eradicating the insurgent presence in and of itself. For although the sea routes had been successfully interdicted, supplies were still coming in via the Ho Chi Minh Trail.

Relying only upon the Ho Chi Minh Trail meant a considerable wait between each supply delivery. In the interim, the Mekong Delta and RSSZ resident VC forces maintained their food stores by raiding or, as they termed it, "taxing" nearby villages. Not only was there a great supply of rice in both areas but also a wide assortment of fruits (durian, longan, oranges, melons, coconuts) and vegetables (white and yellow maize, beans of varying types, cabbage, cucumbers), as well as a diverse array of meat and fowl (pigs, chickens, turtles, ducks), and literally hundreds of species of fish and shellfish. Such a ready supply of foodstuffs made the VC position less precarious. However, it did bring even more hardship into the lives of the region's villagers.

In late March 1966, a considerable amount of intelligence was developed regarding VC activities in an area just south of the large rubber plantation near Phu Thanh, in the north central part of the RSSZ. Some residents from one of the local villages reported that the VC had been severely depleting the village's supplies of food, as well as pressing some of the men into duty as porters and construction laborers. The laborers were being taken to an area on the edge of the mangrove swamp a couple of miles southwest, where the VC were setting up a small camp. The construction was by that time almost complete and seemed to be intended for use not only as a base camp but as a central storage depot as well. The camp sat at the juncture of two streams, both of which emptied into the Song Ba Gioi River to the south.

A SEAL surveillance team was immediately deployed to the site. Over the next three days, they initiated a thorough sweep of the area. Unfortunately, none of the villagers who had supplied the intelligence regarding the base camp were among those who had been pressed into service as construction laborers. Therefore, they had been able to give only a rough estimate of the camp's precise location. By the end of the third day, the team was beginning to think that the intelligence had been of less than optimal value. In fact, they had already begun moving toward their pre-designed extraction point when they came to a small stream and heard the sound of an outboard motor purring in the distance.

The team hastily moved into ambush positions, three of the men on one side of the stream, the remaining two on the other. By that time it was already quite dark and they could see the glow of a lantern approaching along the stream from the east. Within a matter of seconds the bow of a sampan, bathed in the lantern light, crept out of the gloom. As the vessel moved closer, the team could see that it contained four men and what appeared to be several bundles and boxes of varying size. So far, they had not determined if any of the sampan's occupants were VC since no weapons were visible. For that reason, the team leader was contemplating letting them pass, on the chance that the sampan contained only peaceful, local civilians.

But before he could signal the team to that effect, a man in the bow of the vessel stood up to deflect an overhanging branch from the vessel's path with his left hand as he loosely held an AK-47 in his right. That was enough to identify the four occupants of the vessel as VC. Less than two seconds later, as the sampan was within ten feet of the team's position, the team leader fired a burst from his M16, thereby triggering the ambush. The firing lasted only about five seconds but resulted in all of the VC being killed outright. As their vessel slowly drifted to where the nearest SEAL had been positioned, he leaped into the stream to secure and guide it toward the near bank.

Although the VC camp had not been located, the team determined that it was nearby because the sampan contained several sacks of rice, boxes of first-aid supplies and vegetables, one heavy automatic weapon, and a little more than ten thousand rounds of ammunition. Obviously, those supplies could not be intended for use by just four VC. The only possible conclusion was that the four men were taking the material to a nearby camp (probably the very base camp described by the villagers). With that thought in mind, the team leader radioed for a support vessel to move in for extraction and to pick up the captured supplies. A day later, a seven-man ambush team was sent back into the same area and they quickly located the VC base camp and neutralized it, with two VC being killed and another captured. Also seized was a sizable rice cache (approximately half a ton) and several thousand rounds of ammunition.

Shortly thereafter, it was decided that elements of Detachment GOLF would intensify their efforts in the RSSZ and the Mekong Delta. Their purpose was to act in support of Operation Game Warden, thereby deny-ing the VC the secondary means of logistical support found in the peace-ful villages located in both areas. GOLF's ambush teams were deployed quickly along the waterways inside the Rung Sat. By utilizing their own support craft as well as those vessels that had been placed at their dis-posal by Operation Game Warden, GOLF's ambush operations met with immediate success, resulting in a significant reduction in communist riverine activity.

Much of the success of those operations was due to the highly special-ized vessels (SEAL Support Craft) that were utilized by the ambush teams. Speed, mobility, and firepower, three of the most important things necessary for successful ambush operations, also served to define the traits found in GOLF's support craft. The vessels ran the gamut from small rubber rafts or skiffs equipped with outboard motors, suitable for five- to seven-man insertions, to hybrids of Mechanized Landing Craft (LCM-6) capable of transporting and supporting platoon-sized units. Armament on such vessels varied from simple personal weapons, in the case of the rubber rafts and skiffs, to light and heavy automatic weapons (M60, .30-caliber and .50-caliber machine guns), 40mm auto-matic grenade launchers, mortars (60mm and 81mm), and even 106mm recoilless rifles.

The speed of the vessels employed in those river ambushes was critical in that it presented greater potential for capturing VC personnel, vessels, and munitions. During an ambush, intense small-arms and heavy auto-matic weapons fire often caused significant damage to the enemy vessels. Although inflicting heavy losses, in the form of KIAs and wounded, and destroying equipment were important objectives, capturing live personnel, material, maps, or other documents more often than not proved to be of greater value. Each SEAL Support Craft's speed was such that as soon as the kill zone was deemed secure, boats could move in and place a boarding party on any of the damaged VC vessels. The boarding party would quickly assess whether or not the damaged boat could be taken under tow or hastily beached. If the damage was too severe, the boat would be searched, and any live enemy personnel and items of logistical or intelligence value secured.

A good example of effective and speedy support craft occurred in August 1966. A seven-man team had set up an ambush along a narrow channel in the northeast section of the Rung Sat. After waiting throughout the night, the gloom of morning found them still waiting for unsuspecting VC to pass. Since it appeared that they were not destined to have any luck, they decided to break their position and head back to base. A few minutes later they were back aboard the Boston Whaler that they had used to insert into the area. They had moved only about one hundred meters downstream when a sampan rounded a bend in the waterway just ahead. Five men could be clearly seen aboard the sampan, and they seemed to become extremely agitated at the sight of the rapidly approaching SEAL boat.

If the men in the sampan had continued along their primary course, the SEALs would have stopped them briefly to check their vessel. Obviously the five men must have figured that out, because the sampan suddenly swung about, its outboard engine revving wildly as it sped away. The SEAL team leader did not have to give the order to pursue; the helm had already hit the throttle and the Whaler was closing rapidly on the fleeing vessel. Still, the team did not know whether the fleeing craft contained VC or just frightened local civilians. But the question became moot within a matter of seconds when two of the men in the stern of the sampan opened up on the pursuing SEALs with AK-47s.

A SEAL in the bow of the Whaler replied with a sustained burst from his M60 light machine gun while the man just behind him cut loose with a round from his grenade launcher. As the rounds from the machine gun sprayed the sampan's stern and silenced the two men who had been firing on the SEALs, the grenade ripped into the sampan's bow section, stopping the vessel almost dead in the channel. The blast also blew apart much of the bow section, and the vessel began to take on water rapidly. As the chewed-up bow section started to slip under the water, the Whaler roared alongside and three of the SEALs jumped aboard the foundering craft. They determined that only one of the suspects was still alive, although severely wounded.

While two of the SEALs loaded the wounded suspect aboard the Whaler, the other man searched through the sinking vessel's covered section amidships. He found several bundles of clothing, a box of grenades, at least a half dozen carbines, and a medium-sized leather pouch wrapped in plastic. The sampan was going down fast and the SEAL had to make a quick decision about what items he should try to salvage. Just as the water was getting up to about the middle of his calf muscles, he grabbed the plastic-covered pouch and the box of grenades and raced toward the stern of the sinking craft. As soon as he had cleared the covered section, he tossed the items aboard the Whaler before jumping aboard himself. Seconds later the sampan disappeared below the swirling brown water.

The team leader opened the pouch and found it full of waterproof maps and papers. Most of the maps were routine, depicting the general area around the northern section of the RSSZ. But a few of the maps were also well marked, clearly showing the location of several villages, some previously unknown freshwater wells, and a VC base camp. Also depicted on the maps were the locations of local rice caches, and streams that could be used for making hasty retreats if a large Allied force made a sweep through the area. Interrogation of the wounded prisoner revealed that one of his dead comrades had been the logistical officer of the local VC battalion. If the SEAL team had not been able to get to the sinking VC sampan as rapidly as it had, the maps and the prisoner would have been lost to the depths. As it turned out, valuable intelligence regarding the local VC had been obtained.

The capture of enemy personnel and items of intelligence value have always been standard operating procedure for all SEAL field units. A live prisoner may be able to provide valuable information under careful, thorough interrogation. On the other hand, dead adversaries are decidedly difficult to deal with. It also helps to explain why SEAL Standard Operating Procedure (SOP) focused more intently on the acquisition of prisoners than on kills (body counts). But although great emphasis was placed on prisoner acquisition, greater emphasis was placed on the security of the team making the "snatch."

This SEAL philosophy bore immediate fruit in intelligence gathered. Prisoners taken during the first several months of Operation Game Warden and Operation Jackstay provided a clear picture of the VC organizational structure, fortifications, supply net, and long-range operational objectives within the RSSZ and Mekong Delta. One of the earliest pieces of valuable intelligence developed through such prisoner interrogations indicated that the VC presence in the Delta and the RSSZ was far more extensive than had been previously assumed.

When the U.S. Military Assistance and Advisory Group (MAAG) had assumed all training and advisory operations from the French in 1956, all available intelligence indicated that the VC, or Vietminh as they were known at the time, had already established the RSSZ as their safe area in what was to be known later as the IV Corps area of operations. In 1962 the Military Assistance Command, Vietnam (MACV), began to assume many of MAAG's responsibilities, and by 1964 the transition had become complete. Although the prevailing assumption was that the RSSZ was a safe area and a stronghold for the VC, the hard numbers relative to insurgent troop strength, logistical capabilities, and popular support from the regional hamlets and villages had not yet been quantified.

Prior to the SEAL participation in Operations Game Warden and Jackstay, it was assumed that the VC numbers in the Delta and RSSZ combined (full-time guerrillas, part-time guerrillas, political cadre, and other supportive elements) was in the area of 35,000 to 50,000. However, prisoner interrogations during both operations strongly suggested that the actual VC presence in both areas combined was closer to 80,000 to 90,000 (with perhaps 70 to 75 percent of that number being in the Delta). Of those numbers, it was assumed that in the Delta 15,000 to 20,000 were hard-core, everyday guerrillas, with another 10,000 being political cadre. That meant that anywhere from 45,000 to 50,000 were potential part-time guerrillas. Assuming that those numbers were correct, the figures for the RSSZ would have been in the area of 3,750 to 5,000 full-time guerrillas, 2,500 political cadre, and 11,250 to 12,500 part-timers.

Many of the part-time VC operating in the RSSZ hid in plain sight, living and working in the region's scores of noncombatant villages and tiny hamlets. Of course all of these part-timers were not frontline fighters but did provide various other intelligence or support-oriented functions. In fact, a vital function of these part-timers was their role as the eyes and ears of local, full-time VC combat forces. But when circumstances required the mustering of a reinforcing contingent, these part-timers could be mobilized and on line in surprisingly quick fashion.

One Detachment GOLF recon team had an opportunity to observe a typical example of just how well these part-timers performed their job in the early fall of 1966. The three-man team had set up an observation post near a small hamlet on the banks of the Song Dua River, about forty-five miles southeast of Saigon. The area was densely forested. Recently developed intelligence suggested that the area around the hamlet was being used by a local VC company as a staging area. The team had set up just after midnight, positioning themselves in a spot from which they could see not only the hamlet but the river and two trail approaches as well. During the first few hours things were quiet; the only movement came in the form of an occasional pig and scores of hungry mosquitoes.

A few minutes past sunrise, a group of four young boys, each probably eight to ten years of age, came running down to the riverbank and began to wash themselves. As they did, they also seemed to be intently scanning the river, first upstream and then down, as though they were looking for signs of movement. After a few minutes the boys seemed to relax a bit, splashing and chasing each other for a short time before moving under the canopy of a stand of palms about ten feet from the river's edge. For the most part, they stayed there in the shade, one boy always seeming to keep watch over the immediate stretch of river and the two nearby trails while the other three boys played tag, wrestled, or just threw stones.

The team felt sure that the boys were lookouts. The only question was whether they were looking for signs of approaching VC, who might be coming to pillage the hamlet's food stores, or for Allied troops or patrol boats sweeping the area looking for insurgents. If the latter was the case, then the hamlet was obviously under VC control. The team's assumption was just that.

Approximately fifteen minutes after the boys had taken up their position under the palms, an ARVN patrol boat came cruising down the river toward the hamlet. As soon as the boys spotted the boat, they moved into the open and began to act out some sort of mock war scenario, all the while yelling and vocally imitating the sounds of gunfire. They kept up their pretend battle until the patrol boat finally passed their position and disappeared in the distance. Once the boys seemed sure that the boat was well on its way, they began to play a game similar to ring-around-the-rosy for a minute or two, before returning to the palms and their more extemporaneous forms of play.

While the children had been waging their mock battle, the team had turned its interest toward the hamlet. One of the men scanning it carefully with his binoculars saw a group of three men and two women, all armed with automatic weapons and wearing backpacks. The women were carrying bundles and the men were carrying boxes. They exited from a hootch near the far side of the hamlet and disappeared into the trees and thick underbrush. They remained hidden from sight, not only throughout the entire time that the patrol was slowly going by, but also for at least ten minutes after the children had given the all-clear signal with their ring dance. Then the five armed individuals casually walked back into the hamlet as though they had been merely playing a game, just as the children had been doing.

The team decided to move in closer to the hamlet to better size up the situation. They stayed well back under the trees to the east of their objective, all the while keeping the young sentries in view. Because the team members were being so careful in their movements, it took more than half an hour to finally get to within twenty meters of the hamlet's edge. At that moment they saw the boys again run out into the open and repeat their battle scenario. A second or two later, the team suddenly came under intense automatic weapons fire from somewhere directly ahead and quite near the hamlet's edge. The team returned the fire and immediately heard some screams, suggesting that they had hit one or maybe more of their assailants. Their return fire also immediately silenced the enemy weapons.

As the recon team moved quickly toward the hamlet, they could see four people running between the hootches on the hamlet's far side before disappearing into the dense foliage beyond. When the SEALs reached the spot from which the initial burst of enemy fire had emanated, they saw the lifeless body of one of the female VC slumped awkwardly against the side of a hootch in a semikneeling position, her AK-47 on the ground in front of her. Two blood trails started just behind her and then continued on toward the other side of the hamlet where the fleeing VC had made their hasty exit. One of the SEALs grabbed the dead VC's weapon as he followed behind his two buddies in hot pursuit of the other four VC. But when the three SEALs reached the far edge of the hamlet, they stopped and took cover behind the nearest hootch. They knew that rushing into the dense foliage directly along the VC's line of retreat might have led the team into a hastily set, deadly ambush.

As they waited they could hear the sounds of their quarry thrashing along a narrow path in their haste to escape from the pursuing SEALs. One team member moved into the foliage along the path while the other two took a parallel course right through the undergrowth to his left. They moved along quickly and cautiously, scanning the area ahead and to all sides for any sign of an ambush. The two blood trails were clearly in evidence along the path and strongly suggested that the fleeing VC were not interested in wasting time setting ambushes. It was obvious that they had escape on their minds and did not want to have any further contact with the SEALs.

The team had traveled only about thirty meters or so when they suddenly came to a stream. The blood trails grew into a rather large pool of gore at the stream's edge, at a spot where the mud showed the impression of a sampan's hull. The three men squatted down and listened for any sound of an outboard motor or the splashing of a pole as the sampan made its way through the water, but no such sounds were heard. It seemed evident that their quarry had made good on their escape. But the SEALs did have one captured weapon and one dead VC for their efforts. Interrogation of the hamlet's residents by ARVN troops did not result in any worthwhile information regarding local VC activities. However, word spread rapidly throughout the area that even reliable lookouts could not guarantee that a VC village or hamlet would be secure against a surprise visit by a SEAL recon/ambush team.

Still, the hard-core, full-time VC units continued to live in highly fortified hamlets or smaller encampments. They went to great lengths, especially in the Rung Sat, to camouflage their bases as well as many of their sampans, junks, wells, munitions depots/factories, and food caches. In some cases, they also camouflaged portions of a number of their most important escape routes (both land trails and rivers/channels). Paradoxically, it was the extent to which they carried out these camouflage efforts that made their hamlets and other facilities more readily discernible, especially from the air. However, it was not because of any lack of skill in camouflage technique that made the VC positions so obvious. It was that the VC had taken great advantage of the most natural elements of the terrain that made many of their encampments and fortifications stick out like the proverbial sore thumb.

An example of such "natural" camouflage efforts was an area of the central RSSZ four to five miles northeast of Phuoc An. The area was almost circular and about two miles across. It contained a particularly large section of heavily overgrown hardwood forest that had been intentionally left to flourish while the wooded land in the remainder of that sector was being harvested by neighboring villagers. Since wood harvesting was an important enterprise in the RSSZ, wide sections of forest had become denuded. Once harvesting of an area had begun, it was unlikely that prime sections of lumber would escape the saw and the ax. There would have to be a very good reason for the villagers to pass up an opportunity to harvest income-generating hardwood.

Recon teams from Detachment GOLF had begun working through the area in early 1967. Almost immediately they began to notice that the neighboring villagers religiously avoided the heavily overgrown forest area. Fishermen, hunters, and lumber harvesters seemed reluctant to get anywhere near the various streams and trails that led to and then under the thick green double canopy. Obviously, such an area warranted investigation, so a seven-man ambush/recon team was sent to investigate.

After deploying to the area at just a little past 2200, the team moved about a quarter of a mile under the canopy before coming to a stream just wide and deep enough to allow passage by sampans, which made it seem like a good spot to set up an ambush. The team remained in position throughout that night and the following day. But by nightfall they had neither seen nor heard anything that might suggest that any VC were out and about in the vicinity.

Hoping for better luck, the team decided to move their position a little farther east, toward the heart of the area. At about 2100 they broke position and headed east along the meandering stream. By carefully picking their way along its left bank, the going was a little easier than if they had tried to force their way through the dense tangle of foliage. It was also less dangerous than using any of the nearby trails that might be booby-trapped or monitored by VC listening posts. But staying close to the stream also increased the chances of encountering a VC sampan.

The team had been on the move for only about thirty to forty minutes when they heard voices approaching from somewhere to the rear. A few seconds later the dim beam of a flashlight could be seen moving along a trail that was about ten meters to the left. The team took hasty ambush positions but held its fire, everyone watching the dim shapes of two figures walking along the path toward the east. Since they seemed ignorant of the SEALs' presence, the team leader decided to let them continue unmolested. He figured that if they turned out to be VC, following them might result in finding larger quarry, such as more VC, a camp, or a weapons cache. But if the two presumed VC were alone, they could just grab them and see what they might give up during interrogation.

Within less than a minute after the team had begun shadowing the two figures, one of the SEALs lost his footing on a slick spot along the stream bank and fell into the water, making an enormous splash. The sound caused the two men on the trail to turn quickly toward the SEALs' position, their dim flashlight beam sweeping rapidly back and forth over the dense foliage. A second later the air crackled with the sounds of automatic weapons fire coming from the area just behind the flashlight's beam. The team immediately responded, raking the enemy position with their own automatic weapons and shotguns. The firing lasted only five seconds; when it stopped, the enemy position was silent except for the sounds of a man calling out weakly.

"Giup toi voi! Toi bi thuong! Toi dau co!" he moaned in Vietnamese. "Please help me! I'm wounded! My neck hurts!"

Three of the SEALs moved quickly but cautiously over to the two VC lying on the trail. They found that the moaning man had taken hits in the neck, chest, and both arms. His partner was dead. One of the SEALs tended to the wounded man's injuries while another searched the dead man. They were just about to start interrogating the wounded man when two or more outboard motors could be heard in the distance to the east. The other four SEALs took off in the direction of the sounds, two of them running along the trail while the others ran along the stream bank.

It did not take long before the four men came to a small encampment near the bank of the stream, about fifty meters farther down the trail from the ambush. But by the time they had reached the camp, the sounds of the outboards had almost disappeared upstream. One SEAL headed toward the rapidly dying sounds of the motors while the other three men started a thorough search of the camp's immediate surroundings. Satisfied that the area was fairly secure, they turned their full attention toward searching the camp's three hootches. They found that one hootch contained about a dozen boxes of ammunition and several automatic weapons. A second hootch was almost half full of large sacks of rice, plastic-wrapped packets of dried fish, and a modest assortment of medical supplies. The third hootch had obviously been used as living quarters and appeared to have sheltered anywhere from eight to twelve people.

Interrogation of the wounded prisoner revealed that the area was being used to shelter several squads of VC in four or five camps. Although the squads did occasionally ambush an odd patrol boat or two, their main function was to keep the local villagers hard at work providing the VC with produce, livestock, and clothing. The prisoner also said that a larger base camp was being constructed in the western section of the overgrown area to prepare for a significant buildup of forces to battalion strength. He was able to furnish the team with the general location of the new construction site, as well as the locations of nearby bunkers and rice caches. A few freshwater wells were also detailed by the talkative prisoner. Allied forces would have eventually found out about the VC's local camps and activities, but if the team had not decided to check out the overgrown area when they did, it might have gone undetected for several more months.

Such camouflage efforts were better applied in the swampier sections of the RSSZ and yielded far better results for the VC. Still, the scarcity of fishermen, woodcutters, and snake or wild pig hunters was a fairly reliable indication in assessing sites for possible recon and ambush operations. One such sector was the area around Nhan Trach, a wide stretch of mangrove swamp southeast of Cat Lai, portions of which sit astride the more northerly of the two main channel entrances extending from the South China Sea to Saigon. The natural impediments that the terrain offered discouraged pursuit of VC forces into Nhan Trach. The proximity to the channel entrance provided great opportunities for disrupting merchant shipping through channel mining and occasional rocket or mortar fire. Nhan Trach, therefore, was an ideal area of operations for regional VC forces.

During the fall of 1967, recon teams from Detachment GOLF had been operating extensively across much of the northern Rung Sat, especially in and around Nhan Trach. Vietcong activity had continued at a fairly high rate, but so far no one had been able to pinpoint where the local companies were based. Up to that time much of the recon effort had been concentrated in the mangrove swamps and the rubber plantations around Phu Thanh. A few small camps had been located and a few VC had been either killed or captured. Otherwise, the teams had not yet developed any good intelligence that might lead them to the location of the larger base camp, or camps, that they knew must be in that general area.

One particular four-man recon team had been working a section of Nhan Trach a few miles southeast of Phu Thanh. The area consisted of a heavily overgrown section of forest bordered on all sides by swamp and a number of tiny islands covered by nipa palms. It seemed like an ideal area for a base camp because it also was crisscrossed by several narrow but navigable streams. Except for the streams, all other approaches to the forested section would require an assaulting force to slog through the swamp and its oftentimes waist-deep mud. Such natural impediments against possible Allied incursions certainly enhanced the area's appeal as a location for a base camp.

The team had made its way into the area sometime around 2200 and immediately set up an observation post on one of the small nipa palm islands, near the southern edge of the forest. From that location they were able to see two of the streams that led into the heart of the forested section. Because of the lush ground cover and dense overhead tree canopy, the streams were hidden from aerial observation. This made one or both of them ideal entrances/exits for clandestine movement into or out of the forest. Within the first hour that assumption proved to be true when a sampan came gliding past the observation post and into the stream entrance.

The team waited for fifteen minutes before deciding to leave their position and halfwade/halfswim across to the forest through the dark, muddy water. They crawled onto a reedy section just west of the stream and moved inland a distance of ten meters where they huddled together, rested, and listened to the quiet. Hearing no sounds that might indicate that their movements had been detected by unseen eyes, they started to move laboriously through the initially dense ground-level vegetation paralleling the stream. Fortunately, after they had gotten a few meters into the forest, the brush, vines, and other forms of undergrowth thinned out and the going became easier.

As they continued into the forest, the visibility worsened. Even during the brightest part of the day, very little light ever penetrated the dense overhead canopy. Soon the four men were groping their way along, aware of the stream's location only by the sound of the rushing water. After fifteen to twenty minutes of slowly feeling their way through the darkness, the faint sounds of voices and the smell of smoke came from somewhere not far ahead. As the team moved toward the sounds and smells, they noticed that the ground began to rise rapidly and they soon found themselves atop a little knoll. Less than twenty meters ahead on the far side of the stream, they could see a campfire, around which six silhouetted figures squatted.

The team leader directed the point man to move toward the stream to find a good place for the team to cross without being seen or heard. He crawled down the knoll and then swung away from the stream toward the interior of the forest. When he got about ten meters from the knoll he came to a swampy section of ground. Not wanting to make any splashing noises, he turned back directly toward the stream and skirted the mushy area. But he had not gotten far when he thought he heard a strange yet very familiar sound ahead. He stopped, held his breath, and listened carefully. Finally he was satisfied that, indeed, the sounds he was hearing were someone snoring. Then he became aware that the sounds were not coming from just one sleeper but at least two, if not more. The sleepers were to his right, probably less than ten feet away.

He crept forward, then stopped when he could just make out the dim form of a man lying curled up on the ground only a few feet in front of him. And even though it was quite dark and the visibility was poor, he thought he could also make out the forms of three other men sleeping off to the left. Not wanting one of the sleepers to awaken and catch sight of him, the SEAL eased onto his hands and knees and inched his way past the four men. He was careful not to move any closer to the stream, since his present position was now directly across from where the six presumed VC were squatting around their campfire. Even though the fire did not radiate a great deal of light, he was moving on the edge where the light grew faint and the shadows took over.

After crawling parallel to the stream for a short distance, the point man continued his recon of the area, covering another thirty meters before returning to the knoll. He advised the team leader that he had found a good stream crossing only fifteen meters ahead. He added that he had come across the four sleepers situated near the crossing point as well as three others sleeping a short distance farther along on the same side of the stream. Just beyond that spot, he had arrived at a second knoll close to where the stream made a sweeping bend to the left. He said he couldn't be sure, but just before he started to head back he thought he caught a whiff of smoke blowing from the direction of the knoll. And even though he did not investigate further, he also thought he saw a tiny bit of light flickering against the lower branches of the forest canopy above the second knoll.

Based on the point man's observations, it was decided that the team would spend more time doing a recon on their side of the stream before crossing over to check out the six men on the far side. They started along a route parallel to the one that the point man had taken, until they reached the swampy area. There they turned away from the stream and followed the swampy section's perimeter. As it turned out, the boggy area was not very extensive, and it did not take long before they found themselves on its far side, a short distance from the second knoll. Almost immediately they could see another campfire flickering in the distance. It was just far enough away that they could not make out any shapes of people near the fire. Cautiously they moved forward to investigate.

The team managed to get to within thirty feet of the fire, noting not only the five VC around it (at least two of the five were armed with AK-47s, and another held an SKS assault rifle) but also two hootches nearby. One hootch was definitely still under construction; the other seemed ready for use. And stacked a short distance from the unfinished structure was a large pile of bamboo of varying lengths and diameters. Next to that was a pile of palm fronds. Obviously, the VC were in the process of either establishing a new base camp or expanding an existing one. The team figured that since there were new hootches under construction and a number of VC were seen sleeping on the ground, the construction of a new camp seemed very probable.

For the next few hours the team continued to recon the forest area. Not only were they able to observe at least five hootches already under construction (two at the campsite on the near side of the stream and three on the far side, where the first six VC had been seen), but they also saw several areas where pits had been dug and bamboo piled nearby, obvious signs of ongoing bunker construction. During their recon they also counted a minimum of twenty-five men in the area, a few chatting around the two campfires and the rest asleep in two or three nearby locations. Since only eight of the men seemed to be armed, the rest were assumed to be laborers, probably conscripts from one of the neighboring villages.

Since first light was less than an hour away, the team made ready to exit the forest area. As they quietly made their way past the second knoll and turned toward the small swampy section of ground, they happened on a man who was just getting ready to relieve himself at the edge of the bog. Two of the SEALs quickly but quietly pounced on him, one of them rendering him senseless with two rapid punches to the back of his head. With the prisoner in hand and under control, the team exited the forest and made it back to the nipa palm island where their small boat was hidden. After loading themselves and their prisoner into the boat, they got under way, immediately radioing for a patrol boat to prepare to rendezvous with them for quicker transport back to their base at Nha Be.

Interrogation of the prisoner revealed that he was not a VC but a peasant from a village located a little more than five miles east of the forest area. Two days ago he, his brother, and more than a dozen other male villagers had been abducted by some VC who then brought them to the forest. There they were ordered to assist in the camp construction and invited to join "The Cause." He said the VC did not tell them much about what the camp was for, but one of his fellow laborers had overhead some of the VC talking about how well the area would be able to support their battalion. But the prisoner could not furnish any data regarding where the battalion was at present or, more importantly, when it was projected to arrive at the forest camp. Even so, the intelligence developed during the interrogation proved to be solid and resulted in highly successful operations against a VC battalion that moved into the forest area soon thereafter.

The same factors that made Nhan Trach an ideal area of operations for Detachment GOLF also made it extremely interesting for other U.S. units, most notably the 2d Brigade of the U.S. Army's 9th Infantry Division. The 2d Brigade had been assigned to Operation Game Warden as the Riverine Assault Force (Task Force 116, later known as the Mobile Riverine Force). From April to June 1966, the 1st Infantry Division's 1st Battalion, 18th Infantry, conducted Operation Lexington III in parts of that sector, accounting for the destruction of a significant number of VC sampans and pirogues. However, their efforts in finding and engaging VC forces on solid ground, or in locating any of the enemy's larger, heavily fortified hamlets, were far less successful. In fact, the only contact that the 1st Battalion made was with the swamp's totally hostile and nearly impenetrable terrain.

As the men of the 1st Battalion moved deeper into the swampy terrain, they became increasingly aware that the RSSZ was not an ideal setting for conventional troops or conventional tactics. A great deal of their time was spent in trying to cut through the dense, interlaced root network of the mangrove trees, or to wriggle and squeeze between the scrub, saplings, and creepers, along the many small deer and wild pig trails, which seemed to start nowhere and yet to go everywhere. Still more time and energy was expended in trying to deal with an endless sea of mud, which was quite often midthigh to waist deep and extremely thick and gluelike. The weight of flak jackets, rucksacks, and ammunition, coupled with the stubborn terrain, made advancing more than a few hundred meters a significant accomplishment.

February through April are the hottest and most humid months in the Delta and the RSSZ. Temperatures usually soar above ninety-five degrees

Fahrenheit, and the humidity, especially under the forest canopies, hovers around 80 percent, making breathing difficult. The incidence of heat exhaustion increased with the sun's ascent into the afternoon sky. Much time was lost from each day's sweep while stopping to wait for squad members to recover from severe stomach and leg cramps.

In May, the monsoon rains began and there was a modest reduction in the overall daily temperature. The offset was that the daily rains caused the Rung Sat's thick, gluey mud to become more tenacious, gripping and holding fast to the legs of the lumbering troops. As the monsoon season progressed, streams, channels, and rivers backed up, flooding the rice paddies and much of the rest of the surrounding terrain. Each brief daily downpour caused the mangrove roots to become more slick and slippery, making the already-difficult footing impossible. Further, the depth of the mud in some places went from being waist deep to almost midchest level.

For one Detachment GOLF recon team, the mud in the southeast corner of Nhan Trach almost proved fatal. The four-man team had been fortunate enough to spot a VC camp in a wooded section bordered by a broad mudflat on its western side and by rice paddies to the south and east. The north side seemed to disappear into a vast, chokingly dense forest. After examining their options for approaching the camp unseen, it was decided that the best plan would be to cross the mudflat, staying close to its eastern edge. That section of the muddy expanse was dotted with clumps of vegetation just thick enough to offer an occasional area of concealment. It was far better than crawling across the openness of a rice paddy.

The team waited until just before midnight to begin its approach. Initially the going was tenuous due to the mud's fatiguing embrace, but even so, the team was making good time. When they were about a third of the way around the mudflat, the point man signaled that he was in trouble. Until then he had been moving through mud up to the middle of his thighs. But now he was waist deep and unable to move his legs at all. The other three men slowly moved in to help him, but as each man came closer he found himself in the same predicament. Soon all four of them were rocking their bodies back and forth, trying to break the mud's suction in order to free their legs and feet.

Their efforts went on for the next hour or so. There was no real problem yet, but that would change over the next few hours as daylight approached. If they were in the same position when the sun came up, they would surely be seen by the VC. But freeing themselves was beginning to look hopeless. Not only were their efforts exhausting them but they also seemed to be making them sink deeper into the ooze. They continued to look around on all sides for something solid to grip.

The point man had been trying to find a piece of wood to plunge down into the mud around his legs to break the suction. He did see a large piece of shattered nipa palm a short distance to his left, but it was just out of reach. He hit upon the idea of using his shotgun. First, he ejected all of its rounds and then jammed the weapon, butt first, into the mud flush up against his right leg. Over a span of twenty minutes he rocked the weapon back and forth around his leg while trying to twist his leg and foot. Little by little, he could feel his right foot and leg gradually break free of the mud's grip.

He then repeated that same laborious process around his left leg and foot, expending another twenty minutes or so in the effort. Once that side had also been loosened, he jammed his weapon, butt first, into the mud a few feet to the front and pulled hard. Eventually, after much effort, he was able to pull himself completely free of the mud's suction. Then he lay flat on his stomach to prevent his sinking back down into the ooze.

Even though he was exhausted, he did not take time to rest. Instead, he started to pull himself over the short distance to where palms and other vegetation bordered the mudflat. Once he made it to the firmer area, he caught his breath for a few seconds and then moved back a few feet until he was parallel to the SEAL who had been stuck just behind him. That man had also been using his weapon as an excavation tool and had managed to dig himself partially free. The point man reached out so that the other SEAL could grab his hand. After much pulling and digging, the second man was also free. The two SEALs then moved back to help their other two shipmates.

With everyone finally free, the team decided to move back to their former position. They were totally drained of energy and knew that they would not be able to carry out the recon without some sleep.

Of course, not all of the less-than-ideal encounters with the Rung Sat's muddy areas were of such a potentially perilous nature. In fact, a buddy of mine who was attached to Detachment GOLF in the early spring of 1967 told me about one situation that turned out to be downright comical.

He had been a member of a four-man recon team operating on the fringes of one of the rubber plantations located in the upper reaches of

Nhan Trach. The team members had been working the area for three days but had not turned up any significant signs of VC activity. Now they were heading out of the area to a nearby channel where they would extract via River Patrol Boat (PBR). When they were about fifteen meters from the channel, they came to a relatively open stretch of ground covered by only a sparse amount of vegetation. As was the case with most of the northern parts of the RSSZ, much of the soil was a blend of laterite clay and, of course, the ever-present sticky, gummy mud. The first to reach the open stretch was the point man, and he started across toward the near bank of the channel.

There is a strange thing about the area's peculiar mud-clay soil blend. Whenever it gets wet it becomes like a sliding board smeared with grease. The monsoon was in progress; it had been raining steadily for several hours. Unfortunately, the point man was well into the open area before he realized what he was getting into. The realization came when he took a step and suddenly found himself fighting to keep his footing and balance. First, his feet seemed to go in all directions at once, and within a few seconds he found himself flat on his back on the slick ground. He did not lie on the ground for very long. He made it back upright, but his feet immediately began slipping and sliding about, and a few seconds later he was down again, flat on his back.

The three other team members who had been watching the man's predicament were almost incapacitated by spasms of laughter. It took several minutes before they were able to finally control themselves enough so that they could move out across the slippery area to assist their fallen buddy. They did not realize their mistake until it was too late to do anything about it. All at once, all three men started slipping around, their feet churning madly, making them look like something out of a Saturday morning cartoon. Their feet moved wildly, giving them the appearance of running. But they were going nowhere fast, except down to the ground beside their already-fallen teammate, who was now the one convulsing with laughter.

All four of them continued trying for the next several minutes to get into a standing position. As soon as each one was successful in doing so, he would then attempt to gingerly inch his way across the slick surface. But as soon as one of them would take more than a step or two, his feet would again begin skittering about and he'd go crashing back down to the ground in a sprawl. Their efforts were made more difficult because the sight of each other's predicament made each man laugh hysterically.

Finally, after almost fifteen minutes of mud skating, the four SEALs pulled themselves together and shelved the idea of trying to walk out of the slick area. Instead, they lay flat out on their stomachs and crawled, or more accurately wormed their way across the ground to the surer footing near the bank of the channel. Once they had all reached the bank they again erupted with laughter, each recalling how silly they had looked in their idiotic ballet in the mud. When the PBR finally moved in to extract them, the crew shook their heads at the sight of four SEALs totally covered with mud, none of whom seemed able to stop grinning. The team did not find any evidence of enemy activity in the area, but they got a good laugh out of their comical excursion.

By June, it became evident that the VC were not disposed to engage the sizable U.S. force and had elected to remain in hiding. But the 1st Battalion troops did get to experience ongoing, close contact with other inhabitants of the swamp, such as the mosquitoes, leeches, and other critters of varying size and aggressive temperament.

Operation Lexington III came to an end before the end of June. The 1st Battalion was withdrawn and redeployed to Binh Long Province in III Corps. But its time spent in the RSSZ had satisfied MACV that conventional operations in the Rung Sat were ill-advised endeavors. They learned that the VC could have inflicted high casualties on the battalion, whose mobility had been severely restricted by the mud and matted vegetation. But they were just as convinced that the VC could not be allowed to use the region as a safe area. Since Detachment GOLF, along with the other units participating in Operation Game Warden, had enjoyed significant success against the Rung Sat Vietcong, MACV decided that their operations should be increased considerably.

3 MOBLIE RIVER FORCE

By the end of 1966, Detachment GOLF's operational platoon strength had been increased to more than a hundred men. At the beginning of 1967, SEAL Team Two's Detachment ALPHA and its operational platoons had arrived in Nha Be. Both detachments assigned several seven-man squads to duty with Operation Game Warden and its Mobile Riverine Force (MRF), headquartered initially at Vung Tau. The MRF's headquarters was later transferred to Dong Tam, a base set on the banks of the Dai River (the northernmost branch of the Mekong River), approximately five to six miles west of My Tho in the Mekong Delta. Dong Tam was literally created by the U.S. Navy's Seabees, who constructed it on sand and mud that they dredged from the river's bottom. For operations in the RSSZ, the MRF units and their support craft were based primarily at Nha Be.

Those SEALs who were temporarily assigned to the MRF were usually billeted aboard converted LSTs or LCUs (Landing Ship Tank and Landing Craft Utility), which served as barracks ships for the 2d Brigade (9th Infantry Division) troops. Although still attached to Detachments GOLF and ALPHA, the SEALs were temporarily placed under the command and control of the MRF, for whom they provided expert forward echelon services. The SEAL squads would establish listening posts, set ambushes, or perform recon sweeps along the Delta and RSSZ waterways, as well as ranging farther inland to perform the same tasks. When a VC hamlet, group of sampans, or ground unit of significant enough size had been located, the SEALs would then radio the MRF units or call in artillery or air strikes by helicopter gunships. If the MRF units were called on they would be ferried to the hot area aboard LCM-6s, to which they would have transferred prior to the SEAL departure.

Both Task Forces (TF) 116 and 117 were capable of providing almost unlimited support to the MRF units (although TF 117 was the main arm of the MRF operations) and those SEALs operating in the Delta and RSSZ, with a wide variety of vessels. Modified LSTs and LCUs served as self-propelled barracks/supply ships (APB). They also were equipped with steel platforms, converting them to mobile helipads and docking facilities for the many LCM-6s, which functioned as armored troop carriers (ATCs). Originally, there were four of the APBs (USS *Colleton,* USS *Benewah,* USS *Mercer,* and USS *Nueces*) that served as floating bases for the various sections of the MRF. By 1968 only the *Benewah* and the *Colleton* remained on station with the MRF.

The LCM-6s, ranging from fifty to about sixty-five feet in overall length, proved to be highly versatile craft. They passed through a number of permutations, resulting in an impressive array of combat capabilities. Those various conversions found the landing craft functioning not only as ATCs but also as artillery barges, minesweepers, medical triaging facilities, and Command and Control Boats (CCBs). Although those vessels all derived from the same basic LCM-6 structure, they differed greatly in the type of armor, firepower, or other specific structural modifications.

For example, some vessels designated for use as ATCs were equipped with four .50-caliber machine guns and two to four 40mm automatic grenade launchers. Other ATCs utilized one or two 20mm cannons in place of one or more of the .50s. Many ATCs were equipped with steel landing platforms and barrels of helicopter fuel, just as all of the barracks ships were, thereby establishing them as mobile helipads. The helipads were advantageous in extending the range of helicopters serving in operational support of the MRF as gunships or as medevacs. In medevac situations, the choppers could off-load wounded onto the platform of the ATC and then immediately take off again to pick up more casualties. This capability decreased the lag time between medevac missions, greatly increasing the probability of casualty survival.

The vessels used by TF 116 and TF 117 were inland waterway versions of oceangoing armadas. In fact, both task forces came to be called the

Brown Water Navy, because the inland waterways were decidedly brown. Just as oceangoing navies use convoys consisting of troop transports, supply ships, and other support vessels that deploy to an area of operations, such was the case with the vessels of TF 116 and TF 117. I will not provide the technical aspects of all of the various MRF vessels here, since such information can be found in the Glossary. However, there are two specific support vessels that should be described in detail because they were used extensively on all of the waterways of the Southeast Asian theater of operations.

The two types of support craft that proved to be of extreme value to the mission of the MRF were the River Patrol Boats (PBRs) and the Inshore Fast Patrol Craft (PCF, otherwise known as Swift boats). Both vessel types relied on speed as well as specific weaponry in fulfilling various missions, ranging from ambush reactions to the support of convoys. The PBRs have been justly referred to as the true workhorses of the MRF. There were very few operations involving either TF 116 or TF 117 in which the PBRs did not play a significant role. They were thirty-two feet long and were powered by twin diesel water jet engines capable of generating speeds of twenty to twenty-five knots. The earlier PBRs, the Mark I variety, were fiberglass hulled and a little slower than the later Mark II aluminum-hulled model. Their armament included a twin .50-caliber machine gun mount forward and a single .50 mounted aft. The PBRs also carried 40mm automatic grenade launchers and occasionally a 60mm mortar. An obvious advantage of those specific weapons was that they enabled the four- to five-man crew of each vessel to generate a high volume of extremely accurate fire while attacking a target at full throttle.

But the fifty-foot-long, all-metal Swift boats could also generate an impressive display of speed coupled with significant firepower. Those vessels deserved to be called Swift due to their ability to reach speeds of twenty-five to twenty-eight knots. Their armament consisted of three .50-caliber machine guns and one 81mm mortar, which were deployed in a rather unique fashion. Two of the .50s were in a twin mount atop the pilot house. The third .50 was located in the Swift's aft section, mounted atop the mortar. The fact that the mortar was mounted horizontally made it possible for the .50 to sit astride it, piggyback style. This odd-looking system proved to be quite formidable in dealing with the VC's armored riverine and oceangoing vessels, sampans, junks, and shore emplacements. It permitted the piggybacked .50 to maintain a rapid rate of fire (along with the twin mount atop the pilothouse), while the "muzzle-loaded" direct-fire 81mm mortar spit out High Explosive (HE), White Phosphorus (WP), or antipersonnel rounds filled with more than a thousand darts called flechettes.

The speed, firepower, and maneuverability of the PBRs and the Swift boats made them ideal not only for use by the MRF but also for many SEAL operations. They could get SEAL ambush/recon teams into almost any size waterway and do so at startling rates of speed. If a team needed fire support, both vessels could be relied on to lay down enough fire to discourage even the most determined VC unit from staying in range for too long. And the crews of these vessels were gritty enough to do whatever was necessary to get their craft into a hot area, extract a pinned-down team, and then get out of the hot spot, usually before an enemy force could maximize any advantage they may have had.

A typical example of how effective such support could be in extracting teams from precarious predicaments occurred in the fall of 1967. A Detachment ALPHA seven-man ambush team had been working a canal complex a few miles east of Cai Lai in the Mekong Delta. They were sent into the area in advance of a sweep operation the MRF planned to conduct in that sector the following day. A VC battalion was known to be somewhere in the area, and the team's task was to recon the canal approach to locate and knock out any VC bunkers. If the bunkers were not taken out before the MRF ATCs made their approach, the vessels would be extremely vulnerable to enemy rocket, mortar, or recoilless rifle fire from those positions.

Not long after inserting, the team located five bunkers along a narrow canal that made an acute bend to the right. Two of the bunkers were located on one side of the canal just below the bend; the remaining three were above the bend, two on one side and one on the other. Although it was near midnight, raining, and about as dark as it could get, the team could easily see the pale light from carbide lamps burning in all five bunkers. That meant the bunkers were occupied. But they still had to determine how to take out all five without letting any occupants escape. They would also have to take care to eliminate each bunker without letting the remaining bunkers know what was happening. And, of course, they would have to prevent any unwanted attention from other VC forces in the area before accomplishing their mission.

The team was able to silently eliminate the occupants of the two bunkers situated below the canal's bend in short time and without difficulty. But as they made their way toward the remaining three bunkers, they suddenly came under intense fire from just ahead as well as from the opposite side of the canal. The team returned fire and withdrew back toward the first two bunkers. As they did, the enemy fire not only increased dramatically, but the team also began taking heavy automatic weapons fire from the rear as they reached the nearest bunker. Once there, they radioed for immediate extraction and were advised that two nearby PBRs were already en route. The team would have preferred to have tried to make it to a more secure extraction point, but they were surrounded and had nowhere else to go.

It took only a few minutes for the first PBR to move far enough up the canal that the crew could see the raging firefight. They did not have to guess where the team had taken cover because the bunker was now under fire from all sides. As the patrol boat raced up, it began to rake the far side of the canal with fire from all three of its .50-caliber machine guns, as well as lobbing in rounds from the mortar. The vessel came under fire from a position just south of the bunker on the opposite side of the canal. At the same moment the second PBR raced into the fray, its own machine guns spraying the VC position south of the bunker. When both PBR crews put up illumination flares, scores of VC could be clearly seen racing about in the eerily shifting shadows, trying to find better cover.

The second PBR glided over to the near bank where the team was holed up in the bunker. As it swung in close enough, the seven men came out of the bunker and moved toward the vessel, still keeping up a steady stream of fire directed at the closest enemy positions. Four of the SEALs had been wounded during the brief time they had spent in the bunker, but they were still able to move on their own to the PBR. It did not take long for them all to scramble aboard; then both vessels wheeled about and raced out of the kill zone at full throttle. In addition to the four wounded SEALs, two crewmen aboard the first PBR and one aboard the other were hit. Fortunately, none of the wounds were too serious, and everyone aboard both boats could savor their good fortune. Although it was assumed that VC casualties had been significant, there had been no way to confirm the exact nature or numbers.

The MRF's wide array of vessels and the combat ground forces they carried, coupled with the SEAL recon and ambush squads assigned to them, had an immediate impact on the VC presence in the Delta and the

RSSZ. Since the communist vessels were obviously no match for the MRF's armada, they had to concede control of the waterways to U.S. forces. The dusk-to-dawn curfew enforced by Operation Game Warden units quickly proved effective in restricting the VC's ability to freely use the rivers, channels, and canals for troop transport, resupply operations, harassment, and extortion of river traffic. Now they would have to be content with trying to sneak past the MRF's support craft at night.

But even the murky shroud of night could not guarantee that an insurgent sampan, carrying tax collectors, sappers, or ammunition or other supplies, would successfully reach its destination. In fact, night movement soon came to be as risky as daytime excursions had already proven to be. So, the ongoing interdiction of Vietcong river traffic, coupled with the successful sweeping and clearing of mines from the Delta and RSSZ waterways, allowed greater concentration to be turned toward land operations. It also forced the VC into more overland movement and to rely more heavily on indigenous sources of food. That in turn resulted in ever-increasing amounts of reliable intelligence being supplied by the neighboring populace.

In late 1967 the residents of several villages just south of Moc Hoa, located in the northern part of the Mekong Delta, began to provide a stream of reports regarding VC activity in the area. For almost a full month, squads of VC had been raiding the villages, depleting their food stores and taking some of the young men as "volunteers" for construction work at a nearby fortified hamlet. The volunteers were put to work digging bunkers and cutting palm fronds to be used as camouflage for various structures. A few of the young villagers were also pressed to join the ranks of the VC as line soldiers. Some of those who refused were taken back to their villages and publicly executed, as a deterrent to anyone else who might think of refusing the VC's offer to join The Cause.

A Detachment ALPHA seven-man recon/ambush team, attached to the MRF, was sent into the area, inserting several hundred meters north of their objective just after midnight. By an hour before first light they had made their way south and had set up a primary observation post within ten meters of the VC hamlet. They spent a total of seventy-two hours observing the hamlet and searching the surrounding terrain. What they observed was that the encampment supported a sizable force of at least two full VC companies and seemed to be undergoing active expansion. In the area surrounding the hamlet the team also noted more than a dozen existing bunkers and evidence of a like number of others under construction. In a particularly dense section of foliage a short distance east of the hamlet, the team located a cluster of three well-hidden supply hootches.

During their recon of the surrounding terrain the team also noted that there were five main trails leading from the camp, two of which led to the canal less than thirty meters west of the hamlet. At the end of those two trails the team noted a large number of sampans, all thoroughly camouflaged with palm fronds. North of where the sampans were beached, a narrow stream could be seen branching off the canal to the east through dense overhang. They also noted that much of the terrain surrounding the hamlet, especially along all the trails, was heavily booby-trapped.

As the team finally exited the area en route to its riverine extraction point, sometime after 2100 on their final night in the area, they saw at least thirty VC making their way along one of the trails toward the hamlet. The VC were traveling in small groups of three or four, all of them well armed. Now and then a group could be seen carrying makeshift litters piled high with bundles of clothing, fresh produce, weapons, and ammunition. At least one group was carrying an 82mm mortar. From the team's exit route near the canal, they observed other groups of VC approaching the hamlet in sampans. Two or three VC were aboard each one, as well as many large bundles or boxes piled in each boat's exposed well space. Adding that to all of the other observations made by the team during their recon suggested that the hamlet, along with its surrounding terrain, was being used as a battalion staging area.

The team reported their observations upon returning to the MRF's floating base. They paid special attention to the locations of bunkers, booby-trapped trail approaches, VC sampans, and the nearby obscured stream entrance, since it would surely be used by the hamlet's personnel as an escape route in the face of an attack by Allied forces. Based on the data provided by the team, the MRF deployed several companies to the area via choppers and ATCs.

As the companies approached, MRF artillery barges and helicopter gunships pounded the hamlet, inducing the VC to head for cover around the hamlet and the bunkers. The airlifted companies were then dropped off at a landing zone north of the hamlet, from which they made a big show of driving overland toward the VC positions. As they did, the remaining companies were off-loaded from the ATCs along the canal, a little south of the hamlet, to act as a blocking force. The MRF's quick action resulted in the VC being caught off guard. Although a significant number did manage to escape (the VC's knack for escaping from what seemed to be escapeproof situations would have made Harry Houdini envious), a subsequent body count suggested that the battalion had been essentially decimated.

The Delta and RSSZ had provided many ideal settings for the VC to establish and maintain sizable strongholds for their forces. Most such strongholds had lasted because they were located in areas that prevented rapid troop deployment. In the Delta area, some of the most formidable strongholds were situated in the following locations: the region northwest of My Tho, much of the terrain in and around the Plain of Reeds, a section in Go Cong Province referred to as the Coconut Grove, the U Minh Forest, a large section in Sa Dec Province, the Seven Mountains area in Chau Doc Province, and the countryside surrounding Ben Tre. Other important VC strongholds had been maintained for years in the Can Giuoc District of Long An Province, just south of Saigon, as well as in portions of both Phuoc Thuy Province and Bien Hoa Province. And, of course, most of the RSSZ in Gia Dinh Province had served as a long-term haven for large contingents of VC forces.

In all of these areas, a host of VC battalions had established a large number of well-fortified hamlets, complete with extensive bunker complexes, munitions factories, a few tunnels, and even R and R areas. These VC units felt so secure in those regions that they operated quite openly since 1964. ARVN or other Allied units venturing into those areas had experienced either marginal success against the resident VC or, more often than not, had suffered many casualties with nothing of significance to show for them. The reason for the VC's successes against Allied units was because the Allies could not deploy their units and superior firepower rapidly enough to prevent the enemy from melting into the countryside. The joint MRF/SEAL operations, however, drastically changed the situation, beginning in the late spring and early summer of 1967.

In each Area of Operation (AO), the tactics of the joint operational forces followed a similar approach. A SEAL recon/ambush team would be apprised of an area of probable VC activity and provided with whatever fresh intelligence was available, such as recent enemy movements observed by indigenous personnel. The team would examine any available aerial photos and, when applicable, hydrographic charts. Following the briefing session, the team would saddle up and prepare for deployment to the AO, typically via PBR or chopper in the late night or extreme early morning hours. Following insertion into the AO, the team would begin the sweep, being careful about leaving signs of their own presence as they went about searching for evidence of VC activity.

At about the same time that the recon team would have departed, an appropriate number of companies or battalions of MRF troops would begin transferring from the barracks ships to the ATCs. The ATCs would then get under way to any one of several beaches chosen as the most advantageous landing areas. This movement would have been coordinated with the SEAL recon team's sweep of the AO. If the prospects for significant contact were felt to be promising, Monitor Boats (MONs), Assault Support Patrol Boats (ASPBs), or artillery barges would also accompany the ATCs to the preassigned landing areas.

The fact that the MRF units were under way did not ensure that they would actually be landed in support of the SEAL recon team even if the recon team made contact. SEAL units, whether engaging in their own operations or in support of the MRF, were allowed a great degree of operational latitude in the field. If they sighted a small enemy force, they often would not make contact in order to observe the unit hoping that it might eventually rendezvous with a much larger unit, or perhaps lead them to a base camp. The recon unit would not be reluctant to pounce on small units of VC (squads or even platoons on occasion) if that unit was thought to be of great value (couriers, tax collectors, security for operations officers or intelligence/cell officials).

During the late summer of 1967 the MRF received a number of reports from a village in the northeastern part of the RSSZ regarding possible VC activity in the area. The VC were thought to be operating out of a heavily forested section north of the village. On at least two different occasions MRF units conducted sweeps through the forest, but the sweeps were not very productive. The only thing they managed to find on the first occasion was an abandoned hamlet and a few areas where footprints along some stream banks suggested that several people had recently passed through. The second sweep was only slightly more rewarding, netting two small caches of rice. Nothing of greater significance could be found to indicate that the VC were actively using the area. A SEAL ambush team was even inserted into the area to carry out a two- to three-day surveillance, but nothing came of it.

It was decided, however, that a second ambush team should be deployed to check out another smaller but equally dense section of forest southeast of the village. That piece of terrain sat on the edge of a wide expanse of mangrove swamp and had a number of narrow but navigable streams coursing through it. Actually, the characteristics of that smaller section of forest made it a much more likely prospect for VC activity than the more northerly section. But for unknown reasons no reports had ever come in from the nearby village about that area.

The seven-man ambush team was inserted by PBR late at night on the western perimeter of the small forest. The team members decided to head inland a short distance before paralleling the perimeter to the south and then toward the east. Despite the fact that the wooded area was densely vegetated, the going was surprisingly easy; it took less than two hours for them to reach the eastern side. Just as they turned north they caught a whiff of smoke and then saw the soft glow of firelight among the trees a little more than twenty meters off to their left. As they moved in the direction of the light, they came on a stream and heard voices a short distance ahead of them. While the rest of the team held position, the point man moved up to scope out the situation. After going only a short distance he could see two men a few meters ahead unloading a sampan along the stream bank. Not much farther on were two hootches bathed in the light of a nearby campfire.

The point man moved back to report his find to the rest of the team. They all moved forward to check the situation and noted a second sampan beached not far from where the two men were still unloading the first one. A moment later two more men exited one of the hootches and trotted down to join the first two at the stream. It was a fair bet that the team had found some VC, but they were not completely sure since they had yet to see any armed people. The question became moot a moment later when one of the four men reached into the sampan's open deck area and picked up a rocket-propelled grenade launcher. Now there was no doubt that the four men up ahead, as well as any others in the two hootches, were VC, since peaceful civilians had very little need for grenade launchers late at night.

The team leader assumed there might be at most another three or four VC nearby. He decided that the team would take down the camp and its occupants, attempting to capture a live prisoner or two in the process but without undue risk to any team member. So when two VC left the sampans carrying armfuls of supplies to the hootches, three SEALs moved toward the remaining two VC to take them captive or eliminate them quietly. The rest of the team spread out in order to provide covering fire for the capture team should anything go wrong. That was important, because if they were spotted in the open, they would make easy targets for even the worst marksman.

It took only a few minutes for the capture team to reach the two VC and pounce on them. Unfortunately, one of the VC managed to wriggle free and started running toward the hootches, shouting to his comrades to flee. Almost immediately two VC emerged from one hootch while a third was seen silhouetted in the structure's doorway. All three were armed and began firing on the three SEALs, who had already dropped to the ground beside one of the sampans. Two of them returned fire while the other secured his still-struggling prisoner. The rest of the team also took the two hootches under fire, killing two of the VC with their initial bursts. The VC who had been in the doorway continued to fire on the SEALs by the sampans despite the fact that the team's heavy concentration of fire was ripping the hootch to shreds. Then without warning, the hootch suddenly exploded, killing the VC. That explosion was quickly followed by a second one and then a third before things quieted again.

Immediate interrogation of the prisoner confirmed that the hootch had been filled with ammunition and some TNT (the latter was to be used to fashion grenades and mines). The prisoner also said that he and his companions were from the nearby village whose chief had been furnishing the reports about VC activity in the forested area to the north. As it turned out, the prisoner was the chief's son, and one of the two dead VC near the hootch was his brother-in-law. The other dead VC lying on the ground near the disintegrated hootch was a friend. The VC who had been blown up in the explosions was the prisoner's father, the same village chief who was a combination supply officer/tax collector for the local VC. The camp served as a central supply area, which he kept well stocked when he was not busy keeping track of MRF activity in the area.

When the joint MRF/SEAL operations progressed more typically, the MRF units had ample opportunity to engage the enemy. When a SEAL recon team located a VC unit of significant size or, even better, located a fortified VC hamlet, the Radiotelephone Operator (RTO) would immediately relay the coordinates of the sighting to the task force CCB. The data would, in turn, be relayed to the ATCs along with one or more landing area designations. The recon team would then deploy to hinder any possible avenues of escape. From their positions they could also call in air strikes (by both fixed-wing aircraft and helicopter gunships) and select landing zones for choppers airlifting reinforcements into the fray from the ATC helipads. Guarding those potential avenues of retreat often resulted in the capture of higher-echelon VC attempting to flee the scene.

As previously mentioned, these operations were extremely effective in bringing the conflict solidly into the VC's supposedly secure areas within the Delta and the RSSZ. No longer could the VC launch attacks and consistently melt back into the swamps, jungles, and villages, suffering only minimal casualties. They still had their most valuable weapon—an uncanny ability to move their forces in and out of battle more rapidly than conventional forces could react—but now that weapon was being utilized against them by the SEALs and the MRF. They could no longer rely on the hostile conditions of the Delta and the RSSZ frustrating and eventually halting sweeps of their AOs by lumbering infantry companies or battalions encumbered by heavy supplies and artillery pieces.

The sweeps were now being carried out as they should always have been. Efficiently and expeditiously using small ambush/recon teams to locate the enemy and then bringing in well-rested troops greatly enhanced the probabilities of engaging the enemy before they could melt away. With joint SEAL/MRF operations, SEALs proved that small, well-trained recon teams were vital to the success of sweeps conducted in the Delta. But as the operations continued and expanded, 9th Infantry Division Ranger Long Range Reconnaissance Patrol (LRRP) units took an ever-increasing role in performing those recon sweeps. The intelligence developed by such operations made the MRF's larger-scale conventional sweeps much more effective. As such, the MRF's dance card filled up rapidly with its units operating throughout wide sections of the Delta and RSSZ on a fairly constant basis.

The efficiency of these operations soon took on a typical and devastating pattern in their effect on the resident VC forces because the MRF units could close with them before an effective retreat could get organized. When a retreat by the VC did occur, serious casualties could still be inflicted on the enemy force by the accurate and deadly fire provided by 105mm howitzers, 81mm mortars, and 20mm cannons aboard the artillery barges. And helicopter gunships ranging out from Vung Tau,

Rach Gia, Binh Thuy, Dong Tam, and other bases, as well as from the mobile pads aboard some of the ATCs, could maintain surveillance of the retreating VC while utilizing their own weapons to harass and possibly decimate them.

From time to time, a fleeing VC force was allowed to retreat without drawing sustained artillery fire, so that a SEAL recon team could insert into the AO and trail the withdrawing enemy back to its base camp. Upon arriving, the team would determine if the VC force was a lone local unit such as a squad, platoon, or company, acting on its own initiative, or if it were part of a larger force such as a battalion, using the base camp as a staging area. Such observations would allow for the greatest number of VC and their material to be contained in one area. An MRF reaction force could then deploy to the area and get on line before the VC could disperse and escape.

These tactics did not immediately result in large numbers of VC casualties but did result in an immediate and devastating impact on the collective VC psyche in the IV Corps Tactical Zone (IV CTZ). As guerrillas, the VC knew that casualties, even when the numbers occasionally became extensive, were an acceptable risk in attaining victory. To them, the conflict was being waged on a higher plane, well above such trivial considerations as death or injury. That had been the philosophy against the Saigon government from the very beginning, just as it had been against the French, the Japanese, and the Chinese before that.

4 LIFE WITH CHARLIE

The significant increase in SEAL activities throughout the Southeast Asian theater of operations seemed to rattle the VC and put them on edge. The VC had been used to controlling the light and the shadows. They had always been the guerrillas, the bogeymen who sprang from the darkness bringing mayhem, death, destruction, and, most of all, fear to an enemy before evaporating into nothingness. More often than not, VC visits took place with no visible evidence of their coming or going, except for the wounded and dead they left behind. It had been this way for many years, especially in much of the IV CTZ. That changed, however, because the VC were no longer the only guerrillas operating in the shadows.

Since the earliest days of the conflict, ARVN and U.S. conventional units had tried to employ guerrilla tactics against the VC in parts of the IV CTZ at various times. These had met with little or no success because the members of Allied guerrilla units were typically part-timers, drawn from the ranks of line companies and ignorant of the fine points of guerrilla tactics. Their VC opponents were not only lifelong residents of the area but also seasoned veterans for whom being guerrillas was a way of life and not a case of on-the-job training. Aside from some U.S. Special Forces and Ranger units and their ARVN Ranger counterparts, the other

Allied "guerrilla" efforts were quickly restricted to night ambush activities and routine perimeter patrols.

Although the U.S. Special Forces and Rangers had a good deal of success in their guerrilla/counterguerrilla operations, these operations had been conducted primarily in the other CTZs. Their activities in the IV CTZ had thus far been restricted to the westernmost sections of the Delta along the Cambodian border. Thus the activities of the MRF and its Ranger units posed a sudden problem for the resident VC because it meant that a full-time, proficient, Allied guerrilla force would be capable of operating more extensively throughout the IV CTZ. But it was the activities of SEAL recon/ambush teams in support of the MRF, as well as in support of their own operations throughout the Delta and RSSZ, that raised the anxieties of the local VC units to new heights.

One such anxiety was the ability of SEAL units to operate so freely in the heart of VC territory. Not only could SEAL recon teams range widely throughout VC AOs but they did so without leaving much evidence of their presence. More often than not, the only evidence of SEAL presence would be the casualties inflicted on VC units, the destruction of enemy material, or the ever-increasing numbers of VC personnel captured. Despite the degree of activity or the extent of damage inflicted on enemy personnel or equipment, no tracks or other sign were left behind to indicate from which direction the SEALs had come or which direction they had taken in leaving the scene.

The reason for the SEAL successes in Vietnam was due to their ability to appreciate the obvious advantages of the VC's guerrilla tactics and to adopt many of those tactics as their own. Obviously, each SEAL had undergone training in guerrilla tactics prior to rotating to the Republic of Vietnam for duty. And although that training served them well, it proved to be more of a foundation on which the SEALs could refine their skills by observing and adopting those VC tactics that had stood the test of time. The SEAL teams understood that the successful warrior is the one who realizes that adaptation, not ego, is the secret to victory. Much time, therefore, was spent in digesting the VC approach to guerrilla warfare.

Thus far, I have referred to mobility as an integral part of the VC's guerrilla campaigns. Without such mobility the VC would have been defeated with very little fanfare. That mobility proved to be the equalizer in nullifying the Allies' superior firepower and logistical capabilities. It enabled VC units to control wide areas of terrain with small units, keeping Allied units off balance and guessing where they would move next. More importantly, it maximized the effectiveness of the VC's automatic weapons, of varying caliber and size, as well as their use of light artillery.

Automatic weapons were the very cornerstones of most VC units. Such weapons helped to narrow the gulf between their lack of military sophistication and the Allies' vast array of high-tech armaments and superior numbers of field forces. This was especially true in the IV CTZ, where the difficult terrain became an important adjunct to every VC operation, slowing and frustrating Allied units that attempted to pursue the VC into their strongholds. Tanks, armored personnel carriers, and heavy weapons, which provided U.S. and ARVN units with great superiority on firm ground, served only to permit the mud and undergrowth to hold the pursuers in one location. That, of course, allowed the lighter and mobile VC units to pounce on their stationary and exposed foes, ripping into their ranks with high-explosive rounds from recoilless rifles, rocket-propelled grenade launchers, and mortars, augmented by intensely accurate fire from their automatic weapons.

Such scenarios were what the local VC worked hardest to achieve: it meant that they would be confronting their Allied counterparts on an equal basis. This was important not only because the Allies' firepower was vastly superior but also because the VC rarely operated in numbers close to the size of those they would be attacking. Sustained, large-scale engagements were not integral parts of the VC approach to warfare, unless the probabilities for success were extremely high. For them, one or two squads of men or women employing well-practiced tactics of bait, attack, and withdraw were much more efficient and far less foolhardy than sustained engagements against superior forces. And fighting from the shadows, never letting the victim get a good look at who or how many were engaged in the attack, generated fear in the mind of the victim, destroying his effectiveness and sapping his will to fight.

The VC's heavy reliance on automatic weapons and light artillery was also due in large part to basic logistical considerations. Even before the successful interdiction of VC maritime supply activities, the main means of getting supplies to their final destination, the frontline units, was by sampan, bicycle, or porter. (The bikes had been specially modified and reinforced for transport work.) Therefore, consideration was given to the load-bearing capabilities of each vehicle or each porter. This typically translated to each bicycle being limited to 100 to 150 pounds of material and each porter being limited to 50 to 75 pounds of gear. Since sampans vary in size, cargo capacities depended on the sizes and number of sampans available. Even so, the load-bearing potential of even the larger sampans meant that payloads would never be considered significant by Allied logistical standards.

Most VC armaments were either manufactured by communist bloc countries or were copies of such weapons. Some of the more favored Soviet manufactured pieces were the Simonov carbine (SKS), the famous Avtomat Kalashnikovas assault rifle (AK-47), and its Chinese versions, the Type 56 and the Type 56-1. Those weapons were preferred by communist forces because they were lightweight and easily maintained in the field even under the most adverse conditions, and all fired 7.62mm ammunition. This last factor was important because 7.62mm ammo was in great supply in Vietnam and the rest of Southeast Asia.

Light and heavy machine guns were also of critical importance to the VC approach to warfare. Often the type and caliber of a machine gun being used by a particular VC unit gave SEAL recon teams information on that unit's size and probable operational intent. Light machine guns were better suited for the hit-and-run, harassing-type tactics employed by most VC units, whereas the VC's heavy machine guns (comparable to the Browning .50-caliber machine guns utilized by U.S. forces) were far too cumbersome for hit-and-run operations because they were crew-served weapons. The VC usually reserved their heavy machine guns for use as antivehicle or antiaircraft weapons or against lighter armored MRF craft.

Heavy machine guns were most often used by company- or battalion-strength VC units, not only in their perimeter defenses but also during large-scale assaults against Allied positions. Now and then, a VC squad-level unit would take a heavy machine gun into the field, but doing so entailed some risk. For example, a squad having to make a hasty retreat from pursuing Allied forces might be forced to dump the weapon. Such a cumbersome piece could slow them down enough to result in their capture or even death. Since such weapons were far too hard to come by, they seldom ran the risk of losing one during an operation unless there were sufficient potential benefits.

The same considerations were used by the VC in their choice of field artillery pieces. Although a wide variety of mortars, recoilless rifles, and rocket launchers were available to them (albeit on a very limited basis), they usually opted for weapons that provided firepower without restricting a unit's mobility. They found that the very best weapons for day-to-day use in the field were Rocket-Propelled Grenade Launchers (the RPG-2 and the RPG-7). The RPG-7 was the one used most often, not only because it was accurate but also because it fired the B-40 rocket which could pierce ten to twelve inches of armor at ranges of four-hundred to five-hundred meters. They were used extensively against tanks, Armored Personnel Carriers (APCs), all varieties of riverine craft, and infantry. The accuracy and power of the RPG-7 made it one of the most feared weapons in the VC arsenal.

The VC's larger rockets and heavy mortars had greater range, but they were not very accurate. Therefore, they were used primarily for either harassment and interdiction or to pound large installations, such as fire-bases, from long range to remind the Allies that Charlie was still around. However, long-range fire was not of great importance to the VC in the RSSZ and the IV CTZ (Mekong Delta) because their preferred tactic was to fight out of what is known as a "hug." This required that they engage the enemy at close quarters and maintain that close contact throughout the engagement. Such a maneuver was key to the VC's tactics because it neutralized the Allied forces' ability to use artillery against them. In this case artillery fire could not be used without risking Allied casualties from friendly fire.

I have purposely kept this discussion concerning VC weapons very general for two reasons. First, a more detailed listing of the more commonly used VC and Allied weapons is provided in the Glossary. Second, I wanted only to provide a little insight into the VC's approach to weaponry, to enable the reader to better appreciate how SEAL recon teams used such knowledge. Knowing the type of weapons used or stockpiled by VC units could indicate whether they were small units (squads, platoons) intent on making brief raids or larger units (companies, battalions) with larger ambitions. Let's look at a couple of brief examples.

During the heavy monsoon rains of late July 1967, a seven-man recon team was working its way through a particularly mucky section of the northern Rung Sat. It was early in the evening when they came on two hootches on a small island. They searched them and found that one contained only a few articles of peasant-type clothing and a couple of lanterns; the other contained several metal boxes of ammunition. Some of these held a few hundred rounds of 7.62mm ammunition, probably for AK-47s. The remaining boxes contained belts of 12.7mm ammunition (the communist version of .50-caliber ammunition). Also, there was one 57mm recoilless rifle without any rounds.

The team decided to set up an ambush a short distance from the two structures. Even though it was obvious that this was not an encampment, it was just as obvious that it was some sort of supply cache. The ammunition and recoilless rifle, as well as the clothing found in the first hootch, did not appear to have been left there for very long. In fact, all of the items seemed to have been in place for less than a week. If the team were lucky, someone would come along to either pick up the clothing and munitions or to bring more items to the stockpile. As it turned out, they did not have to wait very long.

About two hours after dark, a sampan approached the island and nosed up onto the beach. Two men and a woman hopped ashore and headed straight toward the concealed hootches. Just as they reached the nearest hootch they were pounced on by five of the SEALs. Although all three were unarmed and initially denied being insurgents, one of the men eventually admitted that he and his companions were VC. He also indicated that the island was indeed being used as a temporary supply dump and that a second dump was located inland, four miles to the east. Further vigorous interrogation of all three prisoners revealed that they were members of a VC company operating out of a fortified hamlet only two miles south of the island.

Acting on this information, MRF units conducted a series of sweeps through the fortified hamlet and the area surrounding the second supply dump. A search of the supply dump resulted in the capture of one ton of rice, several thousand rounds of 7.62mm ammunition, and several boxes of crude but effective locally manufactured fragmentation grenades. Unfortunately, the sweep through the hamlet and its immediate surroundings was not quite as productive. Somehow the hamlet's inhabitants must have learned of the MRF's intentions and had made a hasty retreat. All that was left behind were some pigs. Two freshwater wells were found nearby. Less than a week later, however, a second MRF sweep through an area just north of the hamlet resulted in heavy contact with what turned out to be that same elusive VC company. Although the contact was brief and the bulk of the VC managed to disappear into the nearby mangrove swamp, at least five VC were killed and their AK-47s captured. An added bonus was that one of the VC company's heavy machine guns was discovered in a sampan that was poorly hidden along a stream bank.

A second situation took place during November 1967 in an area west of My Tho in the Mekong Delta. A seven-man ambush team was sent into an area near one of the large canals where someone had recently fired on two PBRs and a helicopter. Their crews all agreed that the weapons used in the three instances were .50-caliber-type machine guns. In each instance only a few rounds had been fired. In the attack on one of the PBRs, one B-40 rocket had narrowly missed hitting the vessel's cabin area. Unfortunately, all three sniper attacks had come along a stretch of the canal where the overhanging tree canopy was especially heavy. None of the crews ever saw the positions from which the rounds had been fired.

The ambush team carefully combed through the terrain on the western side of the canal, the general area from which the sniper(s) had fired. Because of the thick, tangled expanse of undergrowth, the going was quite tedious, but after approximately two hours they came across an area well back under the tree canopy, behind a thick screen of young but tall bamboo. The spot was five feet higher than the level of the canal bank and commanded a sweeping view of the waterway. Behind the screen the team found a patch of tall grass flattened as if several people had been sitting or lying there for a long time. In the middle of the flattened grass, the team found three spent 12.7mm (essentially .50-caliber) shell casings. Obviously this was one of the spots from which snipers had fired.

The team found several sets of footprints along a trail farther back under the tree canopy. They followed the trail as it swung around to the east, eventually ending at the bank of the canal some twenty to thirty meters above the spot where the shell casings had been found. The deep impressions in the mud suggested that the snipers had exited the area in a sampan. Although there was no way to determine the direction the sampan had gone, the team did not feel discouraged because the snipers had already come back to the area four times. Perhaps they were feeling cocky and would return to take one more crack at another PBR or chopper. With that in mind, the team went back and set up ambush positions near the area of flattened grass.

A few hours after dark that night, the team heard the faint purr of a distant outboard motor. A short while later they heard voices and plodding footsteps approaching the ambush site. As the VC reached the flattened grassy spot, a SEAL put up an illumination flare, which revealed four VC frozen with fear in the eerie, shifting light. Before the VC could react, the team opened up on them with short but deadly bursts. The ambush proved effective, resulting in two VC KIAs, two moderately wounded prisoners, one 12.7mm heavy machine gun, and a few belts of ammunition. Interrogation revealed that they were a sapper team attached to a VC battalion located less than a mile west of the ambush site. That intelligence was then passed on to the MRF, which launched a series of sweeps against the battalion and inflicted heavy casualties on them.

Although committed to guerrilla tactics, SEAL detachments also relied heavily on weapons that, although lightweight and easily maintained, did not skimp on firepower. Like the guerrillas, SEALs made extensive use of automatic weapons and light artillery, which allowed squad-sized units to attack or counterattack with the authority of a platoon or company. Such weapons allowed SEAL recon/ambush teams to operate as easily and efficiently as the VC did in the difficult and exhausting Delta and RSSZ conditions. A few weapons directly influenced the success of SEAL operations.

Automatic weapons typically utilized by in-country SEALs covered a broad spectrum. The M16 was probably the most widely used because it was highly reliable and lightweight and fired the plentiful Allied 5.56mm round. One of the obvious advantages in using 5.56mm weapons was that ammunition was readily available from U.S., Australian, ARVN, or even Korean units in the field. Even so, SEAL personnel did not restrict themselves to using only 5.56mm weapons.

Proven reliability was an important criterion in the SEALs' selection of armament. Since U.S. units in the Pacific theater during World War II had enjoyed great success with .45-caliber automatic weapons, such as the M3A1 "Grease Gun" and the Thompson M1A1 submachine gun, some SEALs elected to use them as personal weapons. Frequently used 9mm automatics were the Swedish K-40, the French MAT-49s, and the Smith & Wesson Model 76. A few SEALs opted for the Belgian L1A1 FN 7.62mm semiautomatic, frequently carried by Australian and New Zealand military personnel.

The basic light machine gun utilized by SEAL units, as well as by all other Allied forces in Vietnam, was the American-made 7.62mm M60. Although the M60 weighed twenty-three pounds, its cyclic rate of 550 to 600 rounds per minute made it a highly desirable and portable platoon-level automatic weapon. Standard heavy machine guns were the .30-caliber and .50-caliber Brownings. However, due to their bulk and weight, the heavy machine guns were employed only for fire support along the perimeter defenses of land-based positions and aboard riverine craft and some helicopters.

SEAL units also carried a rather unique weapon that seemed to span several small-arms categories. The Stoner M63A1 Weapon System was a multipurpose arm whose basic structure and accompanying component kit contained both belt and magazine feed system variations, butts and pistol grips, and several different barrel lengths. Utilizing the many different components enabled the system to be transformed from a rifle to a carbine to a light machine gun (belt or magazinefed), flexible medium machine gun, or fixed heavy machine gun. The system fired 5.56mm ammunition at a sustained cyclic rate of 650 to 850 rounds per minute. The weights of the different configurations varied from about eight pounds in the assault rifle mode to perhaps eleven pounds in the heavy machine gun configuration. The system's light weight, easy field maintenance, and rapid cycle of fire made it an ideal weapon for guerrilla troops.

U.S. and ARVN firebases provided artillery support (105mm, 155mm, and 8-inch howitzers) for all Allied units operating in the IV CTZ. Artillery support, in the form of 105mm howitzers, was also available from MRF artillery barges and MONs, on station in or near the specific AO. And although the artillery fire was usually quite accurate, that accuracy was totally dependent on coordinates and adjustments provided by forward observers requesting the fire mission. If the initial rounds were not on target, any VC within the target area would have time to scatter and evaporate into the surrounding terrain.

SEAL units relied on lightweight artillery weapons for the same reasons as the VC. Having highly potent, lightweight artillery pieces on hand meant that an ambush team could save valuable time by carrying out its own fire missions. Such readily transportable artillery also increased the potential accuracy of a fire mission because the piece could be brought into close proximity to the desired target. This increased accuracy drastically reduced the possibility of enemy troops escaping unscathed. Taking the designated target under fire from extremely close range often meant that the initial round would be effective.

SEAL units often relied on 106mm recoilless rifles and 81mm mortars to supply many of their heavy artillery requirements. Although those weapons were not actually carried into the field by recon or ambush teams, they were part of the armament aboard SEAL support vessels. The 81mm mortars aboard PCFs could be used as direct-fire weapons against close-proximity targets. Those same mortars could also be used with great effect in a conventional mode against more distant targets. The 106mm recoilless rifle served similar functions as part of the armament carried aboard modified LCM-6s, called Heavy SEAL Support Craft (HSSC).

Two small artillery weapons used extensively by SEAL personnel in Vietnam were the 40mm Mark 19 automatic grenade launcher and the 60mm mortar. Both weapons were highly reliable and easily maintained in the field. Their rates of fire (about 375 rounds per minute for the Mark 19; about 30 rounds per minute for the 60mm mortar), maximum effective ranges (approximately one mile for both weapons), and variety of projectiles (antipersonnel high explosive, armor-piercing high explosive, white phosphorus, flares) made them capable of providing artillery support on the platoon level. Of course, the Mark 19's high rate of fire (fed by belts having twenty- to fifty-round capacities) made it ideal for situations requiring a high saturation of fire. And although both weapons were light enough to be carried routinely into the field by conventional units, they were much too heavy to be carried by SEAL ambush/recon teams. (The Mark 19, for example, weighed about seventy-five pounds). Carrying such pieces into the thick, deep, muddy stretches of the RSSZ or Delta would have been too cumbersome, drastically reducing the mobility and effectiveness of a team. Thus, both weapons were primarily restricted to use aboard the various MRF and SEAL support vessels.

The heaviest of the light artillery pieces occasionally used by SEAL elements was the M18A1 57mm recoilless rifle. Although its overall length was about five feet, the weapon weighed just under fifty pounds. Its maximum range was approximately 4,000 meters and its effective range was in the vicinity of 450 meters. More importantly, the weapon boasted a variety of potent ammunition consisting of High Explosive (HE), High Explosive Antitank (HEAT), and White Phosphorus (WP). And, of course, the rifled barrel (one turn per thirty calibers) meant that the M18A1's accuracy was deadly! If a target was clearly visible to the gunner, the chances for making a direct hit were excellent. The combination of punch and high accuracy made the 57mm recoilless rifle an effective weapon in taking on bunkers or other fortified structures. However, the weapon's weight prevented it from being used by SEAL elements on a day-in-and-day-out basis.

Handheld grenade launchers also proved to be dependable, potent, and highly accurate light artillery pieces that could easily be used in SEAL guerrilla/counterguerrilla operations. Perhaps the best known of the various grenade launchers available to all Allied units was the M79. A single-shot 40mm grenade launcher, the M79 weighed just over six pounds and was capable of firing a wide variety of rounds (HE, HE airburst, WP, illumination flares, CS (Tear) gas, colored flares, buckshot, or flechette-type antipersonnel) with great accuracy at a range of 400 to 450 meters. The cyclic rate of the M79 depended almost entirely on the dexterity of the person firing the weapon, but seven to ten rounds per minute was about average, with fifteen to twenty being possible, although accuracy would be degraded. One of the rationales for developing the 40mm grenade launchers was to provide squads with artillery support similar to the type that 60mm mortars provided for platoon-strength units.

A drawback to the M79 was the fact that the grenadier carried only a revolver or an automatic pistol as backup in situations where use of the grenade launcher was restricted. To carry anything larger than a pistol would have been too unwieldy. However, pistols are far less effective than rifles or carbines in typical SEAL combat situations. As a direct result of the need to give the grenadier a meatier backup weapon, the XM148 and M203 40mm grenade launchers were developed. Those launchers were mounted on the underside of an M16 rifle barrel and provided the same benefits as the M79. They also gave the grenadier the added benefit of having a substantial, rapid-fire infantry weapon. Lightweight, extremely accurate, and capable of being handled by one man instead of by the two-man crew typically required by the 60mm mortar, the XM148 and M203 allowed squad-sized units to employ more than one such weapon routinely, thereby significantly enhancing the unit's operational capabilities.

For unconventional warfare units, such as the SEALs, the idea of multiple grenade launchers was a truly tantalizing one. Such weapons would greatly enhance the potential for success. Having a weapon capable of firing four or more rounds in rapid succession would make it possible to hit an enemy force with what would be comparable to a typical mortar barrage. And even though the rounds used were 40mm, the barrage would quite likely cause the enemy force to assume that it had been taken under fire by an opposing force of platoon strength or larger, utilizing the 60mm mortar. The saturation aspect of such a barrage would also increase the potential for high numbers of enemy casualties or for taking out targets of tactical importance.

Two basic versions of the handheld multiple grenade launcher were given trials by SEAL detachments and other U.S. forces during the Vietnam conflict. One version was a pump-action model; the other was modeled after the workings of a standard revolver. Most of the pump-action models had capacities ranging from four to seven rounds; the revolver models' capacities varied from ten to twelve rounds. Both models were effective, offering a small unit the capacity to seem like a much larger force, even one that had mortar support.

In the late fall of 1967 a SEAL ambush team had an opportunity to appreciate such benefits firsthand. The team had set up an ambush position along a stream known to be a well-used infiltration route, located northeast of Ben Tre and still considered a VC stronghold. Several hours after setting up their ambush, the team intercepted a sampan, capturing its three occupants, cargo of rice, and medical supplies. While most of the team was involved in securing the prisoners and searching the vessel, the point man moved out to look and listen for any evidence of enemy interest in the ambush. Within a short time he returned, with the news that more than twenty VC were rapidly approaching the ambush zone. Although the team had already radioed for PBRs to extract them and their prisoners, the vessels were still many minutes from the proposed rendezvous point.

The point man and four of his mates moved out to meet the oncoming enemy while the other two remained with the prisoners. The five SEALs set up a new ambush position on the edge of a wide grass- and reed-covered meadow that the VC would have to cross to reach the stream. The approaching VC would thus be out in the open, whereas the SEALs' position was well hidden under the outer fringe of the forest canopy. The point man was armed with a shotgun; two of his buddies were armed with M16s and the fourth man held an M60. The fifth man was armed with a seven-shot revolver-type grenade launcher with which the team had been experimenting.

As the twenty-man VC contingent came swarming across the open meadow, the grenadier fired six rounds of HE in a sweeping pattern straight across their path. As he did so, the other SEALs fired short bursts from their automatic weapons. As soon as the first HE round exploded to the left of the onrushing VC, a scream came from the middle of their ranks. As more HE rounds exploded and the automatic weapons fire raked the enemy, more screams of pain were heard. Before the SEALs could cease fire, the VC retreated, those who had not been hit carrying or dragging their fallen comrades.

The brief salvo of HE rounds coupled with the intense bursts of automatic weapons fire had proved too much for the larger VC contingent. The five SEALs held position for a short time, watching for any sign that the enemy was returning, but the surrounding area remained quiet with no signs of movement anywhere. They returned to the original ambush site, and as quickly as possible the entire team, along with their prisoners, moved out en route to the extraction point. As they exited, they carefully monitored their rear and flanks but detected no signs of enemy pursuit. Perhaps the salvo from the automatic grenade launcher had caused the VC to think that they had come on a much larger opposing force than expected. Or maybe the fact that they were outgunned was all that mattered, regardless of which side possessed numerical superiority. In any event, the team and its prisoners made it to the pickup point and were extracted without further difficulty.

Most SEAL engagements during the Vietnam conflict took place at very close quarters, usually within five to fifteen meters or closer. Although carbines and automatic weapons could get the job done during these confrontations, shotguns seem to have been invented for such circumstances. Since the combat shotguns used by U.S. forces typically fired twelve-gauge rounds (either 00 buckshot, consisting of nine .30-caliber-plus pellets, or an antipersonnel load, consisting of eight flechettes weigh-

ing one gram apiece), three blasts from the weapon could result in more projectiles being fired than from a full twenty-round M16 magazine. Shotgun models available to SEALs and other unconventional warfare units were the Remington 870 Express, the Ithaca Model 37 Stakeout, and the Winchester Defender. All these shotguns were pump-action models. Winchester even supplied an automatic version capable of firing upwards of four hundred rounds per minute. The recoil of that weapon, however, when fired on full automatic, made it difficult to keep it trained on target. But such was not the case with the Close Assault Weapon System (CAWS), different versions of which were developed by the U.S. Naval Weapons Support Center and the Limited Warfare Laboratory, among others.

The CAWS weapons progressed through several different versions, ranging from the standard pump configuration to something very near a Stoner or an M16 in appearance. And of the various models available, the Stoner type seemed to be the most enthusiastically accepted, due to its light weight (usually between nine and eleven pounds), cyclic rate (400 to 450 rounds per minute from ten- to twelve-round magazines), assortment of available ammunition (00 buckshot or flechette antipersonnel rounds, flares, and even HE rounds available in some models), and a maximum effective range of 100 to 150 meters. Another big selling factor for the Stoner version was that the perceived recoil was approximately the same as that of the Stoner or an M16. This last factor was very important because it enabled the weapon to be held on target with a minimum of effort when being fired on full automatic.

The VC hated going up against shotguns in ambush situations. This was true whether they had set up the ambush or were on the receiving end of it. The problem from their perspective was that shotguns in the hands of one or more prospective ambush victims meant that the tide could turn against the ambushers in a span of a few seconds. A few quick blasts from one or more shotguns very often resulted in the ambushers interrupting their own fire as they hugged the ground as tightly as possible. As they did so, they would hear lead pellets slamming into tree trunks, pinging off rocks, and generally denuding foliage all around them. Temporarily interrupting their own fire could mean that the intended victims could either make a hasty withdrawal from the kill zone or initiate an aggressive counterattack.

When the VC were on the receiving end of an ambush, shotguns maximized the probability that an initial salvo would result in many wounded or killed victims. As much as the VC hated shotguns, we who used them loved the advantages the weapons offered. For one thing, the very sound they made brought instant fear to those being fired on. Also, the multiple pellets per round increased the probability of hitting the intended target. Best of all, you did not have to aim the weapon carefully. Just directing the business end of the piece toward the enemy was usually sufficient. That was a great advantage in situations in which there was no time to aim carefully and you had to snap off a round or two quickly.

A buddy of mine fondly referred to his Remington 870 as a "shredder." In his estimation (and I totally agree with him) there is no better weapon to have when you need to break out of an ambush. To illustrate, he liked to relate a story about being the point man for a four-man recon team operating near Sa Dec in the western Mekong Delta. The team had spent two days probing a section of double-canopy forest hoping to locate the base camp of a VC company that had withdrawn into the area a few days before. As the team was paralleling a well-used trail through the always dimly lit forest, my friend suddenly heard sounds of movement coming from a tangle of foliage on the far side of the trail. A second later the team came under intense fire from that area as well as from an area directly ahead of them. He wheeled toward the trail and rapidly fired four shotgun rounds toward the ambushers, sweeping the shots from right to left. As he did, the SEAL directly behind him fired a grenade into the ambush position to the team's front. The rest of the team fired their automatic weapons into both areas while carefully reversing the direction from which they had come. But even before they had begun to withdraw, they heard pained screams and the sounds of ambushers scattering in the other direction. The team then exited the area without further enemy contact.

Handguns also played a big part in the SEAL approach to guerrilla tactics. The most common weapons were the .45, .38, .357 magnum, and 9mm pistol. Sidearms were valuable, not only as backup pieces but also for specialized uses, such as eliminating sentries (human, guard dog, or geese; the last were often used as "guard dogs" due to their vile dispositions and loud, challenging honks). Sidearms were also valuable for searching through tight areas (tunnels, interlocking bunker complexes, and belowdecks aboard junks). For sentry and guard-dog elimination, the .38 and 9mm weapons were equipped with silencers (some U.S. Ranger and LRRP units were still using silenced .22s, as their World War II predecessors had). Of all the handguns available, the Smith & Wesson 9mm Model 39 automatic pistol proved to be the best suited for use by SEALs.

The Model 39 was an efficient eight-shot weapon that was reliable and extremely easy to maintain in the field. It had been developed by Roy Jenks at Smith & Wesson, and until 1968 it was the standard sidearm for most SEAL detachments. When the weapon was equipped with a silencer, its discharge was reduced to a loud whisper; use with subsonic ammo further reduced the sound to that of the hammer striking home. In 1968, an improved version of the weapon was made available to in-country SEAL personnel. The new model was equipped with a slightly longer barrel containing a built-in, highly specialized silencer that made the weapon's discharge quite negligible. The silencer made the weapon even more effective for sentry elimination and highly desirable for use in special operations, such as Studies and Observations Group activities and Phoenix Program missions.

The new model also differed from its predecessor in that its magazine capacity was increased from eight rounds to fourteen. (The magazine, however, was usually loaded with only thirteen rounds; the fourteenth round was carried "up the pipe," to prevent the magazine spring from becoming sluggish and contributing to misfires).

The Hush Puppy, as the new model became known, was well received by the SEAL detachments and was used extensively in many situations. Unfortunately, the production of the Hush Puppy never had a high priority, resulting in the weapon seeing extensive use only with SEAL teams.

SEALs used a wide array of fragmentation, smoke, CS gas, and WP-type hand grenades. One grenade that saw far greater use by SEALs than by other Allied forces was the Mark 3 concussion grenade (also called stun or flash-bang grenade). The Mark 3 was especially useful on "snatch" operations for stunning and disorienting designated prisoner(s) and his/her companions. If possible, the prisoner's stunned companions could also be taken into custody; otherwise, they could be more easily eliminated without undue risk to members of the capture team.

All these armaments greatly enhanced the overall effectiveness of SEAL tactics, especially in the IV CTZ. The various types of potent yet lightweight weapons made it possible for SEAL ambush, recon, and capture teams to penetrate deeply into the thickest and most difficult sections of the RSSZ and Delta landscapes in search of VC units and strongholds. And the amount of firepower afforded by each weapon allowed each team to more than hold its own, even in the face of numerically superior VC units. This was very important, because going after the enemy in his own backyard often got sticky. Sometimes the VC backyards turned out to be more like playgrounds, unexpectedly filled with several of Charlie's friends. A seven-man recon team, in such a situation, could suddenly find itself in the presence of an enemy platoon or even a company-sized force.

The ideal situation in recon operations is to develop as much intelligence about enemy emplacements, troop strength, and armaments as possible without being detected. If a SEAL recon team were detected, its array of specialized weaponry greatly enhanced its prospects for holding a position until extraction, fire support, or other means of escape could be provided. Very often the rate of fire and potency of the SEAL weapons in such situations resulted in enemy forces temporarily assuming that they were outnumbered.

The same rationale for using lightweight weapons extended to all other SEAL tactical equipment as well. SEAL elements carried only those items actually needed to complete their task successfully. The equipment had to be lightweight and unlikely to impede the user's movements.

Everything had to be either constructed of camouflage material or be camouflaged easily with indigenous materials, such as foliage segments, soil dustings, or mud smears.

Uniforms were prime examples. The basic field uniform was olive drab in color and constructed of a lightweight, ripstop, cotton blend material especially suited to jungle environs. Leaf-patterned versions (green background with splashes of brown and tan and/or black) and tiger-striped models (tan background with brown stripes, or green background with black stripes) were designed and produced for use by special warfare units, such as SEALs, Rangers, and Green Berets. In general, although the tiger stripes proved to be suitable for use in almost any type of terrain encountered throughout Southeast Asia, the leaf-patterned uniforms were felt to be best in dense foliage.

The term *uniform* was somewhat of a misnomer when applied to SEAL field operations. Clothes worn by SEALs consisted of whatever each man felt would help him and his team to get the job done. Sometimes a man might wear a complete set of standard "jungles." But frequently, a SEAL customized his attire to fit the area's terrain and climate and also to be comfortable. Some men wore standard jungle-patterned pants; others opted for either Navy-issue or Levi jeans (both had a button fly instead of a zipper). Sometimes the jeans were dyed green or black and then streaked or striped with black, green, or brown for added camouflage. In general, almost all personnel took a decidedly nonstandard approach toward what they wore: shorts, cut-off pants, shirts with the sleeves cut off at the shoulders, T-shirts, baseball-style caps, floppy bush hats, and a wide variety of head wraps. Because of that, most SEAL personnel looked more like pirates or swamp bandits than twentieth century, high-tech warriors. And the "look" was magnified because they spent so much time covered in mud. Unfortunately, the "look" also made life a little rough for in-country SEALs because many regular-service types thought that the lack of standard attire indicated a decided lack of discipline. As time passed, that misconception intensified. In many circles we were thought of as being little more than mercenaries, assassins, or even dangerous felons out on parole.

Many regular unit line officers were less than subtle in making sure that their men spent as little time around SEALs as possible. But that was fine with us because there was too much to do to worry about fraternizing with other troops. And if we looked that bad to our own guys, imagine how we looked to the VC and the NVA. Looking like bloodthirsty maniacs as we pounced on a prospective prisoner could sometimes make things a bit easier. In more than a few instances, a captured VC had to be revived, not because they had been knocked unconscious but because his attacker seemed eager to make him the evening's main course. It also seemed to work wonders in eliciting prisoner cooperation during interrogations.

We cannot forget to consider the importance of proper footwear. For the most part, SEALs wore the same standard nylon, rubber, and leather jungle boot used by all U.S. field personnel. The jungle boot was comfortable, durable, secure (the boot's steel insole offered some protection against *punji* sticks), and capable of shedding water and drying out quickly (very important in preventing "immersion foot"). The deep-treaded sole provided superb traction in slippery, muddy terrain. Depending on the situation, however, some individuals frequently opted for wearing "Ho Chi Minh sandals" (constructed from scraps of truck tires, the tread sections serving as high traction soles) or sneakers or even going barefoot.

Some men found that going barefoot was the most efficient way to slog through the tenacious mud of the RSSZ or similar sections of the Delta. Going barefoot offered the advantage of being able to flex one's foot more quickly than when encased in footgear, enabling the foot to break the suction effect of the mud more easily and with less noise and much less energy than a shoe. A well-shod foot pulled from the muck caused a loud slurping sound that could be heard at a considerable distance.

Another important item of field gear was Load-Bearing Equipment (LBE). The standard-issue LBE for U.S. forces was the well-known web gear, versions of which have persisted since at least World War II. One version was the nylon or canvas pistol/cartridge belt and suspenders configuration, to which any number of magazine and cartridge pouches could be attached. Canteens, sheath knives, flashlights, and grenades could be clipped or otherwise attached to the webbing; cartridge pouches proved useful for carrying small items, such as monofilament line, cammo sticks, salt tablets, folding knives, metal signal mirrors, pop flares, and capture gear. The last item consisted of nylon cord, used as lead lines and for securing prisoners' wrists, and cloth, used as gags and blindfolds. However, since many of the smaller items could just as easily be carried in the large pouch pockets of the field pants and jackets, most men found the standard LBE to be redundant.

A far more serviceable item was the tactical vest (tac-vest). Each vest contained many pockets of varying sizes all across the ventral (chest) surface. (If you've ever seen the vests that some professional photographers wear for carrying extra film canisters, spare lenses, and the like, you've seen a close relative of the tac-vest.) Usually, each vest contained on the left side a number of pockets for either magazines or 40mm grenades, and on the right a number of utility pockets large enough to accommodate maps, flashlights, binoculars, flares, marker pens, or cammo sticks. Smoke, concussion, and fragmentation grenades could be easily clipped to various parts of the vest's surface.

There were also flotation packs that could easily and quickly be attached to a vest. The packs were charged by carbon dioxide cylinders equipped with adjustment valves, allowing the wearer to select desired buoyancy levels. Their potential for quick attachment was a vital feature for those team members designated as either the unit's RTO or the M60 machine gunner. Flotation gear was of extreme importance for wading or swimming streams, since both the M60 and the standard field radios all weighed well in excess of twenty pounds apiece.

A specialized tac-vest, equipped with a large pouch built into its dorsal surface, was designed for the RTOs. The pouch was just large enough to accommodate the PRC-25 field radio (or its longer-range but similarly sized variant, the PRC-77), allowing it to sit comfortably just behind the RTO's head. That equally distributed the radio's weight, thereby making it much easier for the RTO to move without undue restriction of his range of motion. The PRC (more commonly referred to as a "prick") had a range of ten- to twenty-five kilometers, allowing the teams to maintain radio contact with supporting elements over considerable distances. Some teams chose to use small, handheld models, such as a survival set made by Motorola, designed for use by downed pilots, about the size of a large paperback novel. They were considered more efficient than standard models in many situations.

5 TRANSPORTATION

The various means of transport used by the teams for their insertions and extractions were of great importance to the SEAL approach to guerrilla warfare. The requirements peculiar to each mission dictated the type of transportation that would be most suitable. For some operations a twelve-foot aluminum "skimmer" or sixteen-foot inflatable Zodiac (both craft were driven by quiet and reliable Mercury outboard motors) might be the ticket, whereas an ASPB might be more appropriate for others.

PBRs and PCFs were used extensively by the MRF and SEALs because of each boat's ability to combine speed, firepower, and maneuverability. For SEAL operations requiring larger vessels and heavier firepower, the ASPBs were usually effective. Some ASPBs were even modified for close-in support by mounting on the vessel's stern an 81mm direct-fire mortar with a .50-caliber machine gun piggybacked on top (the same type of close-in support weapon used on the PCFs). All three vessels were fast (twenty-five, twenty-eight, and fifteen knots, respectively), durable, and highly maneuverable, making them ideal for the sometimes shallow and narrow waterways of the RSSZ and Mekong Delta.

Another craft, constructed with the SEALs' requirements specifically in mind, was the Heavy SEAL Support Craft (HSSC). It was a modified version of the extremely versatile LCM. As with the ASPB, the HSSC was heavily armored, maneuverable, and fast, with a top speed of fifteen knots. Armament consisted of two or more .50-caliber machine guns, a like number of 40mm automatic grenade launchers, and in some cases a 106mm recoilless rifle. A few HSSCs also were outfitted with either an M133 (driven by a gas generator) or M134 (driven by an electric generator) six-barreled minigun, capable of firing six thousand rounds of 7.62mm ammunition a minute. The vessel's spacious open deck area could accommodate more than two SEAL platoons plus a wide array of equipment and supplies.

Also available to SEAL detachments were a wide assortment of other riverine craft, including sampans, pirogues, and Boston Whalers, ranging from ten feet to more than twenty-eight feet in overall length. Two vessels proved to be particularly well suited to Delta and RSSZ operations because they presented a low profile on the water, making it possible for them to be hidden in the thick foliage. Even in daylight hours, both vessels could go unseen by the occupants of VC sampans, until the sampans were almost literally on top of them. A quick burst of fire from the waiting SEAL support craft made VC escape from the ambush kill zone quite unlikely.

The first of these vessels was the Light SEAL Support Craft (LSSC). Originally used as a harbor utility boat, this craft was twenty-four feet long and was specially modified for riverine warfare in the IV CTZ. Equipped with inboard water jet propulsion engines, similar to those used by the PBRs, the LSSC was capable of speeds in excess of twenty-five knots. Its open deck had sufficient space to accommodate a recon/ambush team in addition to its own three-man crew. Usual armament for the LSSC was a 40mm Mark 19 automatic grenade launcher and two M60 machine guns. (Some LSSCs substituted a .30-caliber machine gun for one of the M60s.) The LSSC was also equipped with radar capable of picking up river traffic as well as detecting movement of personnel and vehicles on land.

The second vessel was perhaps even better suited than the LSSC to SEAL riverine operations. Although the LSSC was quick and sleek, the Strike Assault Boat (also known as a SEAL Tactical Assault Boat, or STAB) was every inch a speedboat. An open craft about the same size as the LSSC, the STAB was also powered by inboard water jet propulsion engines and was capable of reaching speeds between twenty-six and twenty-eight knots. There was also sufficient room for an ambush/recon team and its gear to ride along without interfering with the movements of the STAB's four-man crew. Standard armament for the STAB consisted of four M60 machine guns and one 40mm Mark 19 automatic grenade launcher. As with the LSSC, the STAB was equipped with radar capable not only of tracking riverine traffic but also the movements of land vehicles and pedestrians ashore. The vessel's shallow draft of about eighteen inches made it ideal in areas like the Plain of Reeds, where the water level could fluctuate drastically over short distances.

The various SEAL Support Craft were crewed by Boat Support Unit (BSU) personnel, as proficient with their vessels and weaponry in conducting riverine operations as the SEALs were in employing guerrilla tactics. In addition to providing SEAL ambush/recon teams with insertion/extraction capability and fire support, the BSU crews and their vessels saw extensive duty as interdiction units, effectively halting VC use of the waterways in many sections of the RSSZ and Delta. Their swift, quiet, well-armed craft made resident VC stick almost exclusively to the shallowest and narrowest tributaries. This made the insurgents' transport of troops, cadre units, couriers, and supplies a decidedly tedious and precarious process. VC attempting to ambush BSU vessels from shore positions or their own craft afloat quickly found that the BSU crews were far too effective with their weapons for unplanned ambushes against them to be prudent.

One example of how effective the BSU crews and their vessels could be took place in the fall of 1967 near Sa Dec in the western part of the Mekong Delta. A four-man recon team had been en route to a position along a canal where they were to be picked up by a STAB. When they reached the pickup point they immediately came under intense automatic weapons fire from two positions on the opposite side of the canal. In the initial seconds of the ambush, three of the SEALs were wounded, two of them seriously. Still, all four men were able to hang tough and set up a heavy pattern of return fire.

The ambush had been initiated by a group of about twenty VC. As the firefight waged on, five of them managed to cross the canal north of the team's position. Now they had the four SEALs in a cross fire. To make matters worse, four RPG rounds slammed into the ground and overhanging tree limbs quite near the SEALs, spraying all of them with shrapnel.

The five VC who had crossed the canal carefully moved toward the SEALs, getting to within ten meters of their position. They got no closer, however, because hundreds of M60 rounds and several 40mm grenades tore into them, fired by a STAB that had suddenly appeared on the canal behind them. In less than five seconds all five VC were killed. At the same time, the STAB crew was engaging the main ambush force on the opposite side of the canal with withering M60 fire and 40mm grenades. Again after only a few seconds of such intense fire, a large number of VC had either been killed outright or had been wounded. Those who had either escaped injury or had been only slightly wounded melted away into the surrounding foliage.

The VC apparently never heard the STAB as it came racing up the canal at full throttle. It was able to move in without notice not only because of its powerful yet quiet engines but also because the intense firefight helped to cover any engine sounds, so the STAB's crew was able to fire their weapons into the enemy positions at point-blank range. Not only were they able to break up the enemy's ambush, they also totally discouraged the VC from trying to counterattack. The result was that the recon team escaped from a situation that they never should have been able to walk away from; the SEALs could have lasted only another five to six minutes before being killed.

Within a few weeks of that first incident, another took place less than five miles farther east. An MRF ASPB had been cruising along a section of canal when it struck and detonated a floating mine. The resulting explosion severely damaged the vessel, but the crew was able to ease its nose up onto a sandy bank, thereby keeping the craft afloat. They came immediately under intense light and heavy automatic weapons fire from positions along both canal banks. The besieged crew radioed for assistance but were advised that the closest MRF vessels were a few miles away. It would take the other vessels more than fifteen minutes to reach the ambush site.

But less than a minute later, a BSU PBR came racing up the canal and immediately took under fire the VC positions on the far side of the canal. More importantly, the BSU crew maneuvered their vessel so that it was directly between the VC and the stricken ASPB. The maneuver helped to take some of the heat off the ASPB, but it also resulted in the PBR taking a large number of hits from the VC. Despite this, the BSU men held their position and continued a steady stream of deadly accurate .50-caliber and 40mm grenade fire into the enemy positions. Their efforts, coupled with the ASPB crew's equal rate of fire, soon caused heavy casualties among the ambushers.

Most of the VC broke off the ambush and scattered, disappearing into the shadows. However, a few remained just close enough to lob in an occasional RPG round and some harassing automatic weapons fire. Although two of the BSU crew had been wounded during the action, they kept their vessel on line until three MRF PBRs arrived to assist the damaged ASPB and to treat the wounded men aboard both vessels. As soon as the VC snipers saw the PBRs barreling in, they headed for the dense cover of the surrounding forest. An MRF platoon swept through the area later that day, finding more than ten dead VC and evidence that an even greater number of VC had been wounded. MRF vessels continued to work along that stretch of canal over the next few months, but none of them was ever ambushed or even sniped at.

BSU personnel also saw action in the I CTZ as early as 1967. At that time, a few BSU crews and their vessels were sent north, along with a contingent of Operation Game Warden vessels and crews, as part of Operation Clearwater, whose purpose was to provide transportation and security for traffic along the main river corridors between Dong Hoa and Hue. The involved units ensured that traffic along the Perfume, Cua Viet, Cam Lo, and Han Rivers would flow in an uninterrupted fashion. The BSUs also provided the SEALs of Detachment ECHO with the same types of support already being provided to the Delta and Rung Sat detachments by the BSUs attached to CTF (Corps Tactical Zone) 116.

In May 1966, a truly unique form of watercraft was made available for use in the specialized environs of the Plain of Reeds. Two Bell SK-5 Patrol Air Cushion Vehicles (PACV), large and heavy closed-cabin craft that literally rode on a three to- five-foot layer of air, were brought into the country for use by Operation Game Warden forces. The vessels were propelled by prop-driven aircraft engines mounted just aft of the cabin and above the stern. The engines were quite powerful, allowing the vessels to reach speeds in excess of seventy knots. Armament varied but usually consisted of different numbers and combinations of M60 or .30-caliber machine guns, 40mm automatic grenade launchers, and on occasion a 60mm mortar. Much smaller versions of the PACVs, which were simply called airboats (similar to those used by sportsmen in the Florida Everglades) and were armed with bow-mounted .30-caliber machine guns, were also used by Special Forces detachments for their operations against VC units in the Plain of Reeds.

Because the PACVs rode on a cushion of air, they were not restricted to the waterways. In pursuit of a group of VC who had beached their sampans in an effort to escape across land, the PACVs could continue their pursuit onto and across dry land, skimming over mudflats, paddy dikes, scrub brush, or even laterite road surfaces while still maintaining speeds in excess of twenty knots. Unfortunately, the excessive noise generated by the powerful prop-driven engines made it impossible for the vessels to sneak up on enemy sampans or shore positions. But the BSU crews soon found a way to turn that drawback to their distinct advantage.

For example, if a sector of the Plain of Reeds had been selected for activity by SEAL ambush teams, the PACVs could position themselves on the sector's far edge, well away from where VC positions were assumed to be. Then the PACVs would move toward the VC positions at high speed, their engines roaring loudly. (To heighten the vessels' intimidating sound and appearance, eyes and a broad, toothy grin were painted on their bows.) Upon hearing the PACVs coming, the VC would panic and run, usually toward the waiting ambush team, PBR, or ASPB. The plan was based on a similar technique used in India for hunting tigers since the time of the maharajas. In the Indian tiger hunts, scores of men on foot, called beaters, moved toward the quarry while beating on drums; in the Game Warden operations, the PACVs were the beaters.

The fastest and most common means of day-to-day transport in Vietnam was by helicopter. Many were heavily armed gunships, capable of providing high concentrations of automatic weapons and rocket fire in close support of ground personnel and naval vessels, offshore as well as riverine. In areas having terrain such as that found in the RSSZ and Delta, choppers could cover great distances faster than any form of riverine or ground transportation. All of these factors made helicopters a logical means of support for SEAL operations.

The most widely used chopper during the Vietnam conflict was the Bell UH-1 multipurpose utility helicopter (Huey). The gunship version, usually a modified UH-1B Iroquois, was the best suited for support of both SEAL and MRF operations. The Iroquois had a cruising range in excess of three hundred miles and could carry as many as ten fully equipped troops in addition to its crew of four. Standard armament consisted of two door-mounted M60 machine guns, which were handled by the crew chief and door gunner, as well as four fixed M60s mounted outboard, two per side piggyback fashion, on special weapons pylons. As additional armament, a pod of 2.75-inch Folding Fin Aerial Rockets (FFAR) was mounted on each of the weapons pylons, next to the fixed M60s. The fixed M60s and rocket pods were operated by the pilot and copilot.

In the spring of 1967, a light helicopter attack squadron consisting of twenty-two UH-1Bs was based at Vung Tau. Designated as Helicopter Attack Squadron Light-3 (HAL-3) and nicknamed the Seawolves, the choppers and their crews quickly began to prove themselves to be valuable adjuncts, not only to SEAL operations but to those of the MRF as well. Split into detachments of two to three Hueys each, the Seawolves were deployed to several fixed bases scattered about the Delta (Sa Dec, Binh Thuy, Dong Tam, Ben Tre, Rach Gia, Cao Lanh) and also to the APBs, which served as floating bases. Thus deployed, the choppers were able to respond to calls for support anywhere in the Delta or for RSSZ within at most five to ten minutes.

The Seawolves also went on patrols with PBRs from TF 116 in an effort to make the VC disclose their shore positions. In such operations, a PBR would cruise up a canal while two gunships shadowed it, well out of view. If a VC bunker opened up on the PBR with heavy machine gun fire or RPG rounds, one or both Hueys would swoop down to silence the enemy position with automatic weapons and rocket fire. A similar operation was often performed by only two choppers in which one chopper flew low over a suspicious area to invite fire from any VC lurking below. As with the PBR, if VC opened up on the lone chopper, its companion would suddenly appear to take out the enemy position.

Much of the Seawolves' time was also spent providing support to SEAL teams operating throughout the RSSZ and the rest of the IV CTZ. The ambush/recon teams used the choppers extensively for insertions/extractions, fire support, and resupply. Because they could reach cruising speeds in excess of one hundred knots, the Hueys could cover many miles in a matter of minutes, thus extending each detachment's operational range immensely. It also meant that each ambush/recon team was never very far from high-volume, close-in fire support or rapid extraction capability. A quick call put in by an RTO would be followed within a few minutes by the reassuring sounds of rotor blades beating the air as rockets and/or automatic weapons fire slammed into enemy positions.

Ambush and recon were the basic ingredients of most SEAL operations. The degree to which the various weapons, load bearing gear, uniforms, transport/fire support vehicles (both riverine and aerial), and other equipment aided such tactics was critical to the continued success of the SEAL detachments wherever they operated. The true worth of such equipment is best demonstrated by the fact that it gave the SEALs several decided advantages over the VC in the guerrilla tactics employed by each. One obvious advantage was that the Seawolves and the various BSU and MRF vessels supporting SEAL operations permitted the ambush/recon teams to cover wide stretches of terrain in minutes, compared to hours or even days for VC units. It was possible for the teams to appear to be in two places at once, or to come suddenly out of thin air only to disappear again just as completely.

Lightweight artillery and automatic weapons, camouflage uniforms, efficient and compact load bearing gear, heavily armed, fast riverine craft, and equally heavy armed, rapid, far-ranging choppers, certainly served the detachments well in their effort to out guerrilla their communist opponents. But guerrilla warfare is and always has been much more than weapons, transportation, or gear of any type. Successful guerrilla tactics begin and end in the minds of the players. It becomes a matter of who is willing to get dirtier, go farther, sacrifice comfort, or be more patient than one's adversary. It is also a question of how well one can adjust to and work in harmony with whatever kind of terrain the arena of combat occupies. A guerrilla is only as effective as his willingness to sacrifice allows him to be.

6 FLORA AND FAUNA

The tactics employed by U.S. conventional ground force units during the Vietnam conflict were completely understandable, given the fact that their training had not been specifically geared toward waging guerrilla warfare. In fact, their training had a more generalized bent and was geared more toward a World War II approach to combat. On the other hand, the training of SEALs and other special warfare units was geared toward preparing them to not only respond to guerrilla tactics but to actually function as guerrillas themselves. In general, BUD/S, the SEAL basic training regimen, and similar types of special warfare training courses focused on weaponary, camouflage techniques, or land navigation. But BUD/S training also provided less tangible assets, better preparing SEALs to function as guerrillas. The agonies of Hell Week, the long periods spent lying or crawling in bone-chilling surf, running along the strand as you and your team balanced your IBS on your heads, and the many hours of Physical Training (PT) served not only to build physical stamina but also strengthened self-confidence and patience. It was these three factors that, when added to the other tangible aspects of BUD/S training, helped to enhance SEAL guerrilla/counterguerrilla capabilities.

If guerrilla tactics are to be successful, one must allow the animal within to lead the way. Most members of civilized society have a real problem accepting the fact that man, after all, is and always has been an animal. Years of trying to escape from our animal instincts have left us ill prepared, for the most part to exist in our environments without added coverings for our bodies or machines to do what most of us have long since forgotten how to do for ourselves. Although this may be fine in our highly controlled, convenience-oriented societies, it leaves us at a tremendous disadvantage when forced to function under more rustic and hostile circumstances. In these situations, intellectualism definitely takes a backseat to well-honed senses and pure animal cunning.

Guerrillas are predators. Just like any other predator, they must rely totally on their ability to locate their prey (reconnaissance) and then subdue it (ambush). For these reasons, if guerrilla tactics are to be successful, techniques such as stealth and camouflage must be used as effectively as possible. This is especially true in regard to recon operations; if the recon team is detected, the team members stand a high risk of being captured or killed by the enemy. Being detected prior to withdrawing from an AO means that the enemy is given an opportunity to escape before reinforcements can be ferried or airlifted in to sweep the area. Or the enemy force might elect to set more booby traps and shore up any of their defenses that the recon team might have observed. Similarly, if evidence of the recon team's presence is not detected until after the team has successfully exited the AO, the enemy may still be provided with adequate time to effect appropriate countermeasures. Therefore, it is imperative that the team leave no hint that they were ever there at all.

The overall effectiveness of camouflage depends greatly on how, when, and under which circumstances it was used. Wearing leaf-patterned or tiger-striped uniforms and using the proper hue of cammo stick (a double-headed tube containing nontoxic greasepaint in varying shades of light green, dark green, black, brown, and tan) on exposed skin surfaces, although helpful in appropriate terrain, could prove to be a complete waste of time if the wearer did not adhere religiously to all the cardinal rules of camouflage. Camouflage, no matter how well it is applied, is effective only in the right surroundings and situations.

When I was a very young boy, I often went on long walks with my grandfather through the woods that surrounded his farm in rural Pennsylvania. I remember one hot summer day when we had walked for several minutes without seeing any birds or ground animals. Being terribly disappointed, I asked him why no animals were around. At my question, grandfather stopped walking and clapped his hands together three or four times. Almost before the sound of the first clap had merged with that of the second, more than a dozen birds exploded from the trees and shrubbery around us. From the nearby bushes and high grass came the sounds of small critters scurrying and crashing through dry foliage.

"Just 'cause you don't see a rabbit don't mean he ain't there," he'd said. "Most animals are scared of humans, and nature's fixed it so that the color of their fur or feathers lets them blend into the trees and bushes around them. They know that as long as they stay still they won't be seen. Remember, they may be animals but they ain't stupid!"

Among our wildlife brethren, such accomplished hunters as chameleons, tigers, and walkingsticks (insects that are related to the praying mantis) benefit from camouflage that aids them in getting extremely close to their prey, thereby increasing the probability of making a successful kill. More importantly, their camouflage is successful only when employed in conjunction with proper attitude. For example, the chameleon's ability to change color may cause it to blend in with the leaf or branch on which it is perched, but it also must remain still. Coloration paired with stillness (attitude) prevents the prey from seeing beyond the "spell" of the chameleon's camouflage. As a result, the prey winds up "delivering" itself into the predator's jaws.

But if the chameleon moves his head or changes his position from a leaf to a neighboring branch, his movement breaks the spell of the camouflage and makes him as visible to prospective prey as though he was wearing a strobe light. Even insects, although they may not recognize the chameleon for what it is, avoid leaves or branches that seem to move under their own power.

In military applications, attitude plays an equally important role in the successful use of camouflage. Unfortunately, it is all too frequent that field personnel forget that the best camouflage uniform and the most meticulous applications of face paints are useless if the user's attitude is wrong. No matter how closely the camouflage comes to making the wearer appear to be a tree or a shrub, it all goes for naught if the tree or shrub moves or is positioned where a tree or shrub should not be.

Other important attitude considerations are glare, silhouette, grouping, and quiet. Glare can be easily generated by metal portions of gear, sweaty and oily skin, or glass objects such as watch crystals and flashlight lenses. Silhouetting is most often caused by moving along ridgelines or other slightly elevated segments of terrain with your body between a light source and your objective. Grouping deals with the spacing that is maintained between personnel while units in the field are on the move. And quiet, of course, deals with the obvious need to maintain silence during the entire scope of an operation.

Fortunately, metal components on almost all combat gear are glare free. This is accomplished by using special dull-finished metal alloys. Matte-finished paints and rough-textured tape usually prove to be effective in covering up high-buff metal parts. And glass watch crystals, when possible, are either replaced with less reflective plastic or fitted with a makeshift flap of cloth, or even black electrician's tape, to prevent sunlight from glinting off the crystal's surface.

The well-honed camouflage techniques employed by SEAL personnel during the Vietnam conflict enabled recon teams to penetrate into the very heart of VC-controlled areas without detection, thereby contributing high-quality data to their ever-increasing intelligence base. And they allowed their ambush/capture teams to operate in close proximity to VC units, greatly enhancing the prospects of snatching or eliminating enemy personnel successfully. Operating in such close quarters also increased the prospects for capturing significant quantities of enemy supplies, arms, and documents.

Operating so close to enemy positions also required SEALs to go where the VC set up their base camps, to locate the areas where they hid their rice and weapons caches, or to stake out and observe their most secure transport arteries. It meant going into the most difficult sections of the RSSZ and Delta.

For example, recon operations conducted throughout most of the IV CTZ meant that team members would spend a great deal of time wading across small, muddy-bottomed streams and inching their way through almost impenetrable tangles of scrub brush, vines, and reeds. The first ten to fifteen minutes of working their way through such terrain left each team member liberally smeared and caked with brownish green, or brownish black mud. There wasn't any use in attempting to clean off the gooey coating because a few minutes later you'd be just as heavily caked. But more importantly, the coating was actually a blessing, because it made it easier for the team to blend into the operational area's natural surroundings. Should the need to take cover arise, a well-coated team member might only have to squat down among the reeds, hunker down in the shallows, or lie flat in the low vegetation along a mudflat. The stickiness of the mud coating also acted as a sort of magnet for leaves and bits of broken reed or grass, further enhancing each man's cloak of invisibility.

This passive form of camouflage afforded modest relief from the region's thousands of biting and stinging insects. The cool mud also proved to be a natural balm, soothing and taking the itch out of a few of the bites that did occur. Nevertheless, there were still constant buzzing sounds all around our heads from the mosquitoes and flies drawn by our strong odor.

Another serendipitous advantage of the muddy coating was that it functioned as a climate-control mechanism. When still damp, the mud provided respite from the oppressive heat during daylight ops. Even after the mud dried, it acted as a form of insulation, in much the same way that adobe dwellings provide relief from the sun's hot rays. After the sun went down, this same insulating effect worked in reverse, preventing the damp night air from siphoning off too much body heat. Despite the fact that daytime temperatures in the IV CTZ were typically well above eighty degrees Fahrenheit, nighttime temperatures could sometimes dip into the fifties. But even if the temperature fell only into the sixties, you would still feel the chill because of the ever-present sopping humidity.

As stated earlier, sweatbands and hats were always thoroughly soaked with perspiration. But although the odor given off by such items was easily detected by the insects' superior sensory organs, it was not as readily discernible by other humans. This was because of another hidden benefit of the muddy coating: its dominant musty odor. Quite often, the scent of raw sewage was added to the mix. The region's hundreds of waterways were used by the villagers for toilet facilities.

Although the mud offered some relief, the heat continued to be stifling and the insects remained unrelenting in their attacks. The sticky mud, humidity, and strangling tangles of vegetation all could be tremendously taxing for anyone who attempted to master the environs. Without a great deal of patience and a high level of endurance, SEAL operations in the IV CTZ would have been no more effective than conventional force operations had been.

In many ways, counterinsurgency operations are similar to the game of hide-and-seek, which we all played as children. When I was no more than nine or ten years old, we often would play in an area that contained dilapidated, cheaply constructed, deserted, World War II–era row homes. Over the years, dogs had dug little dens under a number of the houses and then abandoned them. The dens were then no more than homes for spiders, beetles, ants, mice, and rats. We would frequently explore and generally gambol about inside the cobweb-filled buildings, but none of us liked to even go near the dens. But whenever we played hide-and-seek, I made it a point to squeeze under a house and hide in a den. It wasn't that I was any less afraid of the creepy, crawly things that infested the dens; it was more a point of hating to lose at any game that we played. And I knew that the others would not try to enter the dens to look for me. This ensured that I would not be caught by whoever was "it."

In the den, I would just lie there telling myself that if I stayed still and quiet, the sources of the scurrying sounds, along with the spiders, beetles, and ants, would eventually go away and leave me alone. Those same thoughts ran through my mind some years later as I lay in the undergrowth on a recon or an ambush operation. But the creepy crawlies that I'd seen and heard in the dens in Pennsylvania would not have made even a passable snack for the creatures that dwelled in the more hostile environs of the Rung Sat or Mekong Delta.

The streams, mudflats, canebrakes, and forests of IV Corps supported a wide variety of animals, beautiful and interesting looking and many extremely dangerous. Anytime you went into the bush you were as likely to see swamp deer, flying squirrels, and monkeys as you were to see cobras, pythons, or kraits. And although the mosquitoes and flies were bothersome, spiders, centipedes, and ants seemed to go out of their way to make life as uncomfortable as possible for anyone in the dense underbrush. It was imperative to ignore all of these creatures, but actually doing so was not always easy. So, coexisting with the local wildlife was the only logical way. It wasn't a question of growing to like being around these repulsive creatures. Instead it was just doing what was necessary. It was also understanding that by enduring such close relations with the local crawlies, you were able to enjoy the advantage of springing on the VC from points of concealment that even he had assumed were too tangled and infested for an ambusher to tolerate.

When children are afraid of something, such as spiders, mice, or snakes, fear makes such things seem to be utterly huge, no matter how small they are in reality. For many, this process persists well into our adult years. Often, people hearing stories by Vietnam veterans about the sizes of many of the Delta and Rung Sat denizens have assumed that fear greatly affected the storytellers' perceptions. In some instances, that may be true, but usually the veterans' recollections about huge insects, rats, and reptiles are completely true. I didn't believe the stories until I got my first glimpse of a spider on a rock beside a drainage ditch. The spider was bigger than a pie pan.

In the bush, the best places for SEALs to conceal themselves were also the very areas where most of the reptiles, insects, and furry critters lived and played. Therefore, you found yourself studying the characteristics and habits of the thousands of forest and swamp denizens at extremely close range. In return, they had opportunities to crawl over and under you and to explore deep within the folds and tucks of your clothing. Of course, there was very little you could do about that because to swat at a spider or to recoil from the sudden appearance of a snake hanging from the branches just above you would almost certainly disclose not only your own position to the enemy but the positions of your team members as well.

Spiders ranging from the size of a penny to about the size of silver dollar were common in the bush. They did not seem to have any real preference for terrain and could be found almost anywhere there was ample ground cover. Most of them were either black or dark brown, some with blue or greenish spots and others with red or orange ones. During the dry months, if you elected to take cover under thick brush well away from running water, you were almost certain to find yourself in the middle of a nest; scores of spiders would scurry back and forth over branches, rocks, and you. Fortunately they did not seem aggressive and were quite content to leave you alone and go about their own business.

Another insect frequently encountered in thick ground cover or areas strewn with rocks was the centipede. Since centipedes avoid direct sunlight, preferring dimly lit or dark and somewhat damp places, you would see them if you accidentally dislodged a rock or jostled a fallen tree limb. Most centipedes were black or bronze colored, perhaps two to three inches long. From time to time you might hear some of the guys talk about running across the odd colossal one that was six, seven, or sometimes well in excess of eight inches long. Regardless of the size of the centipedes, they were capable of inflicting a particularly nasty bite. Often, the pain and swelling associated with such bites persisted from a few hours to two days. Obviously, you tried not to disturb them too much.

One SEAL operating with his ambush team near Can Gio in the RSSZ, during the summer of 1967, found out just how unpleasant centipedes are. He had settled himself into a tangled patch of creeper vines and broad-leafed foliage near a stream bank and was just starting to feel comfortable. As he lay there he became aware of something crawling across his right forearm toward his hand. Looking down he saw that it was a centipede and decided to have a little fun. He began prodding the insect, first this way and then that, trying to confuse it. Unfortunately, he succeeded in frustrating the nasty thing and it bit him in the area between the knuckles of his index and middle fingers on his right hand. The bite was painful immediately and within seconds the area around the wound began to swell.

He tried to ignore the pain, assuming that it would soon begin to subside. And in a way it did. Instead of feeling like a hot pin stabbing the affected area, the pain changed to an intense throbbing. The swelling increased dramatically, causing his hand to soon look like a shiny purplish balloon, the fingers capable of wiggling only slightly. Fortunately, the night passed uneventfully without any contact with the enemy, because his right hand was useless. He could have fired his M60 with his left hand but he would have preferred to use his right hand. He was glad when they extracted and he was able to see one of the detachment corpsmen. Needless to say he had learned his lesson and never again pestered any insects he encountered in the field.

Around that same time another SEAL had a less than pleasant encounter with one of the Delta insects near Phuoc Thuy. He was part of a four-man recon team moving through a mucky stretch of swamp near an abandoned village. As he told it, the team was on its way to the pickup point when he was suddenly bitten above his left eye by some sort of flying insect. The pain was initially very intense but soon eased up. About that same time he noticed that his face was swelling rapidly, at first only around the left eye. That soon changed, however, and within less than five minutes the flesh around both of his eyes had swollen so badly that he could hardly see. He managed to get to the pickup point with a little help from his buddies; once back in camp the swelling quickly subsided. Although he never again had a similar experience, he did have to endure being referred to as "Bugs" by his buddies from then on.

Another group of creatures having a distinct predilection for blood were the leeches. The aquatic variety attached themselves to any part of the body they could get their little mouths onto as you waded across streams, canals, or drainage ditches. The terrestrial types would lie in wait for mammal hosts passing in the damp foliage. If you left them alone, they would eventually drink their fill of blood and then drop off. Pulling them off left a pretty nasty wound. If you could not wait for them to finish dining, the best methods were touching them with a freshly extinguished match or something else hot. For obvious reasons, such methods were not practical in clandestine operations.

Rounding out the insect picture in the IV CTZ were ants, bees, and wasps. Fortunately, ants were a problem only in areas where conditions were not damp. Two or three ant species were vicious and inflicted stinging, burning bites. Some ants were as large as two centimeters in length, but most were usually only a half or even a quarter of that size. The smaller ones seemed more prone to attack in swarms than their larger brethren.

Bees and wasps lived over wide stretches of the region, but they were most abundant in the area in and around the U Minh Forest. That was because the Rhizophora and other varieties of mangrove trees and shrubs were in almost constant bloom. Colonies of wild bees existed naturally in the region, but the local villagers also maintained hundreds of hives, collecting and selling beeswax and honey. The local VC also maintained some hives and wasp nests in strategic areas, using them as booby traps or watchdogs to guard approaches to their strongholds, weapons caches, and food stores.

Of all the creatures encountered commonly in the marshes, rice paddies, and rain forests of Southeast Asia, reptiles probably caused almost as much concern for U.S. forces as did the ambushes, snipers, and booby traps. They came in a wide variety of types, shapes, colors, and sizes and ran the gamut from tiny chirping tree frogs to reticulated pythons, which were known to attain lengths of twenty feet or more. There were monitor lizards, geckos, turtles, and tortoises. (Some tortoises commonly caught by the inhabitants of the U Minh Forest and sold at market weighed in excess of twenty pounds.)

In parts of the Rung Sat and estuaries of the Delta, team members would from time to time come across an occasional crocodile. The Asian-Pacific specimens grow as large as twenty-five feet long. Fortunately, those encountered in the IV CTZ were rarely more than six to eight feet long and seemed quite satisfied to keep to themselves, if they and their nests were given a wide berth. Now and then someone would tell a tall tale about seeing one of monstrous size or of having to fight one off. Even so, I never heard of any documented events in which anyone, not even regional noncombatants, was ever eaten by a croc. But that did not make us any less cautious when operating in areas that looked like home to the extremely territorial and aggressive creatures. A six footer could rip off a leg.

In Southeast Asia, snakes of all types can be found just about anywhere. It was wise to approach most snakes, at least initially, with caution because some snakes are known to be lethal. This was especially true in Vietnam, where herpetologists have estimated that more than 120 types of poisonous specimens reside (the majority of them being cobras, kraits, and bamboo vipers). However, the poisonous snakes were not the only lethal ones around; there were also constricting snakes, chiefly pythons, of varying lengths, with the reticulated python being by far the largest of them all.

Rounding out the list of ever-present, sometimes lethal and frequently unpleasant local fauna were the rats, not the cute little white rats used in lab work or sold as pets, not even the much larger ones scampering about certain sections of substandard housing areas, garbage dumps, wharves, or sewers, but rats the size of well-fed barn cats.

Certainly the fact that the swamps and dense undergrowth supported such a large assortment of animal life, or that much of it would be potentially lethal and/or repulsive looking, should not be surprising. The reason for detailing their types and varieties is not to shock or to offend. It is to repeat the types of conditions routinely encountered and how they could be used to take the resident VC by surprise. In many ways we were employing the same rationale that I had used as a kid playing hide-and-seek.

The VC made similar assumptions about the ways that U.S. personnel approached antiguerrilla warfare. I remember once listening to a VC prisoner tell an interrogator why it would be impossible for us to totally defeat the communist insurgency: Our troops were more interested in staying dry, avoiding leeches and snakes, and trying to swat pesky mosquitoes than in being truly effective against the VC in their inhospitable strongholds. This assumption was generally true, because most grunts were not trained to be guerrillas or to live and thrive under the same conditions as guerrillas.

The VC intentionally set up their strongholds and staging areas where the terrain provided passive perimeter defense. In a typical Rung Sat encampment, one or two sides of the perimeter faced wide expanses of dense bramble and chest-high ground cover that gave way to mudflats and carpets of tenaciously clinging water hyacinth plants floating on the waterways. Such natural terrain conditions presented a conventional force with two big problems. One was trying to negotiate the areas without making a considerable amount of noise. The second was conditions that quickly sapped the strength of conventional forces. Therefore, conventional units avoided such areas, instead opting for more stable approaches to enemy positions.

That was just as the VC had planned. Because they were grossly outmanned and outgunned by Allied forces, they resorted to the most rudimentary means of logistical support and surface transportation. By utilizing the terrain's passive defense opportunities, they could concentrate their manpower and material by actively defending against assaults coming in the more solid sections of the surrounding countryside. Booby traps and ambush positions would not have to be deployed along an encampment's entire perimeter and could thus be more wisely and efficiently deployed along the few well-marked trails that an assaulting conventional force would be more apt to take.

These same terrain features that provided the VC with passive perimeter defenses gave SEAL ambush/recon teams some real advantages as well. Because the VC had become accustomed to the terrain's passive assistance in impeding an assaulting force's progress and heralding its advance, they felt no need to monitor some areas closely. They also assumed that U.S. forces were incapable of putting personnel into the field who were as highly motivated toward getting down and dirty as the VC troops were.

Even so, the VC's passive defense "rear doors" were not really wide open, allowing easy access to their safe havens and strongholds. The thick, gooey mud and almost impenetrable undergrowth had to be negotiated without giving the enemy advance warning of their approach. That meant moving with deliberation and being mindful of all possibilities for creating any needless sounds. This required great patience and the expenditure of a tremendous amount of energy.

Movements across streams and broad stretches of mudflats or other types of open terrain were usually too dangerous to undertake during daylight hours. Such areas were skirted; a team would move along the periphery instead, where overhanging branches, reed beds, or tangled thickets helped provide sufficient cover. Similarly, when more desirable cover was unavailable, those same areas had to suffice as observation/listening posts.

Most movement during field operations was unhurried, which helped you deal with the environment. For instance, you would be better able to identify natural or man-made dangers before stumbling into them. Deliberate movements helped keep your breathing and the sound of your heartbeats sufficiently quiet so that you could better discriminate the sounds of the team's movements from any other sounds that might occur. It also helped to keep you under control and better prepared to take advantage of any options that presented themselves during crisis situations. During the long hours in an observation post, patience helped you to deal with both the tedium of waiting for something to happen and the elements.

In establishing a position to keep a group of suspects or a suspicious area under surveillance, you wanted to get as close as your own adaptive abilities and available ground cover would allow. That could mean setting up more than twenty meters away from the mark, or perhaps getting to within ten feet of it. In doing surveillance work, when you set up a position, all unnecessary movement and sound had to be eliminated. You always assumed that the enemy was lying somewhere in the same area, watching for signs of your presence too.

More often than not, the best positions for close surveillance of an area were also the most uncomfortable, for example, tightly matted thorn or bramble-choked brush, or sopping, soggy turf under a stand of dripping palmetto trees, replete with disgusting animals and insects. Lying quietly in inhospitable surroundings was difficult enough, but the tedium associated with recon and ambush work was another important part of the mix. Unlike movies and novels, in which it seems that the enemy always cooperates by moving into a kill zone a minute or two after you have set up, in real life it almost always takes hours, if it happens at all. Even when the intelligence regarding some proposed enemy movement through an area was excellent, something might happen to delay their plans for a few hours or days, or cancel them entirely. While waiting, the only way to deal with the situation was to keep our minds off the unpleasant weather, insects, or terrain conditions and find ways to divert our thoughts without diverting our attention.

Sometimes, while lying quietly amidst the dense cover, we got an opportunity to closely observe the local animals as they went about their daily activities: a spider constructing an intricate web from start to finish, two big rats fighting over a bird carcass, and a vine-thin tree snake suddenly lashing out from its perch on an overhead limb to snatch a large, brightly colored butterfly from the air in midflight. Once, I witnessed a

bit of comic relief as a small python, about six feet in length, tried to subdue and eat a tortoise the size of a standard military-issue steel helmet.
After about fifteen minutes of adjusting and readjusting its coils, without
any perceivable effect on the hard-shelled reptile, the snake finally gave
up and slithered off beneath the thickly matted undergrowth.

To better appreciate how patience and deliberate movement can aid and
abet stalking and camouflage techniques, picture a tiger or a python on
the prowl. The tiger moves quickly but with an unhurried manner as he
slips through the more yielding sections of thick undergrowth. Because of
that loose, effortless movement, he glides along the ground and is
unlikely to dislodge loose rocks, rustle dry leaves, or snap brittle branches
to announce his passage. He can stop instantaneously and freeze in place
to listen and sniff the air should an odd sound or scent come his way. If it
emanates from a quarry or a foe, he is ready to crouch low for a swift,
sudden attack or to blend with his surroundings until danger passes.

The python takes a very similar approach but adds to the overall picture
his willingness to slide over, under, around, or through obstacles. Such
movement, so effortless and cooperative in its relationship to the prevailing surroundings, helps the snake to conserve energy that will be needed
when contact with prey or a foe finally happens.

What is true for tigers and snakes is also true for man. Actively and
aggressively attempting to impose one's will on nature will surely result
in drawing unwanted attention to one's presence as well as in sapping
mental and physical energy. Mental and physical exhaustion often lead to
rash and dangerous decision making, which in turn almost invariably
leads to lost opportunities or injury and death for yourself and other team
members.

Sometimes, when you do things just as they are meant to be done, a situation can take a funny twist. On more than one occasion recon teams got
too close to an enemy unit. In doing so they actually found themselves in
the heart of a VC battalion's staging area and would have to wait hours or
longer before being able to work their way out. Such situations were,
obviously, quite touchy and could have ended tragically. But if the team
remained patient and moved with proper deliberation, not only would
they get out undetected but they also would have collected a large amount
of hard intelligence.

An example of how strangely comical some situations could be
occurred in 1968. A four-man recon team had been working through an
area west of Long Xuyen, trying to locate a VC hamlet in the vicinity. Just

before sunrise on the second day out, they found the hamlet well hidden in a small, densely vegetated area covered by thick tree canopy and ringed by broad stretches of briar-type shrubs and thorny creeper vines. The hamlet was not too large and seemed to support no more than thirty individuals. It was hard for the team to initially determine how many VC were in the encampment, how many of them were armed, and what type of weapons were on hand. In order to answer those questions, two SEALs moved in to scope out the hamlet from opposite sides.

One man moved around to the eastern edge of the hamlet and immediately spotted three VC huddled together over something out in the open between two of the hootches. They were squatting down, and two of them seemed to be intently watching the other VC, who was sawing or scraping at something on the ground. As the SEAL watched, he was impressed by the fact that several other VC were also watching the trio but from a considerable distance. What were the three VC working on and why were their comrades watching them? Whatever it was it had to be of importance. The SEAL began to move carefully around to the right, to a position where he would be well hidden by a tangle of vines and shrub, no more than ten feet from where the trio was squatting.

As soon as he had gotten into position, the SEAL held his breath and heard his heart begin to pound loudly in his ears. He could clearly see what the three VC were squatting around. It was an artillery round, mostly covered in dried mud. Its size suggested that it was probably one of
the many 155mm rounds that had been fired in the Delta but had failed to detonate properly. But what caused the SEAL to wish he could be almost anywhere else at that moment was the fact that one of the VC was slowly and deliberately sawing on the round, trying to get at the explosive charge inside.

The SEAL wanted to get the hell out of there as fast as possible. But getting into position to view what the trio was up to had been difficult enough. Now it would be even harder to back out, because he was scared and for good reason. The round's appearance looked as though it had been lying around for more than just a day or two. Coupling that with its failure to explode properly made it extremely unstable. With such ordnance, there was no such thing as handling it properly. All he could do was lie there, watch the VC saw into the unstable round, and try to remember all the reasons he had become a SEAL instead of a priest.

As he later told it, the VC finally took a break from their efforts and moved back to catch a smoke. When they did, the SEAL eased his way back out of the undergrowth and rejoined the rest of the team. They remained near the hamlet until that night. Since they never heard an explosion they assumed that the trio had successfully opened the round and extracted the charge. They exited the area and reported the hamlet's position for further handling by other Allied units.

Many benefits obtained from patient, deliberate movement came from the BUD/S advanced training after deploying to one of the platoons following graduation, as well as day-to-day experience in Vietnam. Some of that experience came from conducting occasional joint operations with units attached to the 2d Squadron, Australian Special Air Service (SAS) Regiment, 1st Australian Task Force, based in Ba Ria on the Long Thanh Peninsula, in Phuoc Thuy Province. The SAS units were widely appreciated for their expertise in conducting jungle and swamp operations. They had honed their skills during World War II in combat against Japanese forces in Borneo and later against communist forces in Malaya. Their expertise had been further enhanced because they trained extensively in the treacherous swamps in various untamed areas in Australia.

Joint operations with them were conducted in the area east of Nhan Trach; they proved so successful that VC activities in the sector were quickly and completely suppressed. By employing the python's patient and deliberate movements through such mucky areas, SEAL and SAS recon/ambush teams were able to get on top of their quarry and take them out before they even knew they had been hit. Many VC who survived or managed to avoid capture vacated the region, spreading the word that it was far too dangerous to operate there any longer.

Whether operating independently or in tandem with SAS or other Allied forces, SEAL personnel continued to emulate the python's unhurried, deliberate style. By painstakingly making their way through the very sections of the Rung Sat that the VC had thought anyone else incapable of negotiating, the teams could literally go anywhere they chose throughout the RSSZ. Despite the fact that such movement was far more efficient and less taxing than the more aggressive approach taken by other U.S. units, it still required a great amount of energy. The area's usual heat and humidity coupled with the slightest activity was much more debilitating than digging ditches back in Georgia during mid-August. Just standing around in the middle of the Rung Sat for a half hour at midday would cause one to sweat profusely. Any movement only resulted in greater moisture loss.

Even the patient and deliberate approach was still fatiguing if you were new in country and not yet fully acclimated to the energy-sapping heat and humidity. I can remember quite well what happened after the first couple of times out in the mud. Once we returned, cleaned our weapons, ate, and debriefed, I fell asleep, only to awaken in less than an hour with severe abdominal and thigh cramps. While out that day, I thought I had consumed enough water and salt tablets. But obviously my body was not yet adjusted to the rate at which I was losing moisture. Thereafter, I made sure to ingest more salt around the clock, even when back in camp, and to take an extra sip or two of water when in the field.

It is a gross understatement to say that adequate ingestion of water and salt is of great importance when engaging in extremely strenuous activity in a hot and humid environment. Water and salt allow the body to maintain proper temperature levels under such conditions and prevent the onset of heat cramps, heat exhaustion, and heat stroke. Heat cramps and heat exhaustion can be painful and debilitating; the latter can cause death if not treated properly. All three maladies can be avoided easily by remembering the risk factors and using a lot of common sense. That was essential to the effectiveness of all field personnel but especially for SEALs, because most operated in the field on an almost daily basis.

Most SEALs found that it took one or two times out in the field to begin to adjust to the climate, the terrain, and the pace required in conducting guerrilla/antiguerrilla operations. During that brief period, you would begin to listen to your body and adjust your water intake according to its needs. Most medical experts hold that the average human requires about one to two quarts of water a day to perform adequately. If the symptoms associated with those heat-induced disorders are recognized early enough, they can be treated before gross debilitation sets in.

By far, the most common of the three afflictions was heat cramps, but they could be satisfactorily treated in the field. The symptoms were usually restricted to muscle spasms accompanied by severe pain. Although the muscles most frequently affected were in the calves, thighs, and abdomen, spasms also could attack almost any other muscle group. It was common for a victim to lose temporarily the use of his hands or feet when severe cramping struck the muscles there. Fortunately, heat cramps were easily treated with a short rest, a couple of salt tablets, and several good swigs of water.

Whether you worked out of a land base or from an afloat base, keeping well moisturized internally was easy to accomplish. Water was not only readily available in the form of plain old drinking water, but it was also a main constituent of such typical daily potables as coffee, tea, milk, soda, and beer. Because carrying extra canteens usually was not feasible, you could "camel," that is, make a conscious effort to drink even more fluids than usual, so that your tissues would be well saturated before you went out.

Being able to get enough salt into your system was also easy wherever you happened to be. Typical mess hall chow (and all military rations) contains a significant amount of fats, proteins, carbohydrates, and salt. Salt is a good preservative that increases the shelf life of many food products. It also enhances the flavor of food, especially the bland, wholly unimaginative cuisine eaten when stationed at home or overseas. The sodium already contained in the food, augmented with a few liberal sprinkles from one of the ever-present salt shakers found in military chow halls, could sometimes transform even boring, gummy chipped beef on toast into a fairly palatable and almost tasty repast. Added to this were several types of snack items and scores of indigenous food products, all of which were high in sodium.

Advantages offered in following a more indigenous diet were that it was more readily digestible than U.S. rations. It also helped the SEALs smell more like locals. The odor came from walking through the markets and villages and letting the smell of the wood fires used for cooking and craft work permeate your clothing. Your body began to smell more like that of the Vietnamese because the diet slowly changed your body chemistry. Your sweat, urine, and feces smelled less acrid and pungent (as was normal for American troops because of the heavily meat-oriented diet) and seemed more subtle, almost like flat chicken soup that had been left out too long.

Odor was important when trying to get right on top of enemy positions during ambush/recon operations. If at all possible you wanted to smell as much like the local population and/or the local environment as you could. But if you could not accomplish that, you would try to not smell too out of place. For that reason, you rarely washed your uniform, no matter how grubby or grungy it got. When you did wash your uniforms, or for that matter even yourself, you did not use laundry detergent or soap, no matter how muted its aroma. Although the odor of the soap might seem innocuous in a land-based compound or aboard an afloat base, that same aroma became readily apparent in the field, where it clashed dramatically with the odors of decaying vegetation, raw sewage, and decomposing animal carcasses.

Other precautions had to be taken by those working from afloat bases with the MRF units. Although the teams working from afloat bases did not use any soaps, detergents, aftershaves, or deodorants, their clothing, hair, and skin were not free of such contaminants. Army and Navy personnel aboard the various barracks ships freely used fragrant soaps and detergents, splashed on aftershave, and liberally sprayed themselves with deodorant. Even those who didn't use such products, smelled as though they did after being closed up in a room with someone who used them lavishly.

So, to avoid the possibility of contamination, afloat recon/ambush teams segregated themselves and their accommodations from the other personnel as much as possible. That wasn't too hard to accomplish, since civilized-smelling persons would not want to get too close to SEALs' ripe-smelling uniforms.

In a way, it helped that most conventional force troops thought the SEALs were more than just a little strange. Many of them had heard shocking stories about all SEALs being sociopaths and psychos, trained to kill anything they encountered. Of course such impressions were erroneous, the misconceptions fueled not only by the outrageous appearance of many of the ambush/recon teams but also because of the SEALs' independent and irreverent attitude toward standard military regulations and customs. Saluting was not de rigueur, officers and enlisted men freely fraternized, and most team members did not go in for rank symbols, flashes, or rating badges. In addition, SEALs have always been extremely secretive about the teams and their operations; until 1969 SEALs were a very well kept secret, an organization rumored to exist but about which little was known.

Even though many of the stories that the MRF troops had heard about SEAL operations were nonsense, no effort was made to set the record straight. By keeping to themselves, SEAL afloat teams had more time for sleeping, cleaning, and maintaining weapons, as well as going over maps of prospective AOs. It also meant that they stood a better chance of staying loose, helping the teams to be better prepared to go out on a moment's notice and to stay a step ahead of the VC in the Delta and the RSSZ.

7 SEAL TACTICS

In the preceding chapters we have examined the many tools and techniques that aided SEAL operations in Vietnam and especially in the IV CTZ. We have discussed such things as potent but lightweight weaponry, compact and efficient load-bearing equipment, fast and reliable transport/fire support vehicles, finely honed camouflage/stalking techniques, and even the types of foods that were not only nutritional but also aided in fluid and electrolyte balance. All of those things helped to account for the immediate, convincing impact that SEALs had on the resident communist forces in the Delta and RSSZ. But these items and techniques alone did not make our guerrilla/counterguerrilla tactics "sing." Equipment, arms, and rations are helpful but, as the old saw goes, "It ain't what you got, it's how you use it." So, let's look at the way in which things generally went, using an example of how actual operations were run.

In early May 1967, friendly aircraft conducted a number of reconnaissance flyovers of an area approximately six miles north of Dong Hoa, in the southern Rung Sat. The flight crews reported that for several nights running, the glow of lanterns or flashlights appeared occasionally, filtering up through a rare sparse section of the dense vegetation that covered one of the mangrove islands below. During a flyover conducted just before dawn that very morning, three large sampans, poorly camouflaged by palm fronds and banana leaves, were seen protruding partially from some nipa palms on the island's western shore.

The island was quite large, stretching four hundred meters north to south and six hundred meters east to west. Its eastern shore bordered part of the Long Tau River's left bank; its western shore sat at the confluence of two of the many channels that branched from the Long Tau as it snaked through the Rung Sat to Saigon. This location made it an ideal position from which to conduct mining or harassment operations against river traffic along the Long Tau. The island's shores faced three different waterways, offering multiple avenues for escape should an assault be launched against the island's inhabitants. All of those characteristics made it an ideal location for a VC forward base camp, storage area, or listening post. It was also an ideal area for the SEALs to conduct recon and prisoner acquisition operations.

The Naval Intelligence unit related all of the available data regarding the island and its potential inhabitants to the intelligence liaison officer attached to Detachment GOLF in Nha Be. After a preliminary briefing, the data was turned over to one of the platoons. Thus, at about 0700 one of the platoon's ambush/recon teams received a Warning Order (the first step in putting an operation into motion) indicating that the Platoon Leader's Order (the team's preoperational briefing session) was set for 1000 in the briefing shack. The lag between the two orders was intentional, meant to provide the team members ample time to square themselves away, check their gear, and do any necessary weapons maintenance before the briefing. It was also designed to ensure that all of the team members were notified, in case one or two of them had been away from the area.

The lag also provided some extra time to make adjustments for any errors in judgment. For example, some of the team might have tried to unwind a bit too heavily the evening before over a case or two of beer chased with shots of tequila or bourbon. Or if one of the men had decided to try to really scrub away some of the grime with soap instead of just taking the usual soapless shower, he would have plenty of time to either rinse off the soap's smell in another shower, or he could just take a quick dip in the river or, better yet, in one of the local canals. Either method would be sufficient to remove any lingering aroma that the soap bar had left behind.

The extra time also gave the men an opportunity to check themselves over, both mentally and physically, to make sure that they were ready to go out again. Remember, even though SEALs pulled only six-month tours, those tours entailed going out on ops almost every day or night. Obviously, regardless of a man's condition, such intensive activity would begin to take a toll on his body and mind. So, it was up to him to check in with himself and determine if he were going to be effective or a potential liability to the team. He would have to access any infected wounds or wrenched joints, try to be honest about how much a bout of malaria, dengue, or flu had taken out of him, and ask if he were capable of pulling his weight or just creating more for the team to drag. Now and then, a man wisely admitted to feeling too subpar to help the team. But more often than not, if a team member was not quite up to speed, someone else would have to make that point for him.

In most cases, after the Platoon Leader's Order had been completed, there would still be a few hours before jump-off time. But now and then, there would be only an hour or so. For that reason, once the Warning Order had come down, some team members would also take the opportunity to grab a quick hot meal, a sandwich, or a few pieces of fruit, to build up their energy stores. They might also start sipping on sodas, juices, or cups of water with a salt tablet or two, to keep the tissues well moistened and "salted." No sense waiting until after you got into the field to start maintaining fluid balance. And loading up on carbohydrates, proteins, and fats meant that you would not have to think about carrying anything more than a package of beef jerky if the op was to last only a few hours. The same reasoning applied to the drinking of fluids, either containing sodium or taken along with salt tablets. No sense carrying more than one canteen unless absolutely necessary.

When 1000 arrived, the team mustered at the briefing shack for the Platoon Leader's Order. Once the team was inside the shack, the door was secured and all windows were covered. Outside the shack at least two SEALs, not members of the ambush team, stood security watch to maintain the integrity of the briefing. The rule here was if you were not a member of the ambush team or involved in the planning, you had no need to know what was involved in the briefing. If the operational requirements were such that Seawolf or BSU crews were to play an ongoing, integral role, they might be present for the entire briefing. Otherwise, they would either be briefed separately or would be present for only that part of the briefing actually dealing with their operational role. In other words, all briefings were conducted on a strictly need-to-know basis.

Inside the shack the team leader and platoon leader stood at the front of the room behind a table and in front of a chalkboard. The team members found chairs or stood wherever they felt they'd be able to best see and hear everything that would be discussed. Spread out across the table were topographical maps and aerial reconnaissance photos of the proposed AO; on the chalkboard were sketches of the island and its riverine approaches. After going over those materials and all of the other available data regarding the island and its potential inhabitants, the team was advised that they would be transported to the AO by chopper and inserted at a small stretch of open beach along the island's western shore. The team was also advised that at about the time they would be making their insertion, a PBR would take up a position just south of the confluence of the two channels that faced the island's western shore. The PBR would thus be ready to intercept any attempt by the VC on the island to use sampans to flee and also be available to provide extraction and any necessary fire support if the team made contact with a numerically superior enemy force.

The briefing also dealt with the main focus of the operation, which was to establish the identity and political affiliation (VC or friendly) of the inhabitants and to determine the purpose of their presence on the island. If it appeared that the inhabitants were indeed VC, they would be free to decide if it would be better to take them out immediately or maintain surveillance for a period of time in case they were only an advance element of a larger force. If the inhabitants were not likely to be joined by any other associates, the team was either to take them prisoner or, if that was not feasible, eliminate them. The team was to confiscate as many weapons, supplies, and documents as could be salvaged and bring them back for scrutiny by intelligence units. The briefing concluded with the usual discussions regarding radio frequencies to be used, call signs, status report intervals, and the types and patterns of flares to be used. The final order of business was to police the briefing area, removing all maps, aerial photos, drawings, diagrams, or models used to describe the AO or any other aspect of the operation.

Since the team was not scheduled to muster at the chopper pad until 2100, most of the men took the opportunity to sleep. Later, some of them would hit the chow hall for evening mess and put together their own meal of fish, chicken, or goat and rice; others would opt for just opening a can of tuna or deviled ham and maybe include a few pieces of dried fish. Eventually, everyone would go over their weapons one more time, just to be sure that they were in perfect order. Because so much depended on the reliability of the weapons, it should be easy to understand why last-minute checks of their condition were so comforting.

From the earliest days of BUD/S, SEALs had been told over and over about the importance of cleaning weapons after every use to reduce the possibility of malfunctioning. This was true for all the weapons that were typically used by all in-country platoons but especially for the Stoner. Although other U.S. units had tried the Stoner, they never warmed up to the piece because it required a lot of maintenance. Unlike the communists' AK-47s, which could stand a great deal of abuse and still prove to be reliable (literally, they could be dropped into a muddy stream, left there for several hours, and then picked up and fired without any ill effects), the Stoner needed to be stripped and cleaned frequently. But because of that rather compulsive approach to weapons maintenance, the Stoner proved to be one of the most important pieces in the SEAL arsenal.

During the last hour or so before departure, the team members leisurely went about dressing and then inspecting their gear. Frequently during such final preparations there would be a lot of highly animated chatter mixed with occasional horseplay. Such activity was beneficial because it helped to keep the team loose and let them vent any anxieties. The chatter was usually so animated because with very few exceptions once the team reached an AO they would not utter another vocal sound until after extracting. That could be several hours or even several days. Under such circumstances even the RTOs did not use voice transmissions to make their status reports or to signal for routine extractions. Instead, they used patterns of long and short squelches established during the Platoon Leader's Order briefing.

Whenever SEALs went through the preoperational saddle-up process (strapping on LBEs, slipping on tac-vests, and so forth), it was important that everything felt, hung, and looked right. An item should not hang or be stashed in such a way that it would become painful to the wearer should he have to assume an awkward surveillance position for a few hours. All items made of metal or plastic were checked to determine if they might reflect even the slightest bit of light.

All parts of all weapons, clothing, and gear were checked to see if they created any unnecessary noise, such as a clink, a clank, a rattle, or even the rustling sound of cloth against cloth. So, as the men saddled up they checked themselves over, jumped up and down, twisted quickly side to side, forward and back, trying to elicit any unwanted sound from their clothing or gear. If they succeeded in producing sounds from anything on their person, they rerigged it. Just to be sure, they would help each other out by scanning the other guy's rigging and even critiquing the effectiveness of each other's camouflage efforts, including face paint. If all looked and felt well, they were ready to go.

At just a little past 2150, in the midst of a moderate rain that had persisted since late afternoon, a PBR moved up the Long Tau River toward the island's southern shoreline. As the craft got to within eight hundred meters of the island's shore, it moved over to hug first the right shore of the river, then the left shore and then back to the right shore again. Each of those movements was designed to draw the attention of any watching VC and, hopefully, distract their attention away from the island's northern shore, where the team's chopper insertion was taking place. To better sell the PBR's false insertions, the craft swung quite close to the island's southeastern shoreline and revved its engines loudly before turning about and heading back down the river again. The craft made three more false insertions as it continued on downstream.

At that same moment, on the island's northern shore, the team moved quickly inland several meters and then stopped to crouch in the darkness for about ten minutes, watching and listening for any sign that their arrival had been detected. Satisfied that all was well, they moved out, paralleling the shoreline as it arced around to the east and then gradually southward. After about one hundred meters on that general heading, the team turned due west, moving toward the island's center. As they continued slowly on that new heading, the point man used a red-lens flashlight to scan the proposed line of march and adjusted course to steer the team clear of any significant terrain impediments. Fortunately, the island's thick tree canopy meant that the foliage beneath the treetops was not quite as densely snarled as that in some of the more open sections of the Rung Sat, because so little sunlight managed to penetrate that far down. The dense canopy also prevented a great deal of the steady rain from falling through, keeping the ground from getting too soggy and making the footing a little less tenuous. As a result, the team was able to move freely and to cover some four hundred meters in just a little more than two hours. Then the point man halted their advance after catching a brief glimpse of some kind of light that had flickered for just a second or two about twenty meters ahead. During the brief halt the team "herringboned" (point man facing forward, the next five men alternately facing left and right, the seventh man facing toward the rear) as they waited to see if the light would flicker again.

After several uneventful minutes, the point man and the team leader moved carefully ahead in the direction of the previous sighting. Five minutes later the point man returned to lead the rest of the team to where the team leader lay scanning the nearly pitch black terrain ahead with an AN/PVS-2 Starlight Scope mounted to the bug-out handle of his M16. With the aid of the Starlight Scope, the team leader (sometimes called Honcho, Boss, or the man or by his first name or nickname) could see that there were two hootches and at least three bunkers about ten meters directly ahead of their position. Sitting on the roof of one of the bunkers were two men smoking cigarettes, their backs toward the team and bathed in the faint light of a carbide lantern positioned between them. The team leader saw also that an AK-47 rested on the rooftop next to each man.

Satisfied that the two figures were indeed alone, the Honcho motioned for the team to move forward into a linear ambush formation. The M60 man took up a position at the extreme left of the formation; the team member carrying the Stoner in its belt-fed, light machine gun configuration moved over to take up his position on the extreme right. The Honcho and the RTO, who was carrying a Smith & Wesson Model 76, positioned themselves at about the middle of the line. The point carried a Remington 870 shotgun; the remaining two men, designated as the capture team, each carried an M16 equipped with an M203 grenade launcher, a concussion grenade, and a Hush Puppy.

On a signal from the Honcho, the capture team moved ahead to take control of the two VC while the rest of the team prepared to provide covering fire or other assistance if needed. Once the two suspects were secured and tethered, the team leader joined the capture team to assist in the interrogation of the prisoners while the rest of the team quickly searched the encampment's five structures. During the rapid search, one 57mm recoilless rifle, twenty rounds of 57mm ammunition, three RPG-7 launchers, thirty PG-7 grenades, two KPV 14.5mm machine guns, and several boxes containing approximately ten thousand rounds of 14.5mm ammunition were found. The team also found one 82mm mortar, fifty 82mm HE rounds, and six cases of 7.62mm ammunition.

The two prisoners were so shaken by the suddenness of their capture and the eerie appearance of the SEALs' green- and black-streaked faces that they were anxious to cooperate with their interrogators. They stated that they were part of a squad from the area's VC local force company, assigned to construct a temporary forward base on the island. The construction had been going on for the past ten days and was still several days from completion. In the interim, the squad had begun storing arms and munitions in the two hootches. They also said that the other five squad members would be arriving sometime after midnight with a 75mm recoilless rifle and ten rounds of HEAT ammunition.

The base was to be used by the local force company to create a temporary blockage of the Long Tau River by sinking a large merchant vessel and, if possible, one of the minesweepers that always preceded most forms of shipping up or down the river. If the company was successful, it would then fall back to the bunkers and prepare for the obvious retaliatory Allied riverine assault, which would be launched against the base. That would make the Allied assault craft vulnerable to the rocket and recoilless rifle fire from the VC battalion, which would have established several other defensive positions along both banks of the river. However, the two prisoners did not share the planners' confidence in the operation and therefore were quite relieved to have been taken out of the game.

The team leader had the RTO contact the waiting PBR and advise the crew to pull the vessel back into the south channel, since the detainees had indicated that the other VC would be arriving in two sampans along the north channel. Because the sampans would be carrying more arms and ammunition, the team wanted to wait until the boats had come as close to the island as possible before springing the ambush. That way there would be a good chance that the arms and some of the VC could be captured. To help bait the trap, the team leader would use one of the captured AK-47s to answer the other VC, who would fire three rapid shots from his own AK-47 to signal their approach. This form of signaling was the most common type of communication between small VC units, among whom radios were a rare luxury.

A few minutes past 0100, the rain stopped. A minute or two later, three sharp reports from an AK-47 rang out from the direction of the north channel. Within a few seconds two answering shots came from the island's northeast shore where a narrow, muddy beach lay hidden below the drooping fronds of a cluster of nipa palms. Just as the echoes died away, the sound of the sampans' outboard motors grew louder, and the two boats made for the palm-fringed beach. When they were only twenty meters from shore, a figure seated near the bow of the lead sampan turned on a flashlight and trained its beam onto the beach, probably expecting to see one or both of his two comrades waiting to help with the unloading.

Seeing no one at the landing site and sensing trouble, the VC with the flashlight waved his right arm wildly, directing both craft to veer away and try to make a run for it. The outboard engines growled loudly as both sampans came about abruptly, trying to head back toward the safety of the north channel. But it was already too late, because both craft were now no more than ten feet from shore. An illumination flare fired from an M203 lit up the sky. A second later, the M60 and the Stoner began spraying the farthest boat with sustained bursts as the rest of the team concentrated their fire on the nearer one. Within ten seconds the firing ceased and another illumination round popped over the two sampans. Both boats were still afloat. One was drifting, its outboard having been taken out by the heavy concentration of automatic weapons fire. The other boat's engine died moments later. The point and one of the capture team members dropped their pieces and hurriedly splashed out into the shallow channel to secure the vessels.

Although both sampans, the 75mm recoilless rifle, and HEAT rounds were captured, none of the occupants survived the ambush. Capturing the weapons and other munitions, along with the two detainees already on hand, meant that the operation had been highly successful. The team then blew all of the bunkers and the two supply hootches and boarded the extraction chopper, with the detainees in tow, for the brief flight back to Nha Be.

After landing at the compound, the detainees underwent further interrogation by a team of both U.S. and ARVN intelligence personnel. It was SOP that all indigenous personnel, whether VC, NVA, or civilian, were to be interrogated by, or at least in the presence of, ARVN and/or National Police personnel. That interrogation resulted in what proved to be very valuable intelligence regarding the tactics, habits, locations, and intentions of VC local force and sapper units operating in the southern Rung Sat. It would result directly in several other successful ambush, recon, and prisoner acquisition operations during subsequent months.

After returning to Nha Be the team members were given time to wash up, eat, and clean their weapons (not necessarily in that order) before getting together to debrief so that the after-action report could be completed.

Many times, after a returning team had cleaned up, the men would grab some food either from the chow hall or from whatever each man might have stashed by his rack and then wash it down with a few beers while cleaning their weapons. On rainy nights, some team members would opt for a cup or two of hot coffee before grabbing a cold brew. The coffee was a welcome answer to the still lingering damp chill brought on by the hours they'd spent in the rain and mud.

This was also a good time to let the team's corpsman examine any cuts, deep abrasions, or puncture wounds to determine what type of treatment, if any, was indicated. Ignoring a seemingly minor infection could mean being restricted from going out on any ops until the team's corpsman was satisfied that the infection was almost completely under control. Nobody wanted to watch his team go out on an op without him. After all, going out was what it was all about.

Search and Seizure of a VC Sampan, Bassac River, Mekong Delta, 1967. (Courtesy Don Sheppard)

USN Seawolf Helicopter lifting off from the deck of a barracks/supply ship on the Bassac River, Mekong Delta, 1967. (Courtesy Don Sheppard)

PBR on high speed patrol along the Bassac River in the Mekong Delta, 1967. (Courtesy Don Sheppard)

ATCs (Armored Troop Carriers) moving along an arm of the Bassac River, Mekong Delta 1967. (Courtesy Don Sheppard)

PBRs (River Patrol Boats) return to base after a patrol on the Bassac River in the Mekong Delta, 1967. (Courtesy Don Sheppard)

This enemy trawler was intercepted as it attempted to infiltrate the coast of South Vietnam. It ran aground and subsequently was captured.

A Vietnamese River Assault Group (RAG) stands ready to fire its 40 mm cannon in support of landing parties put ashore in enemy positions along the Bassac River in the Mekong Delta. Five enemy guerrillas were killed in the combined U.S. Vietnamese operation.

A Navy SEAL, his face camouflaged with colored grease paint, watches intently for any sign of enemy activity during a search and destroy operation in one of the Mekong Delta's swampy jungles.

Members of a SEAL team prepare to disembark from an armored troop carrier (ATC) which carried them down a Mekong Delta canal to a staging area some 67 miles southwest of Saigon during operation Crimson Tide.

Two SEALs pause briefly for a drink of water during operation Crimson Tide. This operation resulted in five enemy guerrillas killed, and 153 camouflaged structures and fortifications, 120 sampans, and 75 bunkers destroyed.

Members of a SEAL team are put ashore utilizing a Navy Landing Craft (LCM), to begin a mission in the Rung Sat special zone in South Vietnam.

Interdiction of VC maritime supply routes.

Crewmen ready their Strike Assault Boats (STABS) for a night patrol on the Mekong River.

A Strike Assault Boat (STAB) makes a high speed patrol near the Cambodian border.

Three members of a SEAL team descend from a hovering helicopter by rappelling down ropes, to set up an ambush in the jungles below.

An Assault Support Patrol Boat (ASPB) is damaged by North Vietnamese action in the Mekong Delta area. The crew returns fire while attempts are made to plug up the holes to keep the boat afloat.

A U.S. Navy adviser to Vietnamese Coastal Group 26 keeps his M-14 rifle ready as a civilian fishing sampan pulls alongside to be inspected by the junk patrol. The board and search operations conducted by the coastal group are made in an effort to prevent enemy personnel or contraband from entering South Vietnam.

A U.S. Navy PCF Nine maneuvers around an enemy barrier during a patrol on the Duong Keo River on the Ca Mau Peninsula.

A "junk" patrol searches for a suspicious boat under the watchful eye of U.S. Naval adviser.

Boatswain's Mate First Class W.C. Martin, Gunner's Mate Second Class Andra Catrambone, advisers to RAG-81, and chief warrant officer G.A. Marshall prepare to board the monitor boat of RAG-81.

INTELLIGENCE GATHERING

Capture operations were from the very beginning a high-priority activity for all in-country SEAL detachments throughout the entire course of their participation in the Vietnam conflict. Although some captures were pulled off easily, others could be difficult and unpredictable. The SEALs may have been much larger, better equipped, and better trained in hand-to-hand techniques than their VC adversaries, but that did not mean that the VC threw in the towel and went quietly when caught. Remember, the VC were not regular, uniformed soldiers and were considered to be little more than criminals by the South Vietnamese government. They knew that being captured would usually result in vigorous interrogation by ARVN or National Police intelligence units. Often, interrogation by U.S. troops could be just as dangerous for them. Grievous injury was not uncommon, and death was a definite possibility. Obviously, any clear-thinking individual faced with such dire possibilities would make every effort to resist capture, even if resisting might mean sure death.

The tactics of ambush teams working in the RSSZ and Delta were slanted much more toward making captures than toward the elimination of enemy personnel. To accomplish that objective, most teams set their ambush positions so that the kill zones were smaller than those employed by other military units. That gave team members the advantage of being close enough to any enemy personnel caught within the kill zone to get on top of them and then control them quickly. Doing so meant standing less risk of getting into protracted tussles with the quarry, thereby reducing the prospects of injury for the capture team. If the prospects for making a successful capture proved impractical, working in such close quarters with the enemy also allowed for rapid elimination of "problem" situations. All weapons fire was carefully controlled, keeping bursts confined to only three to five rounds at a time. This increased the probability that the ambush would result in live prisoners with survivable wounds.

Another reason for keeping ammunition expenditure under control was that ambush teams were not line companies going into the field to actively engage enemy units in prolonged firefights. Since the objective of SEAL ambush teams was to move quickly and range deeply into the VC's backyard, the same rationale for keeping equipment to a minimum also extended to the amount of ammunition carried by each man. For instance, team members using M60s might each carry between four hundred and six hundred rounds; those with lighter automatic weapons or shotguns typically had only two hundred to three hundred rounds per man. If a seven-man team found itself in a prolonged firefight with a company-sized or larger enemy force, the situation could quickly get out of control. So, if an ambush team faced a prolonged engagement, it would withdraw when possible or call in Seawolf air support.

If a SEAL team found itself in a position to capture a prisoner, the SEALs had to totally disregard any notion that size automatically meant the upper hand. In a grapple with a potential prisoner, he would not accept that we were the boss. In fact, getting into a wrestling match with a VC was stupid, because trying to control him was like trying to hold down a frightened four year old in the pediatrician's office. Unlike the small child weighing less than fifty pounds, the average VC was somewhat over one hundred pounds and determined to get away at all cost. It was possible when grappling with a potential captive that he might have his own weapon (knife or sidearm), or grab yours, and do significant damage to you or another team member.

For that reason, whenever we decided to take a prisoner down by hand, we dropped him or otherwise smothered his ability to resist effectively as quickly and completely as possible. Of course, if noise was not an issue, a concussion grenade would stun the prospective captive until the capture team could secure him. If concussion grenades were not used, some

SEALs preferred to employ simpler methods such as grabbing the VC from behind and then quickly body slamming him to the ground, stunning him in the process. Other rudimentary stunning techniques included slamming your fist right behind the victim's ear two or three times (one blow usually was sufficient, but the extra ones made sure that the victim's bell had been rung), or perhaps blindsiding him with a vicious forearm to the back of the head. There were many of us who preferred to use saps (small leather straplike affairs, six or seven inches long, filled with a couple of lead weights). I found saps to be efficient and a lot better than cracking a knuckle against some VC's hard skull.

Any prisoners taken during an ambush were immediately segregated, searched, secured (hands tied behind the back with a lead line secured about the neck), gagged, and blindfolded, then moved quickly toward the extraction area. En route, the RTO would contact the chopper or riverine craft designated to make the extraction, advising as to the approximate time of rendezvous. All along the exit route, the team would remain particularly alert. That was not only to be able to react to any enemy attack against the team, but also to protect the prisoners as well. The VC and NVA recognized that their captured personnel could prove to be of great intelligence value. For that reason, VC and NVA prisoners would be higher priority targets for their own forces than the team members. A buddy of mine once related an example of just how intent the VC could be in such situations.

He and his seven-man ambush team had managed to take two VC prisoners after a brief firefight in a small village near Ben Tre in the eastern Delta. As the team hurried their captives toward a landing zone a few hundred meters away, they began to take sporadic sniper fire from their rear. At first the fire was light, but even so it seemed to be directed mostly toward the prisoners and the two SEALs who were handling them. But after a few more minutes passed, the team began to take intense fire from several different directions at once. Once again, even though the entire team was under fire, most of the fire was being concentrated in the area around the prisoners and their handlers. The team returned fire but the VC were not deterred. Fortunately, the team was able to reach the landing zone before the VC were able to set up a more deadly accurate field of fire. The team's sweeping pattern of fire, coupled with a few well-placed rockets from the approaching Seawolf choppers, sent the attackers scurrying for cover. The team extracted safely, and their prisoners seemed, for some reason, to be very interested in cooperating with their interrogators.

If a prisoner had been wounded or otherwise injured during the capture operation, he would receive immediate medical attention, just as carefully as though he were a team member. This was done not only because of the prisoner's intelligence value but also because humane treatment just made more sense. Keeping in mind that a high percentage of VC were pragmatic peasants, motivated more by years of discontent than by political ideology, humane treatment could prove to be the difference between a prisoner remaining loyal to "The Cause" or rallying under the banner of his troubled nation. A brief example of just how grateful a prisoner could be in such situations follows.

In late April 1968 a seven-man ambush team was operating in an area just west of Mo Cay, in the eastern Mekong Delta. At a little past 2300 a VC sampan moved down a channel toward the spot where the team had set up their ambush kill zone. As the sampan's bow nosed into the kill zone, the team opened up and the salvo immediately killed two of the VC. The third one was wounded and fell overboard into the stream. Although he initially thrashed about a bit, fighting to reach the stream bank, he soon tired and slipped below the surface.

The point man, seeing the wounded VC go under, dropped his weapon and jumped into the dark, swirling waters. He dove under the surface near the spot where the VC had gone down and began to sweep his arms back and forth feeling for the body. Luck was with him and within seconds he popped back up to the surface with the wounded man. A few seconds later he dragged himself and the limp VC up onto the stream bank. The team's corpsman quickly bent over the wounded man, examining him and noted that he was not breathing. He was just about to commence Cardiopulmonary Resuscitation (CPR) efforts when the VC suddenly coughed and began to spew a significant amount of water along with a fair amount of his stomach contents. Although he was breathing on his own, his respirations were labored and each breath was accompanied by a gurgling sound. The corpsman noted a bullet wound in the VC's upper right chest and knew that the gurgling sound meant that the man's chest was filling with blood and at least one lung was collapsed. He had what is commonly referred to as a sucking chest wound.

The corpsman placed his hand over the sucking, gurgling wound, rolling the wounded man onto his right side, hoping to stop any further loss of pressure within his chest cavity. He then asked other team members to find a piece of cellophane, plastic, rubber, or anything else that could be used to cover the wound and keep it airtight. One SEAL had been carrying some beef jerky in a small cellophane baggie. Quickly he handed the bag to the corpsman, who immediately spread it over the wound. A battle dressing was then applied over the bag and tied tightly into place. The treatment worked almost immediately, resulting in the VC's breathing becoming less labored and the gurgling sounds diminished.

Yet the VC was still bleeding internally. The corpsman advised the Boss that the prisoner was in really bad shape and already in the initial stages of shock. If he could not be moved to a hospital or aid station as quickly as possible, he would die within a half hour. In this case, the only hope within that time frame would be via chopper. Without hesitation, the Boss had the RTO put in a call for a dust-off, indicating that a suitable Landing Zone (LZ) was only fifty meters to the east. Even as the RTO was sending, the team moved out toward the LZ.

It took less than ten minutes for the chopper to arrive at the LZ. However, during that time the wounded prisoner's condition had deteriorated rapidly, and he went into cardiopulmonary arrest. The corpsman started CPR and got the VC's heart going again. Fortunately, the stricken man also resumed breathing on his own. After the team had boarded the chopper with their wounded prisoner, he arrested again and the corpsman had to bring him back once more. Throughout this entire time, the rest of the team expressed grave doubts that the ministrations would prove fruitful. But the corpsman's efforts did pay off; the wounded VC just barely hung on until the chopper touched down at a hospital in Ben Tre. He was rushed to surgery and everything went well.

Two days later, he was strong enough for ARVN interrogators to begin debriefing him. The team later was advised that the interrogation was amazingly easy, since the prisoner was eager to volunteer all of the information he had regarding the locations of his company's hamlet, their weapons caches, and which nearby villages provided intelligence regarding Allied positions and movements through the area. The prisoner stated that he was giving up all of that data because he was aware that he had been severely wounded and would have died if not for the efforts of the team's corpsman. The interrogators said that many times during the debriefing the prisoner would smile and say how surprised he was that the SEALs had gone to such lengths to save him from drowning and tend his wounds. He knew that we had caused his wounds in the first place, but he also knew that we could have just interrogated him on the spot and then let him die.

As soon as time allowed, at least some limited interrogation of prisoners was initiated in the field, even while the team might be en route to an extraction point. Frequently, such interrogations resulted in information that led to sweep operations being carried out immediately by MRF units in areas adjacent to the original AO. Or they might result in an opportunity to capture a sizable cache of rice or munitions before it could be removed. More importantly, such rapid follow-up operations not only caused heavy VC losses of equipment and personnel, they demonstrated further that SEAL squads and platoons were capable of covering large sections of the RSSZ or Delta at a time. So effective was this ability that some local communist troops assumed that there were many hundreds of SEALs in the IV CTZ. In fact, there were never more than a few SEAL platoons in all of Southeast Asia at any one time.

As another illustration of how prisoner captures were effected during ambush operations, let's examine two more examples. First, we will follow an ambush operation conducted in an area located eight to ten miles west of Dong Tam and several miles north of Cai Be in early September 1967. For some time two VC battalions, the 514th and the 263d, had been conducting significant operations throughout the sector. Their sapper squads and infantry companies had harassed and terrorized the local populace and frequently employed rocket and mortar barrages against U.S. and ARVN forces located at My Tho and Dong Tam. They also had conducted extensive ambush operations against MRF riverine craft along the area's many canals and channels. Although some intelligence about the local VC had been developed, there still was no hard data on how many companies from each battalion were in the AO; nor was there any firm data pinpointing the locations of VC encampments or supply caches.

During the weeks just preceding the operation, other teams had run recons through the area, finding several new trails and noting that many banana and nipa palm trees had been denuded of their leaves and fronds. The new trails meant that there must have been a sudden increase in pedestrian traffic through the area. This was significant, because months before, all the friendly villagers had fled the area and its ever-increasing VC control. The freshly cut banana leaves and palm fronds were significant in that they were two of the VC's favorite camouflage materials, used often to cover secret trail entrances, hide bunkers and supply caches, or camouflage beached sampans. A prisoner captured by one of the ambush teams two nights before revealed that recently he had been pressed into service by the local VC. His job was to cut banana leaves and palm fronds, to be used to camouflage shoreline ambush positions and booby traps, all of which were directed against MRF vessels along the nearby canals and streams. From this information, an ambush operation was planned for the immediate area, with prisoner acquisitions one of its main goals.

As had been outlined during the preoperational briefing, at a little past 2130 the team boarded an ASPB for transport to the insertion point. This was located at a bend of a large channel that branched off from the Tien Giang River (the Mekong River's more northerly branch) and was approximately a mile and a half southeast of the designated AO. The channel was fairly wide in the vicinity of the insertion point, which made the team feel a little more at ease about being afloat. VC ambushes or booby traps employed against riverine craft traveling along the region's waterways were quite dangerous. If the insertion had been planned for a site along one of the many channels or canals where a rock could be lobbed easily from one shore to the other, the prospects were great for the vessel's crew and the team to suffer heavy casualties.

VC ambushes along waterways often were carried out by one or two squads (there were only three men in each VC squad) using RPGs, recoilless rifles, or mortars and at least one heavy automatic weapon. A typical ambush of a single vessel would begin with one or two HE rounds slamming into the boat's wheelhouse or forward gun emplacement. That was then followed immediately by more HE rounds and intensive fire from the heavy automatic weapons. If the vessel and its crew were taken sufficiently by surprise, the VC would maintain contact. But if the vessel's crew responded quickly, directing effective fire against the ambushers, the VC would break off the ambush and filter back into the dense jungle before an air strike or artillery barrage could be directed against them.

Some VC ambushes were far simpler. In some instances a lone VC hiding in the thick vegetation along the bank of a particularly narrow canal or stream might open up on a passing riverine vessel with an AK-47 in an attempt to hit anyone moving about in the open deck spaces. Or a VC mortar team might lob one or two rounds to explode in an air burst above the vessel. Now and then a particularly gutsy VC might run up to a bank as a vessel glided by and lob a frag so that it would burst either above or on the deck, often resulting in several wounded crewmen.

Then there were the booby traps. One of the simplest yet most effective of VC riverine booby traps consisted of several fragmentation grenades. Their pins were pulled and they were bound together with a cord or a rubber band so that their spoons were held in place. Then they were hung in the branches of a tree where they reached out and over a narrow stream or canal. A trip wire attached to the cord or rubber band ran along a branch, down the tree's trunk, and out to the edge of the stream's bank before disappearing into the murky waters. Its other end was tethered to a tree root on the stream's opposite bank. As the vessel's bow passed through that section of the canal, it would hit the trip wire. That in turn released the spoons on the frags suspended above the river boat, and a few seconds later a sizable section of the passing vessel would be raked with shrapnel.

When the VC wanted to do big damage, they relied mainly on command-detonated mines. Most of those devices were built by sappers only a few hours or days before being used. The two most widely used were the DH-5 and DH-10: gas or cooking oil cans filled with five and ten kilos of TNT, respectively, along with ball bearings, nails, or anything else that would create shrapnel on detonation. These were the VC's version of the U.S. Claymore directional mine. Such mines were often hung from tree branches stretched out across the water or draped over well-used beaching areas. When used to their maximum effectiveness, the mines were capable of inflicting devastating and often lethal wounds.

All of these factors made ambush teams feel much safer once they reached an insertion point. On that particular night in September, the team members felt relieved as they moved quickly along the ASPB's deck and then over the side. After first moving inland in a westerly direction for a distance of about twenty meters, they changed their heading several times during the first fifteen minutes ashore. Then they took a northeasterly heading toward the proposed AO located approximately eighteen hundred meters from the insertion point at a narrow Y juncture of the region's two most widely used trails. The operational plan called for the team to recon across country through the darkness, then, on reaching the AO, set up a listening post. There they were to maintain surveillance of the area until at least first light.

The terrain through which the team was moving was a fair mix of heavy scrub, scattered hedgerows, small rice paddies, a few orchards, and two wide expanses of double-canopy forest. The team planned to move through the more densely vegetated sections as much as possible, which meant that the going would be slow. That was fine because it also meant that the team stood a better chance of being undetected as the men moved along their line of march. That modest degree of invisibility would afford them many opportunities to stop and observe any signs of enemy activity.

When the team had come within three hundred meters of the area of interest, the point man stopped to direct the Honcho's attention to the many signs of VC movement through the general area. He pointed out at least four newly formed trails that seemed to begin at the banks of a nearby canal. The trails then extended away from the canal for a distance of no more than twenty meters before disappearing under a section of forest canopy. As the men moved forward and examined the trails, the point man noted that the grass along one trail was still springy and not dry or brittle, strongly suggesting that the trail most likely had been formed during the previous day or two. He also could see, although somewhat faintly, that many of the sandal prints embedded in the bare, muddy sections of the trails seemed much deeper than one would expect of a Vietnamese weighing considerably less than two hundred pounds. Whoever made these sandal prints must have been laboring under burdensome loads, suggesting that the trails were being used by VC carrying weapons or other supplies from sampans beached along the banks of the canal to encampments or supply caches under the tree canopy.

The team had a fair degree of operational initiative, allowing them to pursue targets of opportunity if such targets seemed of equal or greater value than the original objective. In light of all the signs of enemy activity and what seemed to be supply trails leading to a camp under the nearby tree canopy, the Honcho decided that the team should determine what was under the canopy at the trails' end. But before he could direct the point man to take a new heading paralleling one of the trails, the sounds of voices could be heard coming toward the team's position from the direction of the tree line only three to four meters away. The Honcho motioned the team to move forward and to come on line no more than five feet from the trail. A few seconds later, five figures approached along the trail, three of them leading the way carrying AK-47s and flashlights. The other two men were laboring under the weight of a heavily loaded litterlike device, which they carried between them. Since the five VC were heading away from the tree line and toward the canal, the leader had the team hold position and let the procession pass. He decided it would be better to not take down the five men there but instead to follow them to see why they were carrying things toward the canal instead of away from it, if indeed the path was a supply trail.

The five VC stopped when they reached the canal bank. The two litter bearers lowered their burden to the ground while one of the men with a flashlight began to remove banana leaves from atop a sampan beached a few feet away. The SEAL point man halted the team and the Honcho moved up to lie beside the point man. They watched as the three armed VC turned back to scan the area where the team lay watching. These three held their weapons at waist level, their fingers loosely clutching the trigger guards of their pieces, while the other two VC emptied the contents of the litter into the sampan.

The Honcho motioned for one of the two M60 men and the corpsman carrying an M16 with a grenade launcher to cover the team's rear and flanks. He then motioned for the remaining team members to move forward to take down the five suspected VC. The team members had worked together long enough to realize that the preferred outcome was that all five VC should be captured without causing a ruckus. They knew that they should try to take the VC without any weapon discharges, since they were almost certainly in a VC base area. So they moved quickly and quietly toward the canal bank, hoping that they could take down the three armed men before they could realize what was happening and before they could fire rounds alerting nearby VC patrols or listening posts of the team's presence.

Suddenly, one of the armed VC yelled out and then fired three rapid shots from his AK. He and his two comrades began firing wildly in the general direction of the approaching team, sweeping their fire from left to right and then back again. The RTO, the Honcho, and the Stoner man took the three VC under immediate fire, dropping all three quickly with short bursts of automatic weapons fire. The other two SEALs sprang forward to grab the two litter bearers, slamming them to the ground and covering their mouths. The five SEALs then moved rapidly, two of them securing the two live VC with gags, blindfolds, and hands tied behind their backs and tether lines around their necks. While the RTO trained his M16 on the canal's far bank, the Honcho and the Stoner man searched the three dead VC before turning to examine the contents of the litter and the sampan. Everyone moved briskly, knowing that nearby VC would be sweeping through the area soon in response to the sounds of the brief firefight.

The litter and also the belly of the sampan contained a total of twelve RPG rounds and eight DH-10 mines. The Honcho and the Stoner man tossed the three bodies into the sampan, on top of the munitions. The leader had already placed a wad of C-4 in with the mines with its friction fuse hooked onto the belt of one of the dead VC. He hoped that a VC reaction force in discovering the sampan and its dead occupants would move the rigged body, causing destruction of the munitions and killing or wounding several VC troops.

The leader rallied the team and had the point man set out on a heading parallel to the canal. Less than four minutes had elapsed since the first shots were fired. To the left, in the direction of the tree line, were sounds of many men racing through the tall grass only a few meters away. The team turned to form a hasty linear ambush, everyone waiting until the team leader snapped off the first burst. When he did, each man fired into the ranks of the rapidly closing VC. Return fire was immediate, the VC's muzzle flashes flaring perhaps only twenty feet away. The team's M60 and Stoner fired long bursts into the VC position, at a height of only a foot or two above the ground, resulting in immediate silence from the VC weapons.

The team then peeled out, with the last man in line moving up to the front of the column, followed a second or two later by the next man, and so on, those waiting to move up providing covering fire. The point man had already moved ahead to find the best exit route. Since pursuing VC could be heard moving to flank the withdrawing team from the south, the Honcho set up a Claymore mine, aimed toward the south and rigged with a twenty-second delay fuse. Then he and the corpsman each slung one of the VC prisoners over their shoulders and hustled off to follow the point's lead. Twenty seconds later the Claymore went off, but no shouts or moans of pain were heard. Even though no VC were hit, they would still take a minute or two to collect their thoughts before continuing the pursuit.

The point made good use of the two-minute head start, leading the team along the canal bank about fifteen meters before spotting a shaky-looking monkey bridge spanning a section of canal that had narrowed to no more than twenty feet. After halting the team, he quickly crossed the flimsy bridge to do a brief recon of the other side. A minute later he returned, advising the team leader that the vegetation on the other side was thick enough to provide the team with cover and give them time to decide which exit route to take. The primary exit route was the one they would have taken if they had gone on to the original AO. That was now some three hundred meters to the north, however, meaning that they would have to evade the many VC hunter squads en route with two scared prisoners in tow. Or they could call for an immediate Seawolf extraction, but with so many VC obviously in the area a chopper would almost certainly be brought down by enemy fire.

The team slipped across the bridge with the rustling sounds of pursuing VC moving up quickly from the rear. Some thirty meters beyond the bridge, the point led the team into a chokingly dense patch of thorny vines and shrubs a mere fifteen feet or so off the trail. As they all squatted down in a "wagon wheel" (a circle with each man facing outboard and the prisoners in the center), a brief ripple of explosions told them that the booby-trapped mines had been set off back at the ambush site. About that same moment the team also could hear voices and random automatic weapons fire coming from the direction of the bridge.

The leader had planned to have the team take only a short rest in the dense cover until the enemy had eased off a bit on their search. But it seemed that the VC were in a frenzy, the sounds of their voices, movements, and random firing now coming from all directions around the team's position. A few minutes later, the VC to the north of the team's position could be heard pulling back, and the VC to the south started firing randomly again. The team knew that this was the VC reconning by fire, that is, firing into areas where a person might seek cover, hoping that the firing would panic them into breaking cover and running. The VC kept up their firing for a full minute before finishing with three RPG rounds fired near the team position, one exploding just ten feet from them.

When the firing began, the corpsman and the point flopped over onto the prisoners, holding a knife against each frightened man's throat. They got the message and obediently remained quiet. The prisoners and team members all stayed as still as possible, even after the firing had stopped, as six VC came pushing their way through the brush heading straight for the team's position. But the VC stopped a few feet short of the SEALs, squatted down, and started to chat idly. Other voices could also be heard coming from the trail, and cigarette smoke wafted toward the team. Obviously the VC were going to hang around for a while, waiting to see if their quarry might decide to break cover. But after a half hour, the VC trudged back onto the trail, and their voices slowly melted away into the distance.

Everyone waited for several minutes before moving a muscle. The Honcho lifted the canvas flap covering his watch dial and checked the time. It was almost 0330. He decided to have the team hold position for another hour before having the RTO call in a long-overdue situation report and request Seawolf extraction. (Per the preop briefing, situation reports were to be made hourly at fifteen minutes after the hour.) The designated LZ for the extraction was to be an area of high grass and reeds one hundred meters east of the team's present position. By 0530 the team reached the extraction point, boarded the chopper, and lifted off for the short flight back to their afloat base at the mouth of the Delta.

Interrogation of the two prisoners led to some interesting bits of information. For one thing, they claimed that they were not really VC at all but merely two farmers from a local village who had been conscripted as part of a growing labor force. At the time of the ambush, they were told that they were to help the three armed VC in setting DH-5 and DH-10 mines at two particularly narrow areas of the main channel coursing past Cai Lai on its way to the Mekong River. From the way they described it, the section of the channel they were to mine was the very AO toward which the team had been headed. The prisoners were also told that they would be allowed to head back to their village once the mines had been placed and set. The VC were going to set up an ambush position along the channel from which they would fire RPG rounds at riverine targets of opportunity. This information, coupled with that provided by the team in filing their after-action report, led MRF units to undertake several large-scale operations throughout the operational area.

Many ambush operations, no matter how successful otherwise, often resulted in no prisoners being taken. These operations might produce great quantities of captured supplies and armaments, as well as the destruction of many bunkers, sampans, and wells, but no enemy troops or support personnel to interrogate. An example took place during July 1967 in an area northwest of Can Gio in the Rung Sat. An ambush team and two LDNNs were inserted by PBR to conduct an extended ambush/prisoner acquisition operation in an area that had been used extensively by the VC before the onset of the monsoon rains. During the first twenty-four hours, the team discovered an abandoned VC camp consisting of two bunkers along the banks of the channel to the west, several well-hidden hootches, and four camouflaged, sweet-water wells.

Although the camp was deserted, it was obvious that it was being used by the VC. In one hootch the team found neat bundles of clothing, a few pieces of NVA-type web gear, and rags of varying lengths wrapped in plastic (presumably to be used as crude battle dressings). Twenty meters north of the camp they came across another hootch in which they found a dozen large sacks of rice. The hootch was sizable and appeared capable of accommodating scores of rice sacks. The camp was newly constructed, with a large VC unit using it as a base area and storage site.

The team leader had the RTO report the team's findings and advise the base camp that they would set up a listening post to monitor the area. Further recon of the surrounding area revealed three newly formed trails. One led from the camp to a large stream about fifteen meters to the east. A second trail led from the camp to the rice cache, and the third went to the two bunkers. As the team inspected the stream banks to the east, they found piles of varying sizes of bamboo stacked near two freshly dug shallow pits. The pits and their location suggested that two more bunkers were under construction, meant to cover the stream approach to the camp.

Where the trail leading to the stream ended, the team found some wide, deep depressions and several sandal prints in a slightly elevated section of firm mud, under a thick canopy of overhanging vegetation. Because of the canopy's sheltering effect, the depressions and prints were preserved from the monsoon rain. That was obviously the spot where the VC beached their sampans on previous trips to the camp, meaning that the stream bank was the best place to set up a listening post/ambush site.

Since the VC would undoubtably return, it was only a question of when; that night or one after that. Each team member and the two LDNNs set up their ambush positions accordingly, remaining well camouflaged beneath the dense ground cover while getting comfortable enough to cope with what could be a long, tedious, and uneventful night.

As it turned out, the team did not have to wait very long. It was not quite 2230 when the team leader, using a Starlight Scope to scan upstream, picked up the image of a sampan slowly approaching the kill zone. A few seconds later, another sampan slid into view behind the first one. Both boats had thatched cabinlike structures amidship. In the eerie pale blue light of the scope, the Boss could see that each vessel carried three VC. He decided to wait for both sampans to reach the beaching site before triggering the ambush. Since the team had worked together for so long, there was no need to advise everyone how the ambush would be sprung. Everyone waited until the team leader had thrown his concussion grenade before opening up on the six VC who were just pulling their sampans onto the beach. It was all over very quickly; first the flash and ear-splitting roar of the grenade and then the short but deadly spray of automatic weapons fire. Less than thirty seconds elapsed from the time the firing had begun until all was quiet again.

An illumination flare was fired, and the capture team quickly moved to the beaching site. But only four VC, all dead, were found lying on the beach near the boats; the other two were nowhere in sight. Another illumination flare went up and all eyes scanned the stream and the surrounding bank, but the other two were still unaccounted for. There had not been enough time for them to have slipped away, even if they had miraculously survived the deadly concentration of fire. The only other possibility was that they had been hit and knocked back into the fast-moving stream, and their bodies were being carried downstream toward the main channel.

Although the ambush did not result in any live prisoners, the operation was still very successful. A search of the two sampans yielded several cases of 7.62mm ammo, boxes of Chinese-manufactured fragmentation grenades, and a couple of bags of plastic explosives. In addition, there were bags filled with batteries taped together to be used as makeshift "joy box" generators, along with electrical fuses, pliers, crimpers, and other small tools useful in fabricating command-detonated mines. In the cabin area of one sampan, a bag containing maps, diagrams, and other documents was found lying among piles of blankets and empty sandbags. And in the mud near one of the four VC bodies there was a 9mm Makarov pistol, a Russian-made automatic sidearm known to be carried by high-ranking VC officers. It was assumed that one of the dead VC had been a battalion officer who had come along to supervise and inspect the ongoing construction of the camp.

By the late summer and early fall of 1967, the ability of the VC to harass shipping along the main Saigon river approaches had been significantly reduced. SEAL ambush and recon teams continued to conduct extremely successful operations throughout the entire RSSZ, making VC daylight operations decidedly precarious endeavors. VC units also learned quickly that the night was now just as full of dangers for them as it had been previously for Allied units. By early January 1967, VC sapper units operating in the southern part of the Rung Sat realized just how dangerous their work had become.

By that time, Detachment GOLF units had blown up several sweet-water wells, captured or otherwise eliminated a large number of local VC troops, destroyed many bunkers, and captured or destroyed hundreds of pounds of enemy foodstuffs and munitions. All of this resulted in local VC forces having to turn increasingly to neighboring noncombatant villages for food, water, and medical supplies. Since those villages were already being forced to pay "taxes" to local VC units (in the form of rice, livestock, fish, green vegetables, money, sampans, and so forth), the new "requisitions" proved to be too much. This caused many villagers to decide to work actively toward remedying the situation by reporting the location, strength, and movements of local VC forces.

From January through the early spring of 1967, SEAL ambush and recon teams stepped up their operations throughout the RSSZ. Intelligence provided by regional villagers, as well as observations made by recon teams, identified well-fortified VC hamlets located near the villages of Phuoc Luong on the banks of the Nha Be River, Phuoc Khanh on the banks of the Saigon River, and the densely overgrown areas north of Can Gio and near Dong Hoa to the southwest. Teams determined that several heavily fortified encampments, supply depots, and munitions factories were located in the particularly mucky region around Nhan Trach where the RSSZ's northern fringes abutted Phuoc Thuy Province. Reliable intelligence obtained from prisoners recently snatched from that very AO led to an ambush team from Detachment GOLF being sent back in to locate and eliminate any such enemy positions on their own or to call for support from other detachment units if too large an enemy force was present.

For that operation in March 1967, the team was to insert by HSSC along a canal that branched off the Nha Be River and extended into the area just south of Nhan Trach before turning north toward Cat Lai. After inserting, the team was to move overland to an area in the southwestern section of Nhan Trach, some eleven hundred meters from the insertion point. While they were doing that, the HSSC would be slowly coursing along the intersecting waterways, eventually moving back into the canal about a quarter mile north of the AO. There it would remain on station ready to extract the team and/or provide fire support if necessary. The insertion took place at 2200, but because of the difficult terrain that the team had to move through, the projected arrival at the AO was somewhere around 0200.

The team had been ashore for only about thirty seconds when the men and the HSSC came under intense fire from heavy and light automatic weapons and RPG and mortar rounds. All of the fire was coming from enemy positions no more than twenty meters away, quite near the canal bank east and south of the insertion point. The HSSC moved back toward the insertion point, firing its 106mm recoilless rifle, .50-caliber machine guns, and automatic grenade launchers into the heart of the VC positions. With the vessel providing covering fire, the team moved back to the insertion point as quickly as possible, while directing a heavy concentration of fire against the nearby VC. By the time the HSSC and the team arrived together along the canal bank, the vessel had taken several direct hits from the VC's RPGs, as well as a mortar round that hit the craft's still-lowered ramp. This sprayed the open deck area with shrapnel, killing one crewman and wounding several others. Two VC RPG rounds impacted near the team during the initial seconds of the ambush, wounding two SEALs. Fortunately, their wounds were not severe enough to prevent them from returning fire and being able to move on their own.

As soon as the last team member managed to scramble onto the HSSC's ramp, the vessel reversed, backed into the center of the canal, and headed back south along the same route it used in reaching the insertion area. As the craft withdrew, two Seawolf gunships that were responding to the HSSC's frenzied radio calls for assistance swooped down on the ambush site, spraying the VC positions with automatic weapons fire and rockets. The VC initially attempted to fire at the choppers but soon realized that to continue would only make them sitting ducks for the Seawolves' accurate and deadly fire. As the choppers lit up the area with flares, they could see scores of VC hurriedly withdrawing from the ambush site, carrying or dragging a large number of their dead and wounded comrades. During the next several days teams swept through the area, noting many blood trails suggesting that the VC had suffered a large number of casualties in the brief firefight.

As I stated previously, patience is one of the most important elements of stealth, because it is what makes deliberate, careful movement work. If one is not patient, he will soon tire of the time and effort demanded for a particular situation. Instead of moving branches aside carefully and then just as carefully replacing them, he may decide that the effort is too tedious and elect to cut some corners. But patience keeps the mind focused on why care and deliberation are necessary. The careful man is afforded the time to learn the condition of his surroundings and return out-of-place things to proper order. Thus, his movements into and out of enemy territory leave no trace, other than the destruction of enemy structures and supplies and the taking of prisoners.

Another beneficial by-product of patience is that it greatly enhances the ability to remain calm and in control of emotions and actions, thereby intensifying one's senses and self-awareness. Previously I referred to the VC's use of a tactic known as recon by fire, whose purpose was to put small-arms, RPG, or mortar fire into areas where an enemy was thought to be hiding, to induce him either to return the fire or break cover and run. As improbable as it might seem, the best countertactic in such circumstances was merely to hold position and wait out the VC. It was not an easy thing to do, especially when the incoming rounds were nearly on the money. Staying calm and still while small-arms fire cut through the vegetation only inches away from where we crouched, or an HE round hit so near that its explosion literally lifted a SEAL off the ground, was extremely difficult. In fact, I've known some men to lie flat on their faces, keeping their hands completely off their weapons, so they would not be tempted to rise up and return fire.

A patient, methodical approach toward movement through environments such as those in the IV CTZ paid dividends in that we were better capable of interpreting sensory data. As we moved through the forests, swamps, and reed beds, we were being bombarded constantly by sounds and smells. These were often more informative about where we were and what was going on in the area than any intelligence briefing or map reference could be. For instance, during the dry season we might be able to avoid halting a team's march to huddle up while the Boss and the point used a penlight to check a map reference. If we knew that the team's proposed line of march was parallel to an irrigation canal, the scent of raw sewage in the air on a warm night might tell us that the canal was nearby. Such an observation was possible because most small irrigation canals in the Delta also doubled as rudimentary sewage systems for nearby villages. Thus, our noses could tell more about our present location than any single-dimensional grid reference.

A heightened state of awareness was also important for dealing with booby traps, both the natural and man-made varieties. It was tricky to move about the landscape during hours of darkness or half-light, when the potential hazards included not only venomous snakes and poisonous insects but also treacherous terrain features. Some areas had fast-moving streams running beneath the mudflats, which caused the mud and sand to shift and suck below the surface-weighted objects, such as humans trying to make their way across. There were also streams and coastal estuaries that might seem to flow gently but actually possessed strong, swift currents capable of pulling a man under and then whisking him quickly into open water. If he fell victim to such currents without having inflated the flotation rig inside his tac-vest, his chances of reaching the surface again were poor. Being patient, carefully stepping along, and being sure of one's footing were essential.

To illustrate how dangerous and unpredictable the terrain in the RSSZ could be, consider what happened to a member of an ambush team from Detachment GOLF in early 1967. The team was to set up a listening post along the southern fringe of Nhan Trach, where the VC had been operating for a long time. The men were inserted by PBR just after dark on a moonless night along a section of river densely packed with nipa palms, vines, and other low ground cover. As the PBR slid in toward the right bank of the river, the seven men were to slip over the side one by one into the shallows, scramble onto the embankment, and melt into the undergrowth. Less than two minutes passed when only six of them had made it to the rally point; there was no sign of the seventh man, the point.

They did not have to wait long to discover what had happened to him. In the stillness of the night they could hear someone snapping his fingers (one of the nonverbal forms of communication used by teams in the field) somewhere back in the direction of the insertion area. The team moved out quickly toward the sounds because the snapping grew more rapid, indicating that the man was in danger and needed immediate assistance. It took only about fifteen seconds for them to reach the spot where he was, immersed to his upper lip in the water only a foot or two from the bank. His right hand was holding his shotgun high above his head and the fingers of his left hand were snapping wildly. He had managed to find a particularly deep section of mud along the river bottom, at the spot where he was to climb onto the riverbank.

Two of the team members eased carefully into the water on both sides of him to help him pull free. But they had to quickly back out when they found themselves also sinking rapidly into the ooze. Instead, they each grabbed one of the trapped man's arms and began pulling him as they leaned back against the riverbank. At first he did not budge, but, as he gradually rocked his body from side to side, the suction slackened a bit. This went on for twenty minutes before they were able to pull him onto firm ground. As he emerged from the water they saw that his pants were down around his ankles. He had sunk to his waist into the mud, which had seeped down under his waistband and filled his pant legs, holding him fast like an anchor. He was finally able to break free of the mud's grip because his belt had snapped, allowing his pants to slide down and release the mud.

If the team had not reached him as quickly as they had, he soon would have slipped under the water and drowned, leaving no trace of his passing. If he had attempted to struggle free by himself, his movements would have aided the mud in pulling him deeper and deeper into its firm embrace. But he had stayed calm and used his head, remembering that by staying still the mud's pull on him would be slowed, giving him extra time to alert the rest of the team. Knowing that the team would notice his absence quickly and search for him immediately made staying calm easier.

The VC (and before them the Vietminh) had spent their lives not only fighting in such conditions but also learning to scrape out a living in the RSSZ. Their understanding of the mudflats and sections of quicksand was intimate. They knew how to use the swampy region's ground conditions to their best advantage. Often, they would set an ambush in an area where their enemy would have only one direction in which to retreat from incoming fire, directly into a mudflat or a patch of shifting sand. Once the victim had stumbled into such an area, the VC could lie back and watch him trying to extricate himself from the sucking pits of ooze and grit.

Staying calm enabled SEALs to quickly appreciate and take advantage of all available options in extricating themselves from tight situations. In the previous example the best option would have been to move quickly toward a possible exit from a kill zone while staying calm. That way, the point would have been able to note changing ground conditions and turn the team toward firmer ground if mushy footing was encountered. Following a possible extrication, the team could then retreat back along the approach route or, better yet, attack the ambush line, a tactic that usually surprised the enemy so much that he would break contact and leave the area.

Many dangers encountered in the field were natural, but most were man-made. For example, in early 1967 in an area several kilometers west of Moc Hoa, the VC were assumed to be using the site not only as an R & R facility but also as a supply depot and staging area. An ambush team was sent into the AO to scope it out and acquire a prisoner or two, to get more definitive information about what was going on.

The team could move through the area fairly easily for most of the night and saw many signs of recent VC activity. An hour before dawn, they came across a small, well-fortified hamlet located only a few meters from the Kinh Phuoc Canal. As they approached they came under mortar fire from the north. Each man crouched down immediately and slowly turned his head from side to side, trying to get a fix on the direction of the mortar fire. If the team had been part of a conventional unit, they might have dispersed and sought cover. To have done so would have kept them in the center of the kill zone, allowing the enemy eventually to zero in on their position. There must have been an enemy spotter adjusting the fire, because the rounds were marching directly toward the team's position. As soon as the point man determined the direction of the rounds, he stood and directed the team out of the kill zone on a ninety-degree heading away from the line of incoming fire. The team escaped and called in an air strike, which obliterated the hamlet and several occupants.

Most communist and Allied forces drastically restricted their actions to defense during the monsoon season (May through November). The VC knew that the foul weather impeded the Allies' aerial observation. And the mud became more gooey from the daily rain, making it foolhardy for the Allies to put large, cumbersome units into the field. So the VC devoted their energies to repairing and strengthening their fortifications. They trained their personnel in the manufacture of armaments and conducted recon operations in preparation for future campaigns.

The monsoon season also presented the SEALs with significant tactical opportunities. Among other things, movement through difficult terrain was facilitated because the incessant rain muted the telltale sound of a misplaced foot slipping off a slippery cajeput root and splashing noisily into the water. And tracks left in the mud would soon fill with water, making them disappear into the shifting ooze.

These advantages also came in the company of some rather great disadvantages. The teams would have to navigate through terrain that when dry was already an orienteering challenge. Even during the relentless onslaught of the monsoon rains, the recon teams had to maintain long periods of motionlessness, since they elected to operate in such close proximity to enemy infiltration/exfiltration routes and encampments. This meant that they had to endure long hours of cramped muscles, with the discomfort intensified by the wet conditions. After prolonged exposure to such conditions, some men found themselves still feeling wet for hours after getting back to their warm and dry camp.

There were many ways to make lying around in the mud and rain a little more tolerable during ambush/recon operations. We might be able to position ourselves under some banana fronds or other broad leaves. These made fine natural umbrellas, providing minimal relief against the pelting rain. On an extended operation, those not standing watch would huddle close together to share body heat. It was not the same as sleeping in a warm, dry bunk, but it was better than curling up alone and shivering before it was time to stand watch or move out again.

Staring is something everyone does from time to time, often when you don't know you're doing it. But it can be a problem if an enemy soldier happens to look at you and manages to "pick up" your eyes. Although it might not seem likely to most people, it is surprising how clearly the whites of a person's eyes stand out when viewed against the dark background of dense foliage. After all, you cannot camouflage the whites of your eyes; you can only hope that the shadows cast by the surrounding foliage or the brim of your hat might mute sufficiently the brightness of your big American eyes.

When you stare at some person too long and too intently, he can often pick up your vibes. Most of us have had the experience of being in a restaurant or ballpark and becoming aware of the steady gaze of someone. With that experience in mind, imagine how much more intense the feeling would be if that stare emanated from someone planning to arrest you or do you great bodily harm. So if you made the mistake of staring too long, you had to be prepared to divert your gaze at the first indication that the person under surveillance was becoming uncomfortable and was about to turn to look in your direction.

The overall accuracy and scope of SEAL intelligence gathering broadened with the ever-increasing expertise in stalking and conducting swamp and jungle operations. Ambush and recon teams became adept at maneuvering so closely to enemy positions that they were able to exceed by far the observations made by other U.S. and Allied recon units. Whereas other Allied recon units reported enemy troop strength, armaments, food stores, and types of structures located within enemy hamlets, SEAL recon teams were capable of making far more expansive observations.

The teams would work so closely to enemy positions that they could not only see troops, structures, and material but could make other valuable observations based on what they could hear or smell, such as the type and quality of rations, general morale (such as from animated chatter, laughter, or bickering), permanence of the encampment (size of latrine facilities, depletion of indigenous fruits and produce), or the presence of fresh munitions (aroma of Cosmoline in the air). By listening carefully, team members could listen in on tactical briefings or casual conversations. Many SEALs were fluent in Vietnamese, and some teams included some LDNNs or other Vietnamese personnel.

During an ambush operation along the Kinh Te Canal, north of its intersection with the Can Giuoc Canal, listening in on enemy conversations paid big dividends. The team, accompanied by two Vietnamese LDNNs, came on three VC hunkered down in a recently constructed, well-hidden bunker along the canal bank. The VC had one RPG rocket launcher and a dozen rockets they planned to use against passing river traffic. Instead of taking down the VC immediately, the team members worked to within ten feet or so of the enemy and listened as the three men chatted idly. One of the LDNNs made eye contact with the Honcho and signaled that, if possible, the VC should either be taken prisoner or taken out as silently as possible. Although the Honcho did not know what the LDNN had heard, he immediately nodded agreement and signaled the rest of the team to move in on the VC.

The capture team and the two LDNNs pounced on the VC and secured them before they could react. The VC's conversation had revealed that a VC paymaster was due to be coming down the canal after midnight that night. The three VC were then interrogated separately; each confirmed that the paymaster and a small security force were expected in a few hours. The team then set up an ambush at the position where the VC had planned to fire on passing Allied river traffic. It was a little before 2200 and was raining heavily; it was still raining at 0230, when a sampan came into view.

The Honcho watched the sampan's approach through a Starlight Scope and waited until the vessel was well inside the kill zone before triggering the ambush. He fired a burst from his Swedish K-40 into the sampan's bow, followed by two flares that lit up the area. Bursts of automatic weapons fire then poured out from the team's position, raking the VC craft fore and aft. The firing lasted less than ten seconds, after which the capture team moved into the stream quickly to secure the craft. Unfortunately, all seven occupants of the sampan had either been killed or were near death. As had been expected, the paymaster was among them, along with canvas pouches containing cash, pay records, fake identity cards, and other types of documents of intelligence value. Although the team had not been lucky enough to take the paymaster alive, the pay records were a real coup because they contained the names of many local VC who resided and operated in the surrounding area.

If a recon team was operating in advance of one of its own platoons, Game Warden units, or the MRF, their observations about enemy troop movements and encampments would be transmitted to the main force. They then could elect to move in to engage an enemy force or camp, or to bypass it if a target of greater interest had been located elsewhere. The hamlet or camp would be earmarked for future action. In certain situations in which the recon team felt sufficiently confident in its ability to overwhelm the enemy camp and its personnel, it might elect to move on its own initiative. Such operations often proved successful, resulting in the capture of VC personnel, equipment, and valuable documents that otherwise might have slipped through the cracks. The intelligence value of the prisoners and documents taken in such operations would usually make the risks seem quite reasonable. Risks could be offset by heavy fire support from helicopter gunships, which could be on station within minutes following a team's hasty radio request. If the team was to be extracted by a riverine vessel, supporting fire could be provided by its heavy weapons.

The information supplied by prisoners further enhanced the SEALs' ever-expanding intelligence base. They combined such information with that obtained from other MACV sources, other U.S. and ARVN units, area villagers, and their own firsthand observations. This gave the SEAL detachments a much clearer picture of VC structure, tactics, locations, and overall strength in both the RSSZ and Delta provinces. Their widening intelligence base paid off, not only in high-impact raids against VC units but also in the steadily increasing confidence exhibited by Rung Sat and Delta villagers for their own safety. This resulted in a steady increase in the cooperation and assistance of villagers in campaigns against the resident VC.

Villagers throughout all of South Vietnam were engaged in a much higher stakes kind of game than the actual combatants were because they were in the midst of the action. All too often their villages, fields, livestock, and other possessions were inadvertently struck by small-arms fire, short artillery rounds, or off-target bombs. Sometimes, firefights between opposing forces would wind up involving a nearby village and its inhabitants. And local VC or NVA units would often use villages as resupply areas, listening posts, caches for weapons or food, and sources of young conscripts.

Villagers often found themselves being the unwilling pawns of combatants on both sides. Local communist units pressured villagers to act as early warning systems, passing along word of Allied troop movements in their areas. The VC dealt harshly with villages failing to comply with their requests or found to be cooperating with Allied forces. Kidnap, torture, and assassination of village officials and their entire households became a common method of exhibiting VC displeasure with a less than compliant village, effectively keeping the inhabitants in check.

Unfortunately, many villagers also found themselves being terribly mistreated by ARVNs or other Allied troops. Although such treatment was not the norm, nor was it sanctioned, it did occur and resulted in many "fence-sitting" villages deciding to cooperate more with the VC than with the Allies. They knew that to cooperate with the VC meant possible incarceration or severe treatment by Allied personnel. But they also knew that if the VC learned of any cooperation with the Allies, an individual and his or her immediate family would be subject to torture and death. The fate of the victims would be carried out in such a way as to serve as a potent object lesson in the need for silence.

It was also understandable that most of the rural civilian population had little motivation to cooperate with the ARVN troops or their Allies. This was due to the fact that ARVN units did not maintain a significant presence in most of the RSSZ or IV CTZ. They typically operated in close proximity to large population centers, venturing into the rural districts only during infrequent sweep operations. Many U.S. troops took such dearth of activity to indicate that the ARVNs were less than motivated toward engaging the enemy. But when ARVN forces did engage VC units, they usually proved themselves effective in dealing with the situation.

A more likely reason for the lack of aggressive operations by ARVN units throughout most of South Vietnam was that they were not just fighting a war, they were engaged in a civil war. As with Union and Confederate forces during the U.S. Civil War, troops are somewhat more circumspect about rushing to do battle with an enemy unit whose ranks might include their own relations. So as long as resident VC units did not pose too great a threat to an ARVN force's immediate area of responsibility, there would rarely be a need for the two groups to face each other in the field. This arrangement worked out badly for the rural civilians because it left only the Regional Force (RF) or Popular Force (PF) to keep the VC wolf from their doors.

The RF/PF units often operated out of large, well-fortified complexes. Some consisted of neighboring villages situated around old, abandoned three-cornered forts, the type the French had built during their long period of occupation. They consisted of three high, slightly inward-slanted walls with sentry towers located atop each corner. The perimeter around the forts usually consisted of two or more concentric triangles of concertina wire. Bunkers, Claymore mines, and sometimes *punji* sticks were placed at strategic intervals in the bare areas between each wire triangle. A few forts even set drums of phougas (a gelatinous, highly flammable gasoline product) into sections of the outer walls at points where an enemy assault would be most likely. When fired upon, the phougas erupted in a napalm-like fireball, engulfing everything in its path in a sea of intense flame. Needless to say, the VC preferred to give such fortified positions a wide berth. They were not averse to throwing a few rockets or mortars at the forts, but an all-out assault was a rarity. For that reason, the occupants of outlying villages sought shelter around RF/PF forts whenever the VC were on the move in their neighborhoods.

When conducting recon overflights of western Delta districts where forts existed, SEALs could readily tell when the VC were active in an area by taking note of the numbers of newly constructed hootches in the villages surrounding an RF/PF village. Or they could see how many sampans were beached along the banks of nearby streams at the height of the day instead of on their way to market or out in search of a day's catch. These indicators were frequently enough to consider sending an ambush team into the surrounding countryside, even with no other sign of enemy activity. The people might still have been reluctant to provide the Allied forces with hard, overt intelligence, but their need to seek safety was equally informative. Even MRF forces would commit a unit to an area because of such indicators.

Because of the extensive jungle canopy and/or dense ground cover prevalent in the RSSZ and the Delta, it was difficult for aerial reconnaissance to be of much help in getting a fix on VC personnel or structures.

Although overflights might show signs of probable VC activity, greater reliance was placed on information from recon operations or cooperative villagers.

Ambushes set up along the canals branching off the Long Tau resulted in the elimination and capture of scores of VC personnel, sampans, documents, and weapons. Sweeps conducted in the areas north and west of Dong Hoa were also successful.

Those sweeps also uncovered several well-camouflaged hootches containing large stores of TNT, C-4 and assorted fuses, primer cords, and blasting caps. There was also a strange array of metal items such as empty Coca-Cola cans, milk or gas cans of varying size, cooler chests, and the large, rectangular orange and white Foremost dairy products signs that could be seen tacked to the sides of dockside buildings along the waterways. The larger metal items were used to fabricate mines used against river traffic or Allied land forces. The Coca-Cola cans became crude but effective fragmentation hand grenades. Gas cans were made into the VC's favorite mines, the DH-5 and DH-10, used in much the same way as were the U.S. Claymore directional mines. These successful operations continued throughout the remainder of the year, especially during August through December, resulting in the capture of large quantities of enemy material as well as the destruction of many VC structures and the elimination or capture of scores of the enemy.

The reduction in the numbers of active VC in the Rung Sat was important because many were sappers. Sappers were often Dac Cong, the VC's special forces; they were well motivated and extremely efficient practitioners of sabotage, terrorism, and infiltration. For a time, the Dac Cong were viewed by most U.S. troops in the same way that all VC were viewed—small, ill equipped, poorly trained, and no match for the technically superior American GI. But that proved to be invalid; the Dac Cong mines made passage along the Saigon River approaches a high-anxiety endeavor. They made it necessary for all merchant vessels to be ushered along by minesweepers.

The hundreds of deadly booby traps that the Dac Cong had sown along the region's trails, riverbanks, and rice paddy dikes made each step an adventure. The Dac Cong also proved adept at crawling undetected through the perimeter wire surrounding Allied positions to turn the Claymores around so that they'd blow back in the faces of the defenders. Their frogmen were continually trying to attach mines and other types of explosive devices to MRF barracks ships, so those standing deck watch often dropped fragmentation grenades over the side whenever anyone thought they had seen a swimmer or a wake in the water. This was understandable, especially after a team of Dac Cong swimmers scored a major coup in 1967 during the construction of the MRF base at Dong Tam. They used limpet mines to sink the *Jamaica Bay,* which was one of the largest river dredges in existence.

While Detachment GOLF's personnel were conducting their sweeps in the RSSZ, Detachment ALPHA SEALs were engaged in successful operations in several parts of the Delta. Their sweep and ambush operations were conducted over wide areas, resulting in heavy enemy losses. From the start, the operations concentrated on areas that had long been considered Charlie's territory. As had been the case in the Rung Sat in Gia Dinh Province, VC forces operating in the Delta provinces of Long An, Go Cong, Kien Hoa, Dinh Tuong, Vinh Long, An Giang, Chuong Thien, An Xuyen, Chau Doc, Vinh Binh, Phong Dinh, and Sa Dec found that conducting business as usual entailed a decidedly increased element of risk.

This was made abundantly clear in sections of Kien Hoa and Vinh Binh Provinces. Wide areas around Ben Tre, Mo Cay, Ham Long, and Cho Lach had for years been under control of the VC operating from well-fortified positions along the Rach My Tho and Rach Mo Cay Canals and the Ham Luong and Co Chien Rivers. The VC in those areas operated largely in the open, their troops moving about with their weapons in plain view. Their sampans used the rivers and canals freely to supply their units in outlying sectors or to ferry political cadre, tax collectors, and paymasters between large encampments.

In early December 1967, for two nights straight Game Warden river units noted an increase in VC activity along the southern section of the Rach Mo Cay Canal. On the first night, an ASPB neutralized two VC bunkers that had attacked it with RPGs and heavy machine gun fire. During both nights, several sampans were stopped by patrolling PBRs along the same stretch of water. One of the sampans carried four people, three AK-47s, a few hundred rounds of 7.62mm ammunition, a large box containing what appeared to be stolen antibiotics, and a large canvas bag filled with surgical instruments. Interrogation of three of the sampan's four occupants was not very enlightening because they simply refused to answer any questions. However, one man was far more cooperative and stated freely that he was a doctor en route to what he had been told was a large VC base camp located somewhere northwest of Mo Cay.

An ambush team was therefore inserted along the banks of the Rach Mo Cay Canal the following night. This happened just south of Mo Cay, a few minutes before midnight on a clear, moonless night. The terrain conditions were not bad, and the team was able to move quickly, covering more than eight hundred meters in less than an hour. It was not yet 0100 when the point halted the team after they crossed a small stream. As they lay quietly, the sounds of voices and the smell of wood fires wafted toward them. The Boss signaled for the point to continue toward the source of the sounds and smells, and two VC were heard walking along a trail about ten meters to the team's left.

Everyone held position, turning to face the oncoming voices. Unbelievably, the two VC continued to approach the team's position, stopping in front of the crouching point man. As one VC squatted down and passed a cigarette to his companion, two SEALs sprang from cover and quickly secured them. A hasty but hushed interrogation revealed that one of them was the nephew of the headman of a nearby village as well as being a low-ranking officer with the local VC company attached to the 308th VC Battalion. The prisoners said that the team was only thirty meters from a large base camp serving as the temporary tactical operations center (TOC) of the 308th VC Battalion.

Before the prisoners could be interrogated further, the team came under intense automatic weapons fire from the direction of the camp and also the left flank. The SEALs returned fire, peeling off and dragging their prisoners with them as they withdrew. The RTO called for an immediate extraction and requested an air strike after providing the coordinates of the base camp. Five minutes later, a Seawolf helicopter swooped down and the team climbed aboard just as two Cobra gunships began raking the base camp with rockets and minigun fire. A recon of the area the following day showed that the camp had been almost completely destroyed. There was ample evidence that many of its occupants were killed or wounded by the Cobras' high volume of accurate fire. Although it could not be proven conclusively that the camp had been a battalion TOC, the large number of resident VC strongly suggested that it must have been the hub of an important activity.

The trails and waterways around VC-controlled sectors were always dangerous, due to the booby traps ringing those areas that also doubled as early warning systems. The booby traps ranged from simple shallow holes, designed to cause ankle injuries, to large unexploded artillery rounds or bombs set with pressure-sensitive triggers used as land mines.

A favorite booby trap among the VC in the Delta was grenades and cans set along trails or at stream crossings. A grenade, its pin pulled, would be placed inside a can wide enough to accommodate the grenade but narrow enough to keep the spoon in place. One end of a trip wire would be attached to the neck of the grenade, the other tied to a tree root or limb on the other side of the trail or stream. Along a trail the trip wire would be set at midshin level; at a stream crossing the device and trip wire would both be underwater, the trip wire at about knee or thigh level. When the victim tripped the wire, it pulled the grenade free of the can, releasing the spoon and detonating. Although the grenades could and did cause death, the VC aimed at causing painful and debilitating wounds, requiring a dust-off (medevac by chopper) and causing fear among the survivors.

Most VC hamlets were well camouflaged and heavily fortified with bunkers, spider holes, and several fallback points from which to mount counterattacks or delaying actions. The encampments had wells, live-stock, produce gardens, and storehouses full of rice.

Because of the tremendous VC presence in those areas, in December 1967 platoons from Detachment ALPHA conducted Operation Crimson Tide in Vinh Binh Province. It proved to be one of the war's most success-ful one-day sweep operations. Platoons were transported to the AO by HSSCs, ASPBs, and helicopters, which remained close at hand to provide fire support if the SEALs made heavy contact with the enemy. Although the operation resulted in only five enemy KIAs or prisoners, large num-bers of food caches, weapons, structures, and other material were cap-tured or destroyed. After-action reports listed 75 bunkers, 153 hootches (troop quarters, munitions factories, and supply huts), and 120 sampans destroyed or captured.

Despite the success of Operation Crimson Tide, platoon-sized sweep operations were abandoned by the SEAL detachments in favor of smaller-scale recon and ambush tactics. Not only had such tactics already proved their worth in the RSSZ, but ambush/recon teams from Detachments ALPHA, GOLF, and the more recently formed BRAVO (discussed in the next chapter) had greatly reduced the numbers of VC cadre and infra-structure operating in the upper Delta. During the last half of 1967, SEAL recon teams operating in support of MRF units provided high-quality intelligence on VC positions and troop strengths. From this information, MRF units averaged at least a hundred VC KIAs a month and great numbers of destroyed sampans, bunkers and other structures, captured personnel, documents, and supplies.

These successful operations fostered another beneficial and much welcome outcome. The local citizenry gradually warmed to the idea of placing trust in MRF and ARVN units. The Allied presence had ceased to be a purely transient one. No longer was it usual for an ARVN or a U.S. unit to conduct a two- or three-day sweep, then move out of the area, quickly followed by the VC meting out punishment to those who had cooperated with government "puppets." The local residents could now rely on Allied troops staying in the area, their bases positioned within sight of several villages. Those villages a little farther off the beaten track could get quick response to a call for assistance from helicopter gunships or monitor boats. The newfound security gradually paid dividends in reliable intelligence being provided on the activities of neighborhood VC units.

Other factors influenced the local citizenry to decide to participate more actively in their own defense. These were the various civic action programs (CAP) carried on by most Allied units, including SEAL detachments. These CAPs offered medical assistance (holding sick call in villages and transporting the severely ill and injured to areas where more sophisticated treatment could be provided), engineering expertise (repair/construction of bridges, housing, roadways, and wells), and agriculture/livestock/fisheries management (supplying refined fertilizers and pesticides, advanced veterinary medicine techniques, and principles of fish farming). Equally practical aspects of CAPs included assistance in the training of RF/PFs and village militias, advice on how to strengthen perimeter defenses, and providing valuable intelligence. The most important thing that the CAPs offered was a demonstration that Allied units were residents of the various AOs, not just transients who did their sleeping elsewhere in relative safety while villagers were left in fear.

9 TET-68

At the end of January 1968, the texture of the war's fabric changed dramatically, especially in IV Corps and the Rung Sat. Beginning in the late night hours of January 30 in I Corps and II Corps (the early morning hours of January 31 throughout most of the rest of South Vietnam), communist forces launched the Tet Offensive, or Tet-68, the greatest military effort yet undertaken by either side. Both NVA and VC units took part in the offensive, aimed at most of the major Allied military installations; they targeted thirty-six out of the country's forty-four provincial capitals. Major sustained engagements took place in and around Quang Tri, Hue, Ban Me Thuot, Nha Trang, Bien Hoa, Saigon, Ben Tre, My Tho, Ca Mau, Soc Trang, Vinh Long, Chau Phu, Rach Gia, and several other large cities. As media footage demonstrated vividly, sizable sections of Hue, Chau Phu, and Ben Tre (also known as Truc Giang) were held by communist forces for days before U.S. and ARVN units could regain control. Much of Ben Tre was destroyed in the effort.

From the earliest hours, it was clear that the communists were committed to wresting as much territory as possible from government control. After-action reports and interrogation of communist intelligence officers revealed that the NVA and VC put more than 100,000 troops into the field in support of the offensive, with thirty-four battalions committed to the III and IV CTZs. Troops swarmed across the countryside of III Corps and the Delta and into the cities, establishing solid defensive positions before ARVN and U.S. defenders could respond adequately.

The first few days of the offensive saw U.S. forces getting their first taste of house-to-house fighting since World War II. ARVN and MRF battalions, along with ambush teams attached to platoons from Detachment ALPHA, spent much of those initial days rooting out elements of the 261st, 263d, and 514th VC Battalions in My Tho and the 306th, 308th, and 857th VC Battalions at Vinh Long and Ben Tre. It was obvious that the VC had not planned to take large sections of these cities as a diversion; they definitely had intended to stay. So tenacious was their defense of their positions in My Tho that the city was not retaken by Allied forces until February 2. At Vinh Long the VC held on until February 8 before hurriedly withdrawing.

A somewhat smaller but equally volatile engagement took place in Chau Phu, the capital of Chau Doc Province, located east of the Cambodian border. VC platoons swiftly moved into the city expecting that it would be easily taken, assuming that any area Allied units would be reinforcing other units to the east or south. The VC were unaware that an ambush team from Detachment BRAVO and personnel from Detachment B-42 of the U.S. Army Special Forces had been conducting Phoenix Program operations in the area. The SEALs, Green Berets, and their respective Provincial Reconnaissance Units (PRUs) divided their personnel into several ambush teams and quickly moved against the enemy positions. The VC attempted to hold their positions but eventually acknowledged that they were severely outclassed.

Realizing that they were in an extremely tenuous position and that attempting to fight their way out was at best suicidal, they decided to withdraw, taking civilian hostages as shields. The VC also set a large portion of the residential section of the city afire as a diversion. Tragically, scores of the hostages and other civilians were killed during that maneuver, some in cross-fire situations and others by the VC. Although the engagement was not as large as those at My Tho, Vinh Long, or Ben Tre, the loss of civilian lives and destruction of property was proportionately as devastating.

A large number of the communist losses in the Delta came from Allied artillery and close-in air support. The high concentrations of artillery, rocket, and automatic weapons fire constantly pounded the VC positions inside the various beleaguered cities, making it impossible for the VC to regroup or even relax between assaults by U.S. and ARVN troops. When the insurgents had finally had enough and attempted to retreat into their strongholds, the artillery and gunship fire persisted, further thinning their ranks.

The Tet Offensive was also an ambitious attempt by the NVA and VC to induce the civilian populace to rise up against the government while dealing a crippling blow to as many ARVN and U.S. units as possible. Although the communists were somewhat successful in causing confusion and holding several villages and towns for a brief period, they did not achieve their major objectives. The populace did not join the communists, and although the offensive did catch the ARVN and U.S. units off guard, the large-scale engagements played to the Allies' strength. Once the initial shock of the attacks had been weathered, U.S. and ARVN units quickly turned the tide, causing huge numbers of enemy casualties and taking thousands of enemy prisoners.

Although the NVA took its lumps, by far the largest of the communist losses were suffered by the VC. Estimates range as high as forty thousand to fifty thousand dead and seven thousand to nearly ten thousand captured. During the first week alone of the Tet Offensive, the MRF and SEAL detachments operating in the Delta accounted for well over seven-hundred VC KIAs. It would be several weeks before MACV would digest fully the scope of communist, Allied, and civilian losses: ARVN, in excess of twenty-five hundred killed, eight-thousand wounded, and five hundred missing; U.S., eleven hundred dead and more than six thousand wounded; civilian, fourteen thousand dead, more than twenty thousand wounded, and well in excess of five hundred thousand left without homes. About this time, the U.S. government would feel the first real rumbles of unrest among the American populace, now disenchanted with what it viewed as an immoral and unjust war.

But the ARVN and the other Allies had proven that they could weather any large-scale engagement with their communist opponents and do so handily. In the Delta, SEALs soon learned that the losses had left the resident VC forces too thin to control as much territory as they had previously. The best indication that the tide had turned in the Delta AOs was the fact that merchant travel along the Mekong, Bassack, and other rivers now moved with little harassment from VC ambushers or "tax" collectors. National Route 4, which had been closed by the VC to any form of extensive transportation, was now open for commercial use for the first time in more than four years.

As a result of the Tet Offensive, the VC nearly ceased to be a useful military arm. Not only did they suffer huge personnel losses, but their all-or-nothing effort required them to come into the open. When they saw that they were not going to be successful, they had to salvage as much of their remaining forces as possible, quickly withdrawing them to their base camps. They had no time to retreat carefully and surreptitiously; therefore they were observed by numerous villagers. These observations provided fairly reliable intelligence on communist troop strengths and locations of strongholds, which previously had been well shrouded in secrecy.

One large VC stronghold was located in Dong Thap District, just north-west of My Tho. Following the siege at My Tho, large numbers of VC moved toward Dong Thap on foot and by sampan. The area was known to the MRF because SEAL ambush teams had conducted recon operations there in the fall of 1967. From intelligence provided by the teams, MRF infantry battalions went to the area, engaging two VC battalions (the 514th and the 263d). At that time, the VC had fired RPGs, heavy machine guns, and 57mm recoilless rifles from well-fortified bunkers along the banks of a large canal that intersected the Mekong River. The VC forces experienced heavy losses, but the bulk of their troops managed to escape during the night. Following Tet-68, however, the two battalions came close to being prisoners in their previously formidable sanctuaries.

Ambush teams found that the VC still had many bunker complexes commanding several narrow points and tight bends in the canals. These were ideal ambush points because MRF vessels had to reduce speed to negotiate the tight bends, making them vulnerable to enemy fire. The SEAL teams tried to neutralize the bunkers with grenades, rockets, or recoilless rifle rounds. They also designated fire missions by Seawolves (aerial rockets) or by prop-driven A-1 Skyraiders (low-level napalm runs). By neutralizing the VC ambush positions, MRF battalions could move into position more rapidly, cutting off the VC's avenues of escape.

SEAL ambush teams were active in the Plain of Reeds, the U Minh Forest, the Seven Mountains area, and the countryside surrounding Ben Tre. The VC still had some effective battalions in these sectors, but after their huge losses, they did not wish to commit them in large-scale engagements. Instead, they reverted to their old and reliable ambush and withdraw tactics. They saw that their best bet was to use hit-and-run tac-

tics until NVA forces could be brought into the area to resupply and reinforce them.

During those early weeks, SEAL recon teams and listening posts were
able to gain valuable intelligence on which subsequent ambush and prisoner acquisition operations would be based. Detachment ALPHA personnel conducted highly successful ambushes in and around Bay Nui, the
once-impenetrable VC stronghold situated between That Son and the city
of Long Xuyen. Bay Nui was important because it was in the midst of one
of the most productive rice-growing sections in the Delta. It afforded easy
access to the Hau Giang River, the Kinh Mac Can Dung and Kinh Cai
Son Canals, and dozens of lesser tributaries. This provided excellent
cover for ambushing river traffic and providing the ambushers with
speedy escape routes. The countryside around Long Xuyen and across the
Hau Giang River was lush with vegetation and fruit trees. There were
fresh-water wells, livestock thrived in local villages, and fish and shrimp
flourished in the waterways.

In late February 1968, platoons from Detachment ALPHA conducted
extensive ambush operations throughout most of the area around Long
Xuyen. One team visited an RF/PF fort near Lai Vung and found it bursting at the seams with newly arrived refugees. Most had come in from
neighboring villages on the scores of islands dotting the Hau Giang River,
between Thuan Hung and the Kinh Mac Can Dung Canal. Some villagers
happily cooperated with the SEALs and pointed out a VC-held village on
a large island north of Long Xuyen. They thought that twenty to thirty VC
had been there for the past two weeks. Several refugees added that they
had seen sampans moving toward the island within the previous twenty-
four hours.

Late that night, the SEAL team boarded a STAB and quietly inserted
along the island's southern shore. In an hour they arrived at a tree line fifteen meters south of the village and scanned the compound for signs of
activity. After keeping surveillance for a half hour, two men moved into
the village for a closer look. They were a few meters from the nearest hut
when an RPG round impacted to their right, slightly wounding one of
them in the hip and thigh. The blast was followed immediately by automatic weapons fire coming from the two nearest huts and the area
between them. The team returned fire with three grenades, taking out both
structures. In less than a minute the VC positions had fallen silent, so the
SEALs moved forward to assess the situation.

Eight dead VC were found around the two shattered huts, but the rest of the village seemed deserted. The team, however, could hear people crashing through the thick vegetation west of the village heading toward the river. The SEALs set out in pursuit, firing illumination flares as they went. They reached the river and saw two sampans moving swiftly toward the opposite shore. They began firing at both craft, causing one sampan to be blown nearly in half by a well-placed round from a grenade launcher.

When the firing stopped three SEALs dropped their weapons, inflated their flotation vests, and dove into the river to snag the one sampan still afloat. Two VC were aboard, one of them dead, the other alive, although he had sustained multiple wounds in his upper back. No one knew how many VC had been in the other sampan, but one badly mangled body was seen drifting downstream.

The surviving VC was removed from the sampan, and his wounds were immediately tended by the team's corpsman. The RTO called for a hasty extraction by Seawolf helicopter while four team members went back to search the village. This turned up several hundred rounds of 7.62mm ammunition, a few weapons, and a rucksack filled with maps and documents. The maps showed the location of VC camps, many of which had existed prior to the Tet Offensive but had since been abandoned. Careful examination revealed the names of local VC operatives, one of whom was a village chief. Others named were prominent merchants, doctors, and military personnel, including two or three officers. The documents and the wounded VC prisoner were turned over to the National Police for further questioning.

The VC strongholds and sanctuaries now became like small sections of a once-raging forest fire, not yet out but starting to become more manageable. The devastating losses the VC had suffered made them reluctant to think in terms of company-sized or larger engagements, preferring to retreat or even surrender than to suffer larger numbers of casualties. That did not mean wholesale surrender. Quite the contrary. Their sapper and ambush activities increased for a time, but eventually more and more VC became disenchanted with their situation and feared that they would soon join their comrades, captured or killed by SEAL ambushers who seemed to be everywhere at once.

SEAL ambush teams were experiencing great success during those early post-Tet months. What had at one time been highly contested areas of the Delta now seemed to be more akin to private hunting preserves for

SEALs, Special Forces units, and the MRF. Each month saw larger numbers of VC being killed or captured, scores of enemy bunkers and sampans being destroyed, and huge caches of rice and armaments falling into Allied hands. For many VC the handwriting was on the wall, and more and more of them were taking advantage of the amnesty offered to those joining the government's Chieu Hoi Program.

These *hoi chanh,* as the Chieu Hoi ralliers were called, added greatly to the ever-expanding Allied intelligence base, resulting in even greater success for SEAL ambush teams in the Delta throughout the rest of the year. Allied troops were more capable of locating the enemy as they began to withdraw farther into such areas as the Seven Mountains region, the U Minh Forest, the Plain of Reeds, and the areas on both sides of the Cambodian border. Many *hoi chanh* became Kit Carson scouts, actually leading SEALs and other Allied units into VC territory.

In late March and early April, VC units began to mass for what would prove to be one last effort at taking Saigon or severely crippling those ARVN and other Allied units directly responsible for the capital's defense. Interrogation of recently captured prisoners indicated that a new communist offensive was imminent. Rather than waiting for the VC to make their move, ARVN Command and MACV set about deploying their forces in a series of concentric AOs, sweeping the various Saigon land and riverine approaches for VC units and emplacements. That joint operation was known as the Toan Thang (Total Victory) Campaign, using ARVN units as the innermost circle, with U.S. and Australian troops making up the outer circles. MRF units were responsible for sweeping Long An Province and portions of Kien Tuong and Hau Nghia for signs of VC activity. That was, of course, a wise choice since the MRF had already been working extensively in those very AOs for a long time.

Detachment ALPHA ambush teams assigned to the MRF conducted extensive operations in and around Can Giuoc, Binh Chanh, Ban Luc, and Can Duoc. During their patrols they soon discovered that the area around Can Giuoc showed the greatest signs of enemy activity, with large numbers of bunkers and food and weapons caches. They also located two areas containing new medium-sized tunnel complexes. The bunkers and other fortified structures were destroyed, as were the food and weapons that could not be transported readily out of the area.

A sizable number of VC were found in the area, and several were taken prisoner by the SEALs. When company-strength VC units were located and their positions relayed to MRF battalions, the VC would consistently attempt to run rather than stand and fight. Prisoners taken during such operations said that their units had all been ordered not to engage in company-sized or larger actions with Allied units. The VC did not want to experience any more losses on the order of what they had during Tet-68.

In early May of 1968, however, the VC did attempt one last massive assault against Saigon, its road approaches, and the Tan Son Nhut Air Base. For a few days, the VC battalions involved in the multipronged attack were able to at least hold sections of Saigon's Cholon District and a small area adjacent to the air base and to impede traffic along the roads leading toward Bien Hoa, to the east, and the bridge and roadway linking Saigon with the Nha Be District. But the limited successes of the assaulting communist forces were short lived, and by the early part of June the entire area had been retaken by ARVN units. ARVN success in dealing with the threat, especially in retaking Cholon from the tenacious VC attackers, restored confidence in their abilities as a viable combat force.

10 U MINH AND CA MAU

With the increase in reliable intelligence and the regional VC units staying closer to home, Detachment GOLF and ALPHA ambush teams significantly increased the scope of their operations. Ambushes set up along well-known and newly disclosed VC infiltration routes produced an increasing number of enemy KIAs and prisoners. In the Plain of Reeds area and Seven Mountains region, teams inserted by STAB, chopper, or PBR conducted extended recon patrols and listening post operations of several days' duration, locating VC positions and assessing troop strengths. The information passed on resulted in a tremendous reduction in VC supply capabilities in the western Delta by the beginning of the 1968 monsoon season.

In the U Minh Forest sector, VC units had operated without much interference from Allied forces for most of the war. In the weeks and months following Tet-68, communist units operating and residing along the Trem, Ong Doc, and Kinh Quan Lo Canals as well as along the Cai Lon River became the focus of SEAL ambush and prisoner acquisition operations. The terrain was ideal for the ambush teams, being in many ways similar to the Rung Sat. One great difference between the two areas was that the trees of the U Minh Forest were much taller (often forty to sixty feet), thicker, and more dense. The area is the second-largest mangrove swamp on earth (after the Amazon of South America), covering more than a thousand square kilometers. It is a most inhospitable area and supports the lowest population concentration in the Delta.

During Tet-68, VC local force units mounted sizable assaults against the naval base and airport at Rach Gia and the city of Ca Mau (also called Quan Long) and its airport. They had been no more successful, however, than their comrades in other parts of the country. They did not suffer the same number of decimating casualties as other communist units. They were more realistic in assessing their capabilities for taking their objectives and opted to return to the security of the swamps before many of their troops were sacrificed. They therefore were left with most of their forces and supplies intact, capable of continuing with operations in much the same way as they had before.

The idiosyncracies of the region's terrain made it an ideal locale for them to conduct guerrilla operations against local village militias, RF/PFs, and Allied bases. For instance, the mouth of the Cai Lon River was just south of the naval base at Rach Gia, allowing VC sappers to make quick forays against RVN and U.S. vessels there. Attempts to follow the VC were at best frustrating and at worst deadly. Pursuing forces were at a distinct disadvantage because there was neither rhyme nor reason to the way navigable channels ran into the sudden beginnings of impenetrable stands of timber and choking carpets of lianas, small ferns, and underbrush. To be hung up in such areas meant that within seconds the surrounding vegetation would erupt with small-arms and automatic weapons fire from waiting VC ambushers.

SEAL ambush teams in the area used the terrain against the resident VC forces. The cajeput trees, growing everywhere, especially along the edges of waterways, offered great spots from which to spring ambushes. These trees often grew in such a way that a sampan going along a canal had to move at a snail's pace. A well-camouflaged ambusher could be only a foot or two away and not be seen by the prospective victim. Getting on top of passing VC and controlling them before they could escape or offer strong resistance resulted in highly successful prisoner captures. These operations proved so successful that less sophisticated VC began regarding the SEALs as some sort of demons or other supernatural creatures. Many began referring to the SEALs as swamp demons, "men with green faces," or "the ghosts that live among the trees."

Controlling the area in and around the U Minh Forest, as well as the rest of the Ca Mau Peninsula, was of critical importance in reducing communist supply capabilities. The eastern, southern, and western coastlines were ideal areas for clandestine insertions by sampans ferrying in supplies from junks they had met well off the coast. Because the coast area was extensively etched by streams, rivers, and canals, the sampans had many opportunities to move quickly inland and then disappear into the countryside. If such craft were to be intercepted by PBRs or ASPBs, this would have to occur before the sampans could make it to the coast and the protection of the mangrove swamps.

SEAL ambush teams offered an ideal way to deal with the problem. By setting up ambush sites along these very channels from the coastline, the VC sampans would not have to be chased or searched for, because the VC would inadvertently deliver themselves and their cargoes into the hands of the people they were trying to avoid. Ambushes in these areas met with great success and resulted in large numbers of prisoners, KIAs, and captured contraband. The effectiveness of the SEALs' operations gradually caused the VC to abandon their smuggling efforts and other activities in the Ca Mau Peninsula. The VC finally accepted that supplies entering the Delta would have to come from the Ho Chi Minh Trail or not at all.

One example of how effective SEAL ambush teams were in interdicting VC supply operations in the Ca Mau Peninsula was an extended recon/ambush operation carried out during early May 1968. An ambush team from Detachment ALPHA was sent to Ca Mau to follow up on hard intelligence obtained from two recent VC defectors. They said that they had spent the past week helping to transfer weapons, ammunition, and other supplies from their camp near Thoi Binh to a larger camp deep in the heart of the U Minh Forest. Since they had helped only with loading the material into sampans and had not made the trip to the new camp themselves, all they knew was that the camp was situated along one of the many narrow channels that branch from the Ong Doc Canal a few kilometers south of Can Du. They did know that more supplies would be moving along the canal, en route to the new camp, for the next several nights.

Armed with that information, the team was inserted by chopper late that night along the west bank of the canal, north of Can Du. For the next two hours they worked their way slowly south, paralleling the canal. Whenever they came across a narrow channel or stream branching from the canal, they followed it a short distance, checking for signs of recently cut vines or reeds, indicating that the VC had passed that way recently. Just after midnight, they found a tangle of freshly cut vegetation that seemed to have been placed intentionally across the mouth of a narrow channel.

The team moved carefully around the pile of vegetation, noting and avoiding several booby traps.

They had traveled only a short distance when they heard voices a few meters ahead. They moved to within a few feet of the voices and found three VC behind a squat semicircular wall of sandbags, under a partially fallen cajeput tree. While two team members moved to take the position from the rear, the Boss inched forward, training his Hush Puppy on the three chatting VC. The two-man capture team sprang forward and grabbed two of the VC while the Boss put down the third one with three quick and silent rounds from the Hush Puppy. The two VC resisted for only a few seconds and then submitted to being secured. If they had not, the capture team would have taken them out silently with their knives, or the Boss would have dusted them with the Hush Puppy. Eliminating the sentry position quietly was essential, so as not to draw the attention of any nearby VC or scare off any sampans approaching the stream.

Interrogated by the Boss and the corpsman, both fluent in Vietnamese, the two VC were willing to cooperate, but initially it was hard to calm them enough to question. They were worried that the SEALs would kill them and chop them up, as they had been told by their local political cadre. One babbled briefly that the SEALs were only half human, lived in the mud, and enjoyed eating their victims. Having been captured so quickly and seeing seven large men surrounding him and his hapless companion seemed to bear out the stories. Finally, the corpsman was able to calm him, saying that he would be treated well if he cooperated fully and answered all questions.

From the brief interrogation, the team learned that the camp was located thirty meters farther upstream. Although there was one other sentry position on the far side of the camp, no other VC were yet in residence. The camp would eventually support two companies of VC now located at platoon-sized camps on the outer edges of the U Minh Forest. Although more supplies were supposed to be delivered to the camp before sunrise, no VC troops were slated to arrive for several days. Since the two prisoners could offer no more information, they were gagged and stashed behind their sandbag wall. The capture team and the corpsman stayed with the prisoners while the rest of the team set out for the camp and the other sentry position.

It did not take long for them to loop around to the other side of the camp, where the second sentry position was located. But when they got to the small sentry bunker, they found it deserted. They assumed that the VC who were supposed to be manning that position had headed for one of the nearby RF/PF or ARVN units to turn themselves in, as many of their comrades had done. A quick recon of the camp revealed that it too was deserted. It consisted of six finished hootches and several other structures under construction. Although the huts were not searched thoroughly, a brief peek revealed that two contained many sacks of rice, about two hundred pounds' worth, along with several bales of clothing. But since the team was expecting two or more VC sampans filled with supplies to be moving down the stream toward the camp, they returned to the first sentry post to prepare for the ambush.

The ambush would be simple because the stream was less than twenty feet across at its widest point. Two SEALs were deployed in the water amidst the reeds along the far bank while three others went to the opposite bank a little farther from the stream's camouflaged entrance. The Boss and the corpsman continued to stay with the two prisoners. From time to time, the Boss would scan the area with his Starlight Scope, but there was nothing to see.

It seemed as though the sampans would not be coming, since by 0500 there was still no sign of them. The Boss was just about to have the RTO call for a PBR to move in for extraction when the sounds of outboard engines could be heard. A few seconds later, they sounded as though they were idling right at the stream entrance. The SEALs assumed that the sampans had stopped to remove their camouflage before pressing on. Sure enough, less than a minute later the engines revved up and the first sampan slid into view.

There were two VC in the lead sampan and three in the second. In ten seconds, the first boat moved to the center of the kill zone. All five VC appeared totally relaxed; one man in the lead sampan smiled and called out a greeting to the sentry position. At that same moment the outboards on both boats were shut down, allowing them to drift toward the bank just below the sentry position.

When the lead sampan came to within a few feet of the bank, the Boss flipped a stun grenade into its bow. A second later there was a loud bang and a blinding flash of light. Three team members jumped quickly from the bank into the second sampan as the two SEALs in the water reached up over the side of the first boat and pulled two VC into the water. In less than two minutes all five VC were dragged ashore, quickly secured, and gagged. One by one, each VC was taken aside and briefly interrogated, but nothing of value was learned.

The lead sampan contained one 12.7mm heavy machine gun, several SKS assault rifles, two RPG grenade launchers, and a large covered kettle containing tortoise meat. The second had several cases of 12.7mm and 7.62mm ammunition, a few more SKS assault rifles, and a number of RPG rounds. Concurrently, three SEALs returned to the camp and searched the remaining huts thoroughly. They came up with a 60mm mortar, more than a dozen mortar rounds, and a thousand rounds of 12.7mm ammunition. The RTO then called for PBRs to extract the team and remove the captured material.

Until 1965, Delta VC units received 70 to 75 percent of all their supplies by junk or sampan traveling along South Vietnam's South China Sea coastline. Through the efforts of Operation Market Time's picket line of many ships and aircraft, the percentage of supplies dropped to less than 10 percent by early 1968. Prior to 1965, supplies coming down the Ho Chi Minh Trail had accounted for only about 30 percent. By the end of 1967, the trail had become the main supply artery, with huge storage areas on both sides of the Cambodian border.

Detachment GOLF platoons served on a rotational basis with the Market Time units. The platoons spent much time boarding hundreds of junks each week, searching the vessels for contraband and checking crews and passengers for proper identity cards. Such boardings were usually uneventful and tedious, but sometimes just as the boarding craft closed with a suspicious junk, automatic weapons fire or an RPG rocket might slam into the picket vessel. At other times a search belowdecks of a suspicious junk might erupt suddenly in a fierce but brief firefight when undocumented infiltrators foolishly chose to attack the boarding party. And there were the fanatical and suicidal smugglers who felt it better to blow their vessel, themselves, and the boarding party out of the water rather than be taken captive. Such situations could serve to ruin the boarding party's whole day if not handled properly.

The SEALs attached to Operation Market Time were not restricted to boarding operations. They also carried out ambush, recon, and prisoner acquisition operations at various points along the coast, extending from Vung Tau to the small but craggy islands just north of Nha Trang. The islands and irregular sections of coastline offered many havens for smugglers, sappers, and small local force units. This was especially true for the area just north of Nha Trang, because the many islands offered fine bases from which the VC could launch sapper attacks against the logistical facilities in the harbor at Nha Trang and the major supply port of Cam Ranh Bay, fifteen miles to the south. Although an unsuccessful attempt to take Nha Trang by the NVA's 18th Regiment occurred during the early morning hours of Tet-68, communist forces were never very successful in establishing a significant, ongoing, large-scale military presence in the area. Sappers did continue to work the sector, intermittently, until the final American withdrawal in 1975.

SEAL operations had become so extensive that VC and NVA prisoners came to assume that there had to have been many hundreds of SEALs in country, especially in the Delta and RSSZ. Actually, there were never more than a couple hundred SEALs in all of South Vietnam at any one time. But the in-country personnel were constantly in the field, in one capacity or another, rarely spending more than a day or two at a base camp. Since one of the main purposes of the SEAL mission was to out guerrilla the guerrillas, that could be accomplished only by attacking the situation in the same way that the VC did—on a constant basis. But full-time activity in Vietnam's hot and humid climate was thoroughly taxing and physically debilitating, no matter how well conditioned an individual might have been. Even the VC and NVA troops found that constant activity sapped their strength; they welcomed the beginning of the monsoons, knowing that activities by forces on both sides would be greatly diminished.

Because of the high level of activity expected of SEAL detachment personnel, the usual tour of duty was restricted to only six months. Theoretically, SEALs could have served the standard twelve-month tour, like other U.S. troops, but the extreme stresses of SEAL tactics, considering the type of terrain in the RSSZ and IV Corps, made the six-month program more logical and practical. Even so, it was common for SEAL personnel to request and receive permission to remain in country as replacements for units losing men to stateside rotation or attrition. Other SEALs would take the more circuitous route of returning to the fray after a brief stay stateside.

For the remainder of the spring and summer of 1968, SEAL detachments continued to move aggressively against communist units throughout the country and at sea. Special interest continued to be devoted toward interdicting supplies being smuggled into the country.

But in March of that year, President Lyndon Baines Johnson announced that he would not be running for reelection to office. Antiwar demonstrations in the United States proliferated and became increasingly more violent, making it clear that the people had had enough of the war and wanted the troops home as soon as possible. In May the first peace talks of the war got under way in Paris. To increase the possibility of success in those talks, President Johnson announced on October 31, 1968, that he was calling a halt to all bombing of North Vietnam. On November 5, Richard Nixon defeated Vice President Hubert Humphrey in the 1968 presidential election and shortly thereafter announced that he wanted the entire war effort made the exclusive responsibility of the Government of South Vietnam (GVN), freeing U.S. troops to return home as soon as possible. He dubbed this process "Vietnamization."

In preparation for Vietnamization, President Nixon resumed Operation Rolling Thunder, the bombing of targets within North Vietnam. U.S. forces were also instructed to diminish gradually their overt participation in ground actions. At the same time an increasing emphasis was placed on air support for ARVN field forces. In February, the U.S. Navy was instructed to begin the South East Asian Lake Ocean River Delta Strategy (SEALORDS), a project that turned over hundreds of motorized junks, PBRs, and other riverine craft to ARVN forces as a part of Vietnamization. U.S. Navy personnel, including SEALs, acted as advisers to ARVN riverine forces, providing them all the expertise necessary to make the transition smooth.

One of the main responsibilities of SEALORDS units was the ongoing interdiction of supply and troop movements into the Delta area from the Cambodian frontier. SEAL ambush teams and BSU crews played major roles in that effort, employing the skills already honed during previous campaigns in the Delta and Rung Sat. Ambushes were set on rivers and canals using STABs, PBRs, and airboats, as well as on land, along trails and roads. Many operations run from Moc Hoa and Sa Dec resulted in the capture of large quantities of enemy material and many VC and NVA personnel. Some were couriers, tax agents, paymasters, and operations or intelligence officers at battalion level or above. Such losses were both devastating and disheartening.

VC infiltrators, using sampans and motor launches in attempting to slip through the SEALORDS net, learned quickly that their boats were no match for the STABs and other river craft. The SEALORDS vessels had the edge in speed and firepower and had engines that ran so quietly that they could get very close to an enemy sampan before its occupants could hear them coming. Ambushes were sprung quickly and completed with the enemy vessel either in tow or burning, eventually sinking below the dark, muddy waters of the river. ARVNs, LDNNs, and other indigenous personnel proved to be quick studies in grasping all that the SEALs and BSU crews had to pass on.

With the rivers and canals heavily patrolled, SEAL ambush teams were able to devote more time to instructing LDNN personnel in guerrilla/counterguerrilla tactics. The LDNNs were highly effective in ambush tactics against Delta VC units, especially along the Mekong River near Sa Dec. In that section of the Delta there are numerous islands that the enemy used as indoctrination centers, munitions factories, boat repair facilities, supply and troop staging areas, forward bases, and R & R centers. On a couple of islands the VC had hamlets that cultivated crops and raised livestock to provide a ready and constant supply of food for their troops. In the early years of the war, the VC made no effort to conceal the fact that the hamlets were theirs, but by late 1967, the islands' residents portrayed themselves as poor peasants totally averse to aiding the local VC.

On several occasions, Detachment ALPHA ambush teams and their LDNN counterparts made clandestine insertions on the islands, setting up listening posts and keeping the area under close surveillance. They observed that many island hamlets were anything but peaceful. Accordingly, successful ambush and prisoner acquisition operations were initiated. Many prisoners provided vital information on the location of VC local force and sapper units. More importantly, they identified scores of espionage cell members working near Sa Dec, Cao Lanh, Ap Phung, and even Dong Tam and My Tho. With that information available to ARVN units, the VC experienced a sudden reduction in the numbers of effective operatives. As time passed, the LDNNs tried to prove their ability to handle all counterguerrilla operations in the Delta as well as the RSSZ and other sections of III Corps. By the summer of 1969 the LDNNs were capable of carrying the ball on their own.

Until 1968, Ba Tri, An Thuy, and Dong Xuan, in Kien Hoa Province, were at the mercy of the local VC, who depleted the villagers' food stores and routinely conscripted the area youth. Fishermen and merchants traveling along the rivers and canals had their catches or cargo "taxed" heavily. If the tax could not be paid, the VC would confiscate the sampan. By the fall of 1968, however, Ba Tri and its neighbors found that they were no longer the local supermarket for the VC. Traffic along the rivers, streams, and canals moved freely, allowing the area residents to take their produce and wares to market. By the time the wet season rolled around in 1969, the entire area was secure and the residents committed to the Saigon government.

SEAL ambush teams in the U Minh Forest area also noted a significant reduction in VC activity. By early 1969, the VC presence there had been reduced seriously, prompting a quick resurgence in the local economy. The number of mortar and rocket attacks on the airstrips at Ca Mau city, Duc Long, Kien Thanh, and Rach Gia decreased. Full use of the region's navigable rivers and canals was now possible, as well as Highway 4, snaking its way north from Hong My. The reduced VC presence meant that villagers felt more secure about their lives and possessions. The VC no longer had sufficient strength to send squads to the villages to collect "taxes" or draft young men as replacements.

SEALORDS operations now dominated much of the SEALs' activities in South Vietnam. Ambush teams working with BSU crews gradually tightened the net about those areas still containing VC units of company size or larger. They made the movement of communist supplies and reinforcements risky undertakings. The interdiction efforts of SEALORDS units caused an almost total cessation of riverine insurgency by communist forces. They also reopened the Vinh Te Canal, connecting Chau Doc, and Hatien, and the Thoai Ha Canal, running between Rach Gia and Long Xuyen. The same was true for the rivers and canals around Tri Ton, Cai Lai, Moc Hoa, Phuoc Xuyen, Tan Dong, My Tho, Ben Tre, Can Giuoc, and Dong Hoa. It became evident that 1969 would be the year when the Delta, the RSSZ, and many sections of III CTZ would be considered under government control for the first time in many years, if ever.

The year 1969 would also be the beginning of the end of overt involvement in the war effort by U.S. forces. In March, President Nixon authorized the bombing of NVA and VC base camps and supply depots within Cambodia. Although some major engagements continued between communist and Allied units, for the most part the NVA and VC lay back, continuing the reinforcing efforts they had begun in late 1968. As the bombing of North Vietnam and the Ho Chi Minh Trail gradually intensified, June saw the first of Nixon's promised U.S. troop withdrawals. Vietnamization had begun, and the most intense period of the Vietnam War was drawing to a close. The years 1967 to 1969 had seen the most violent military confrontations, the greatest loss of civilian life, and the greatest expenditure of men and material in the history of the hostilities.

As did other U.S. units, SEAL personnel continued to serve in country until 1972. For the most part, U.S. personnel returned to a more advisory capacity in support of ARVN forces and avoided as much as possible actual participation in day-to-day military engagements. But SEALs who advised indigenous forces had to go into the field where hostilities occurred. Not participating would have been impossible and completely foolish. SEAL personnel, therefore, continued to operate in the same fashion as they had from their first days in the Rung Sat. The only difference was that they did it in gradually decreasing numbers, until the last personnel officially left the country in 1972.

11 WATCHING THE TRAIL FOR SOG

Through the centuries, almost every war has presented the combatants with an assortment of circumstances that required a degree of special handling. The circumstances were often of a social, political, or logistical nature, frequently due to the impact that war has on the populace within a theater of operations, as well as on the populace of adjacent countries. This has been true in conventional wars and even more so in civil wars. Thus, the Vietnam War, being not only a conflict between the independent governments of the North and the South but also involving armed strife between the NLF and the Saigon government, was obviously a prime candidate for special handling.

Although conventional forces and tactics were used in varying degrees by all combatants during the war, unconventional approaches were key elements of the conflict. This was especially true for the NVA and VC. Unconventional approaches were perhaps most evident in their supply apparatus and the VC infrastructure's (VCI) three-man cell organization. To respond adequately to the communists' unconventional supply and intelligence networks, ARVN and MACV units had to respond unconventionally. To coordinate that response, Allied forces relied primarily on the Studies and Observation Group (SOG) and the Phoenix Program. The two groups were separate organizations and command structures, but they shared common purposes and strong ties with the Central Intelligence Agency (CIA).

SOG, sometimes also called the Special Operations Group, was extremely active and multifaceted. First organized by MACV in 1964 to undertake clandestine operations against communist forces throughout most of Southeast Asia, SOG took an amoebalike approach to the communists' free-form system of warfare. SOG units used a decidedly unconventional approach in their operations. For the most part, the exact nature of those operations remains highly classified, with no after-action reports having been maintained. Therefore, many SOG operations remain shrouded in rumor, conjecture, and hyperbole. But I will provide not only examples of operations that have been reported officially but also some that are only rumored to have occurred.

An in-depth study of SOG operations would be inappropriate at this point, but I feel that some brief background information will be helpful in understanding the role played by SEAL personnel. Originally, the SOG relied almost exclusively on U.S. Army Special Forces personnel to run its operations. But by 1966, it also included Ranger LRRPs, U.S. Air Force personnel, SEALs, U.S. Marines, ARVN Special Forces personnel, and a wide variety of mercenaries of varying ethnic backgrounds. Employing thousands of personnel, the SOG hoped to cover the enemy's multipronged efforts (propaganda, infiltration of troops and supplies, political assassination, training of cadre, and so forth). To facilitate their efforts, the SOG was divided into four basic operational units (Psychological Studies Group, Maritime Studies Group, Air Studies Group, and Ground Studies Group). Even though the four units were separate in their designed functions, they often overlapped and contributed greatly to one another's day-to-day functions.

The Psychological Studies Group (PSG), operating mainly out of Tay Ninh, had the responsibility for disrupting enemy morale and conducting disinformation-type projects. It relied on radio transmissions, air-craft, and field personnel in carrying out its missions. Propaganda materials were often dropped over known enemy infiltration routes (especially the Ho Chi Minh Trail and Truong Son Corridor), strongholds, or other such haunts by C-47s, dubbed Bullshit Bombers. (Although a number of C-47s were earmarked for use as Bullshit Bombers, most of these aircraft were on loan from the Air Studies Group or the U.S. Air Force 5th Special Operations Squadron out of Nha Trang.) Some of these C-47s were also equipped with powerful loudspeakers for broadcasting propaganda messages.

The PSG field personnel carried out most of the disinformation operations. These frequently took the form of falsely coded radio broadcasts between Allied units that were designed to be easily broken by VC and NVA monitors, who would then use them to their detriment. False documents would also be left around heavily trafficked enemy areas. Since communist units had no reliable means to check out the authenticity of the information they were "intercepting," they occasionally took it at face value, with predictable results. Even when they did not believe the false information, they often found themselves too confused and unsure to risk any operations for varying periods of time.

The Maritime Studies Group (MSG) conducted its operations along the coastlines of South and North Vietnam, their inland waterways, and portions of the Cambodian coastline. SEALs figured prominently in recon missions and amphibious raids. These happened, of course, in the Mekong Delta and along the coast of North Vietnam. Forward listening/observation posts were maintained on several islands just outside the entrance to Haiphong Harbor. The craft used by the MSG included the same type of vessels employed by Operations Game Warden and Market Time units. Additionally, larger ships attached to Task Force 77, an operational unit of the U.S. Navy's Seventh Fleet, maintained a staging area at Yankee Station in the Gulf of Tonkin during the war.

By far, the Air Studies Group (ASG) and the Ground Studies Group (GSG) carried out the greatest number of SOG operations. Both directed many of their activities against enemy infiltration routes inside North and South Vietnam, along the DMZ, and inside Laos and Cambodia. They were diversified, covering everything from electronic surveillance to long-range reconnaissance patrols all along the Ho Chi Minh Trail. Some recon missions were performed deep inside North Vietnam. Operations inside Cambodia and Laos had to be conducted with great care, because both countries had taken firm positions of neutrality toward the war. Such Allied military operations were strictly forbidden, but some latitude was allowed for hot pursuits.

The ASG devoted much of its time to deploying and monitoring electronic surveillance equipment along infiltration routes. Common monitoring devices were the ADSID (Air Delivered Seismic Intrusion Detector), the ACOUBUOY (sound-sensitive intrusion detector), and the ACOUSID (sound and seismic-sensitive intrusion detector). The information produced by these devices was valuable in assisting both air and ground units in interdicting communist movements along well-known infiltration corridors.

These detectors were rocket-shaped devices about two to three feet in length and weighing about twenty-five pounds. They were usually airdropped by U.S. Navy Neptunes or U.S. Air Force F-4 Phantoms. ADSIDs embedded themselves in the earth upon impact, leaving only a small antenna visible; ACOUBUOYs and ACOUSIDs, dropped by parachute over areas covered by dense forests, became snagged in the trees and remained suspended above an infiltration corridor. People, large animals, and vehicles passing through areas seeded with monitoring devices triggered their seismic and/or sonic sensors, causing a signal to be beamed upward toward a constantly patrolling monitor and communications plane. If sizable enemy activity was suggested, a preemptive air strike or recon patrol would be ordered.

GSG operations were primarily coordinated and run out of Danang, Ban Me Thuot, Kontum, and Saigon. Typical operations were long-range reconnaissance patrols and searches for U.S. and other Allied prisoners. They interdicted infiltration routes, rescued downed aircrews, sabotaged enemy structures and equipment, and conducted surveillance of enemy units. As did the ASG, the GSG concentrated many of its activities along the roads and bike/footpaths of the Ho Chi Minh Trail. GSG units ranged widely throughout Cambodia, Laos, and North Vietnam. The success of their operations depended on well-coordinated working relationships between the GSG and the ASG. Without this, both groups would have been far less effective.

Evidence of significant enemy activity in a certain sector often resulted in GSG recon teams being deployed into the area to evaluate the situation. Their ability to deploy rapidly into an area of interest and then furnish visual assessments of a sensor's transmissions greatly enhanced successful interdictions of enemy movements. Air strikes called in had better chances of success because the strike would be pinpointed and adjusted by ground troops observing the target.

SEALs were especially suited to the unusual demands of SOG operations. Clandestine operations were always an integral part of SEAL activities. SEALs were also experienced in conducting long-range operations far from base camps. The main SEAL unit supporting SOG operations (mostly in support of the MSG) was Detachment ECHO, based in Danang in the I CTZ. ECHO conducted commando-type operations against shore positions (sometimes farther inland as well) located along the coastline of North Vietnam and its offshore islands. Their missions included ambush operations and prisoner snatches against NVA units near the DMZ. Since they also acted as advisers to the LDNN, their Vietnamese counterparts often took part in their operations. The LDNNs worked well with their SEAL advisers, so such joint operations were consistently effective. The SEALs and LDNNs conducted successful guerrilla actions against NVA base camps and supply staging areas well inside North Vietnam. Although the actions were not reported in the media, the NVA definitely received the message that their own tactics could easily be used against them inside their territory.

Other MSG operations carried out by Detachment ECHO and LDNN men included mining of the Haiphong Harbor approaches (limpets were used inside the harbor against bona fide military targets), raids against coastal radar facilities, and demolition of railway lines. On occasion, demolition teams destroyed large numbers of Haiphong Harbor lighters, seriously tying up commercial and military traffic. (Haiphong Harbor was a shallow-water harbor, so deep-draft vessels had to load and unload their cargo at lighterages outside the harbor entrance.) Teams also established short-term observation posts on offshore islands near the mouth of the harbor.

SEAL support of the GSG operations was provided by personnel from Detachments ALPHA, BRAVO, ECHO, and GOLF. Detachment ECHO teams worked mainly along the DMZ and the Laotian segments of the Ho Chi Minh Trail. Teams from the other detachments worked against the Cambodian sections of the Ho Chi Minh Trail. They also worked hard at disrupting traffic along the Sihanouk Trail, a secondary communist supply route originating in Cambodia's main seaport city of Sihanoukville (Kompong Som) and stretching northeastward before ending in several staging areas located in the Parrot's Beak, Angel's Wing, and Fishhook sectors. A huge staging area and bunker complex would eventually be uncovered in 1970 by U.S. troops in the dense jungle surrounding Snoul, just north of the Fishhook.

The Parrot's Beak, Angel's Wing, and Fishhook were extremely important to the enemy from the beginning of the conflict. The Parrot's Beak and Angel's Wing are oddly shaped stretches of Cambodia that extend deep into Vietnam about fifty miles northwest of Saigon. The Fishhook was approximately sixty-five miles northeast of that area, about fifty miles northwest of Saigon. Since all three areas were close to Saigon, as well as to the northern sections of the Mekong Delta and War Zones C and D, they were ideal sanctuaries for regional communist forces. SEALs who worked there spent much time searching out communist supply areas. All GSG troops working in and around the Parrot's Beak and Angel's Wing constantly searched for any information on the location of the Central Office for South Vietnam (COSVN), the NVA headquarters that directed most Vietcong activities. The search for COSVN was frustrating and unsuccessful because the office was highly mobile. No matter how close the searchers got, they never could find anyone at home.

The primary mission of the GSG remained the disruption of troop and supply movements southward along the Ho Chi Minh Trail. This was, of course, critical if South Vietnam was to have any chance of defending itself against the combined NVA and VC onslaught. SEAL teams would shadow enemy units moving down the trail to determine the infiltration routes being used most often. They would actually pick up an NVA supply or troop convoy as it exited the Mu Gia Pass and keep track of it for several days or more. During that time, they would catalog the many limestone caves in the mountains and foothills along the route used by the NVA as primary storage depots. Locating and keeping track of the trail's many supply depots and rest areas were key factors in determining how best to neutralize its importance to the NVA.

To better understand the trail's importance, one should first understand that by 1968 fifty thousand to sixty thousand troops per year had moved southward along the trail. It has also been estimated that the communists were bringing down more than one hundred tons of material a month. The trail was as important to the communists' logistical efforts as Danang Air Base or Cam Ranh Bay were to the Allies. Therefore the trail was as well maintained and defended by the communists as the Allies guarded their own supply areas.

Bombing of the trail had been going on since the winter of 1964, when the United States launched Operation Barrel Roll, a clandestine action aimed at destroying the trail's Laotian sections. Since bombing of the Cambodian sections had been prohibited for years, effective interdiction was so much wishful thinking. But in 1968 the United States launched Operation Commando Hunt, a combined effort of U.S. Air Force, Navy, and Marine Corps aircraft. They pounded at the main infiltration routes extending from the Mu Gia Pass section of the North Vietnamese panhandle, southward to the Laotian/Cambodian border. Although these bombings resulted in many casualties and lost supplies and equipment for the enemy, they did not seriously interrupt the trail's routine traffic flow.

One of the first pieces of important intelligence developed by GSG units was that aerial bombing destroyed no more than 10 percent of the enemy's supplies and troops on the trail, largely because much of the trail lay obscured beneath dense forest canopy. Further, communist truck convoys and foot traffic moved quickly between well-fortified rest areas, many of which were below ground and surrounded by formidable bunkers. Once the trekkers made it to a rest area, most were able to weather the most intensive bombing sorties. The overall accuracy of U.S. bombers operating along the trail was drastically reduced because only high-altitude bomb runs could be made. Low-altitude runs carried the risk of being shot down by the extremely accurate antiaircraft artillery defending most of the trail's rest areas. That was especially true in the mountains and foothills of the Laotian panhandle. During the early spring of 1967, one team operating a few kilometers northeast of Tchepone noted just how formidable NVA air defenses could be.

Some of the limestone caves used by the NVA throughout the mountains and ridgelines of the central panhandle were fairly small, only the size of a hut; others were immense, giving rise to scores of tunnels that led to other equally large chambers. Working with a contingent of CIA-recruited Hmong tribesmen, a SEAL team found one such large cave complex and moved in carefully to develop as much intelligence as possible about it, its inhabitants, and especially its overall purpose.

Within the first several hours of their surveillance, they learned that the complex was of major importance to the NVA, not only in that immediate area but also in much of the I CTZ as well. The main cave was situated along the west wall of a small valley; the cave's huge entrance was just beneath an enormous overhanging ledge. Trucks loaded with munitions, medical supplies, diesel fuel, and other material moved in and out throughout the day. And although the team did not see any tanks or other tracked vehicles, the road surfaces were clearly marked with their unmistakable tread patterns.

Several smaller caves seemed to house the complex's personnel as well as provide areas to serve as kitchens, aid stations, and communications centers. One or two caves were used to assemble or manufacture weapons, explosive devices, and clothing. Most interesting were the caves and overhangs located along the higher levels of the valley's walls and surrounding ridgelines. Positioned inside these caves were antiaircraft artillery and large-caliber heavy machine guns, deployed to blanket the entire portion of the valley with intense interlocking fire. This was most important because the valley walls made it difficult for high-altitude bombing to be effective against the complex and its personnel. If an aerial assault were to be effective against the complex and the trail running through it, the aircraft would have to make low-altitude runs. These would guarantee large numbers of Allied planes being lost, as was proven later when some low-level raids were flown against the NVA there.

GSG units also discovered that any damage to the trail caused by U.S. bombers was usually repaired within a matter of minutes following the attack, because each rest area and corresponding section of trail was maintained by an NVA engineer company. Their expertise and ingenuity in creating roadways was rivaled only by their ability to repair destroyed road sections rapidly. They accomplished this by utilizing the copious amounts of splintered timber and pulverized rock that the bombing runs produced as incidental by-products. Although some engineer companies were later supplied with bulldozers, most were quite capable of achieving excellent results with indigenous water buffalo or elephants.

Typically spaced at intervals of fourteen to twenty kilometers, the rest areas served as base camps for the trail's maintenance/defense units, known as the Binh Tram. (Many of the original trail engineers had come from Binh Tram, a village in North Vietnam.) The rest areas also provided the troops, truckers, and "people's porters" with places where they could stop, eat a cooked meal, bathe, and rest before continuing on their trek. In many encampments there were aid stations or even well-equipped hospitals complete with triaging rooms, beds for twenty or more patients, and operating rooms, maintained in the most sterile conditions possible.

The Binh Tram, like all NVA or VC personnel and equipment, was multifunctional and adaptable to almost any situation. The engineer companies and battalions had created and maintained the trail's road surface and had also constructed the rest areas. The rest areas that contained aid stations or hospitals were provided by the Binh Tram with necessary medical staffing. Medical supplies, such as surgical instruments, anesthetics, and drugs, were brought in with the supply convoys or purchased on the local black market. Herbal remedies and large quantities of fruits and vegetables were grown in well-tended, expertly camouflaged gardens carved out of the jungle near each rest area. A few camps even maintained live-stock and "farmed" fish in man-made ponds or diverted streams.

Classrooms were set up in each rest area where films or lectures dealing with military tactics, first aid, weapons maintenance, and political ideology were presented. In some trailside camps in Laos and Cambodia, members of local communist guerrilla groups also attended the classes and reported on their own operations. To make the lessons more interesting for the less educated members of the largely peasant audience, plays, skits, and minimusicals, heavily laden with communist ideology, were well-used teaching aids. All presenters came from the ranks of the Binh Tram.

Another valuable function performed in the rest areas was the assembly and manufacture of weapons, sandals, clothing, and ammunition. Since much of the material coming down the trail, especially in the years prior to 1968, was transported by the people's porters on their backs in baskets attached to carry poles, or on specially modified bicycles, load weights had to be adjusted accordingly. Bulky items, such as rockets and launchers, mortars, and antiaircraft and field artillery, had to be broken down into easily handled loads. Many were disassembled into three loads with further adjustments being made for the larger artillery pieces. When artillery pieces designated for the defense of a rest area arrived, the Binh Tram quickly set to work cleaning, assembling, and deploying them.

Other supply shipments contained the raw materials for manufacturing weapons. In the trail's early years, these included rifle barrels, shell casings, black powder, and cases of lead balls. By late 1967, however, most rest areas in southern Laos and Cambodia had evolved into fully functional munitions factories, complete with machine lathes and tool and die equipment. They were capable of turning out hundreds of automatic weapons, grenades, and land mines, as well as thousands of rounds of ammunition a month. This meant that supply convoys had to carry fewer numbers of small arms and ammunition and could devote space to artillery pieces, high explosives, spare truck parts, and fuel.

As the NVA began to rely more heavily on trucks to transport supplies along the trail, fuel became vital. Initially, each truck had to carry its own extra fuel, sacrificing valuable cargo space. Later, fuel trucks were a standard part of each convoy. Finally, a pipeline originating in northern Laos and running between each of the trail's rest areas extended all the way down to Snoul, Cambodia. It was constructed primarily out of large-bore rubber pipe. Some sections were repaired with or replaced by lengths of hollowed-out bamboo, the universal tool in Southeast Asia. (The NVA and VC used bamboo to make a wide variety of items such as *punji* sticks, cooking pots, water pipe, canteens, bangalore torpedoes, and even throw-away mortar tubes.) The pipeline, built and maintained by the Binh Tram, greatly facilitated the flow of truck traffic down the trail, resembling a busy highway in some sections by 1969.

Along with manning rest area antiaircraft artillery batteries, Binh Tram personnel were also responsible for each camp's ground defenses and general security. Their units manned recon patrols, aircraft spotting stations, and listening posts. Ambushes and booby traps were set up to prevent compromise by U.S. or ARVN recon units. The units also established and maintained communications links between the rest areas. Although radios were available and were used to contact patrols and convoys, most communications between roadside camps was conducted via telephone lines, to prevent monitoring by Allied forces.

The GSG understood the critical importance of the Binh Tram and the rest areas to the trail's ongoing efficiency, so their units tried to locate, monitor, and, where practical, neutralize them. But since the rest areas were focal points of activity, they were also targeted for intelligence gathering. Supplies, troops, sensitive documents, high-level military officers, and intelligence cadre passed through the camps on an ongoing basis. As the GSG saw it, the situation was like studying ants. The best way to view ants and note their habits is to watch an anthill. The best way to rid an area of ants is to destroy them as they move to or from the anthill. On the trail, the Binh Tram were the ants and the rest areas were the anthills.

Surveillance of and actions against the rest areas called for small mobile units proficient at camouflage and stealth and capable of delivering a knockout punch. The GSG knew that SEAL ambush and recon teams possessed such qualities and quickly put them to work conducting operations against the rest areas and the sections of the trail running through them. The operations were diverse in nature, although the greatest proportion of them were recon oriented, as was much of SOG's work. Developing hard-based, dependable intelligence was far more valuable than kills.

The tactics that the SEALs had been using in operations elsewhere in South Vietnam were the same as those the GSG employed in their cross-border activities. Recon and ambush teams routinely used helicopters for insertions and extractions and had engaged in extended operations far from base camps and logistical/fire support. Their weapons had been selected to give team members maximum mobility without sacrificing firepower. Similarly, their packs, radios, and load-bearing gear facilitated mobility and speed without sacrificing operational effectiveness.

To illustrate how important and effective surveillance of certain trail-side rest/staging areas could be, I will describe two operations conducted in Laos during late 1968 and early 1969. The first involved the cave complex northeast of Tchepone. When that complex was located, it would have been possible to contain the area, methodically annihilate resident NVA forces, and capture or destroy all their equipment and supplies. But the resultant damage, no matter how significant, would have only been transient, at best. By keeping track of the supply convoys and troop movements through the area, the SOG teams were better able to disrupt the enemy's efforts. Such surveillance directly resulted in heavy NVA troop and equipment losses in eastern Laos and the western I CTZ. That was especially true in those areas extending from just north of Hill 861 (northwest of Khe Sanh) southward into the heart of the A Shau Valley and beyond.

Several GSG units were involved in these monitoring operations. One was a team consisting of three SEALs, two South Vietnamese nationals, and six Hmong tribesmen. They spent three days shadowing two NVA companies that left the cave complex in late December 1968 and headed south along the trail. On the first day the two companies remained together and seemed to be heading toward the next rest area some eighteen kilometers away. But after marching only three kilometers, one of the companies left the trail and began heading almost due east through the heavily forested rolling foothills toward the border. Meanwhile, the other company kept moving south along the trail. Since the company trekking into the foothills was moving actively toward the border, it was obviously the more tactically important object of interest, since South Vietnam was where all NVA troops and material were ultimately headed. That company was also more interesting because it was carrying four Chinese 7.92mm Type 24 heavy machine guns, used frequently by the NVA as antiaircraft weapons. Therefore, the team elected to follow that company.

The team paralleled the course taken by the NVA as they snaked up and down the steep, densely vegetated, double and triple-canopied hills. The NVA unit was being extremely cautious, frequently stopping to send out scouts on both flanks as well as to the front and rear. On two occasions, it even circled around, heading toward the main section of the trail before resuming a southeasterly heading. It was obvious that the unit was either trying to shake off or get the drop on any possible pursuers. Then, about half an hour after nightfall, the company halted a little less than ten kilometers north of where Route 9 crossed the border into Laos. After setting up a hasty perimeter a short distance from a lazily flowing stream, the unit set up listening post/ambush positions about fifty meters out on both flanks. The men then cooked a quick meal after which they sacked out for the night.

The following morning, they set out again. But this time they headed due east and maintained that heading for an hour before looping around to the south and then back east again. That course took them into a much steeper area in the far more densely forested foothills of Co Roc Mountain (the NVA's primary artillery base, used effectively in their long siege of Khe Sanh), making their progress far more difficult. They stopped several times, taking fifteen-minute breaks, before pressing on again. Finally, five hours after leaving their overnight position, they came to a freshly constructed narrow dirt road. The company followed the road into the thick forest on the eastern slope of a steep hillside. A few minutes later the company came to a wide clearing that appeared to be of recent vintage.

It was more like a bald spot on the hillside's eastern slope, strewn with many large outcroppings of ragged rock and a few isolated scraggly trees. The NVA continued northward on the road as it coursed along the clearing's upper periphery, carefully staying well under the tree canopy. Five minutes later, they moved into a camp area situated ten to fifteen meters from the clearing's eastern edge. As the weary marchers strode into camp, they were greeted by twenty NVA who were already there.

The camp was still in the early stages of construction, several hootches having been erected already and some bunkers well on the way toward completion. Also there were four pitlike bunkers, each surrounded on three sides by sandbags. The pits were the type usually used as emplacements for howitzers and other artillery. Farther back under the dense forest canopy, thirty meters east of the camp, four ZILs were parked in another clearing under a broad canopy of camouflage netting. (ZILs were Soviet versions of the U.S. 6x6 trucks, often used for cargo and troop transport.) Three trucks had twin 37mm antiaircraft guns in tow; the fourth towed a 130mm gun, the NVA's favorite long-range field piece.

The entire picture was clear to the team. They had come upon an NVA forward firebase only a day or two from completion. Although only one 130mm gun was in evidence, the four gun pits under construction signaled that three more large pieces were to arrive soon. The heavy machine guns, along with the three 37mm AA guns, suggested that the firebase was permanent, not designed merely to toss a few rounds at a U.S. firebase or base camp. The base's location was ideal on the eastern slope of a large hill from which Route 9, lying a mile to the south, could be monitored easily by the camp's patrols. It was also well within range of the U.S. Marine firebase at Khe Sanh, as well as other U.S. and ARVN positions on or near Hill 881 North, Hill 881 South, and Hill 861A.

It appeared that the NVA intended to keep the fieldpieces under the tree canopy until they were used for a fire mission. If Allied aircraft were to attempt an air strike against the small firebase, they would have to come in from the north or south due to the base's steep hillside position and the nearness of the equally steep slopes of the facing hill to the east. Such an approach would bring the planes into the very teeth of the camp's AA weapons. If there were other AA emplacements on the facing slope, the assaulting aircraft would face an intense and deadly cross fire. Therefore, the Boss felt it imperative to recon the facing slope. He wanted to determine whether other AA sites were in place and also to locate the firebase's forward observation (FO) position, which had to be on the top or far slope of the facing hill because it was one hundred meters higher in elevation than the firebase's position. Without an FO on the facing hill, the firebase would be virtually useless against Allied positions across the border.

While the Boss, one of the South Vietnamese nationals, and two of the Hmongs continued the surveillance of the firebase, the rest of the team set out to recon the opposing hillside. It took them more than three hours to make their way down into the narrow gorge between the two slopes and then up the facing hill. Within minutes of reaching the top, they located the Observation Post (OP), well camouflaged and dug in between two large jagged outcroppings of rock. The three observers inside commanded an expansive and unobstructed view of the border area and the strategically important Allied-controlled hills beyond.

Once the OP had been located, the team quickly saw two AA positions. As had been expected, they were located between ninety and one hundred meters below the OP, down the slope facing the hillside where the firebase was positioned. Locating the AA positions was easy because the team saw communications wire running from the OP to each AA position. More wire extended from the AA sites into the ravine and up to the firebase. This was typical of NVA units in and around the trail; field telephones provided them with better communications security because Allied aircraft and ground units were monitoring radio traffic continually. The recon team did note that two field radios were inside the OP position, probably for emergency use or to maintain communications with surrounding NVA patrols and camps.

By the time the recon team made its way back to where the Boss and the others were keeping a tight watch on the firebase, it was almost 0200. After digesting all the information found on the far slope and hilltop, the Boss had the team withdraw to the top of the hill, then moved half a mile south along the hilltop where it bent around slightly to the east. Using a Starlight Scope, the Boss scanned both slopes, pinpointing all four NVA positions, noting that each had buttoned up for the night. He had determined already that he was going to call for an artillery fire mission against the firebase, the two AA positions, and the OP on the hilltop, to be followed by an air strike. He decided to wait at least until sunrise, to be better able to adjust the incoming fire and to assess damage afterward.

After sunrise the RTO called in the coordinates of all four positions, requesting that the fire mission against the NVA firebase precede the air strike. That transmission was received by a surveillance/communications relay aircraft circling high above the trail. It was then relayed to the nearest U.S. firebase across the border. In less than five minutes, four marker rounds (white phosphorus) slammed into the slope just above the firebase. The RTO then called in the necessary adjustments, and the base was obliterated by an intense saturation of HE rounds.

The sounds of the last few HE rounds had barely died away when the first U.S. Air Force jet swooped down on the hilltop, laying down a carpet of napalm that vaporized the OP. Three other jets then dove, blanketing the firebase and the other two AA positions in napalm. During their first run, the lead plane drew some AA fire from the positions below the OP. But the first load of napalm was right on target, because all was quiet on the ground, except for several secondary explosions indicating that ammunition and fuel had been hit. As the Boss scanned both slopes with his binoculars, he could see that all weapons, vehicles, and personnel had been taken out and large sections of both slopes were on fire. The bomb damage assessment was listed as better than 90 percent.

A similar type of surveillance operation took place during the early spring of 1969 in an area just inside Laos, some seventy-eight miles southeast of the cave complex near Tchepone. It was assigned because of a tremendous amount of foot and vehicular traffic, presumably generated by NVA troop and supply transport movements. These were detected by ACOUBUOYs recently seeded throughout the area. A seven-man team was dispatched to the sector to determine what the NVA troop presence might be. Since there was a strong desire to get the team into the area as quickly as possible, they were inserted by helicopter.

Because cross-border incursions into Laos and Cambodia by U.S. units were not officially sanctioned at that time, such insertions had to be accomplished creatively. For operations near the border, the units involved could merely walk in. There was no need to go to any extravagant lengths to mask such incursions. Helicopter insertions, however, were another matter. Often they were assisted by Air America personnel and their wide array of aircraft, ranging from Huey-type helicopters to Caribou transports. Air America, an alleged civilian airline engaging in commercial passenger and cargo flights throughout Southeast Asia, was also on the scene. It was actually an arm of the CIA, and its aircraft were used in Cambodia and Laos to transport CIA and SOG personnel and provide them with logistical and tactical support. Their aircraft routinely flew in and out of remote areas, often utilizing airstrips and landing zones almost too small to be considered safe by most other pilots. For this operation, however, since time was a little short, the team boarded a U.S. Army Huey. Due to an unfortunate navigational error, the helo strayed about five miles across the border before realizing the mistake. Somehow the team was left behind on the ground when the chopper lifted off again.

The team's accidental insertion occurred just past 2200. As soon as they hit the ground they moved quickly through the jungled and hilly terrain on a heading that, after more than four hours of almost continuous movement, brought them to the AO, one mile east of the Kong River and about six miles west of the A Shau Valley. Within the first few minutes after arriving in the AO, they heard and saw numerous signs of a large NVA presence. Since sunrise was only an hour away and the team was exhausted from working through such rugged terrain, they moved back into a dense section of vegetation a short distance from a frequently traveled trail. Their well-hidden position allowed them to sleep in two-hour shifts while maintaining a close watch on the trail and surrounding terrain.

During the next five days, the team ranged widely over the area, noting scores of footpaths leading toward the border and the A Shau Valley beyond. They also found four narrow muddy roads along which trucks of various types rumbled, carrying supplies of rice, weapons, ammunition, and troops. As they traced one of those roads back toward the east, they discovered a staging area large enough to support a battalion. Streaming into that encampment were NVA troops on foot, people's porters pushing bicycles packed with more than one hundred pounds of material, and trucks covered from hood to tailgate in palm fronds and other types of foliage to camouflage them from aerial surveillance.

That staging area was located only three miles from the border and appeared to have been in place for up to a year. The team noticed that the NVA troops arriving on foot were carrying only their weapons, a very small amount of ammunition, and the uniforms on their backs. When they departed the camp toward the border, they were loaded down with large quantities of ammunition, disassembled antiaircraft weapons, rockets and launchers, mortar tubes, rice and other food staples, shovels and other tools, and spare parts and other types of maintenance items for trucks. The team had found not only a staging area but also a main supply depot for the NVA base camps inside the A Shau Valley. To destroy such an installation would create significant logistical problems for A Shau Valley NVA units until a replacement staging area could be set up.

The team withdrew back toward the east, heading for a high ridge located a half mile from the border. It was on the northern slope of a higher peak astride the border, offering an unobstructed view of the surrounding countryside. More importantly, the ridge was located a little more than a mile from the staging area, so it would be a safe location from which to call in air strikes or artillery. Saturation bombing or artillery barrages would be necessary to get at the staging area because it was located under double-canopy jungle. B-52s would be carpeting the area, and fighter jets (Navy, Air Force, and Marine) would be mopping up with napalm. The team had to stay as far out of harm's way as possible while being in a position to direct fire missions and later perform bomb damage assessment (BDA).

After the RTO called in the target coordinates, the team scanned the surrounding countryside, noting the main NVA truck route across the border. Also noted was an area less than three miles farther east where several trucks were parked under the trees on the edge of a wide stretch of high elephant grass. The coordinates of both sightings were also radioed in as targets of opportunity once the primary objective, the staging area, had been compromised. Ten minutes later, the first artillery rounds impacted on target, splintering the trees around and above the NVA encampment. Following a barrage lasting several minutes, B-52s could be heard approaching from the southwest.

The B-52s passed over the AO quickly, laying a thick, broad carpet of 500-pound and 750-pound bombs across the terrain. Although their time on target was fairly brief, the degree of devastation was tremendous. Just before their sweep, Air Force jets swooped down onto the truck park across the border and the road leading to it, firing rockets and dropping napalm. That same scenario was repeated against the staging area following the B-52 strike. Multiple secondary explosions were noted around the staging area and the truck park. Later that day and part of the following day, the team conducting a BDA of the staging area noticed extensive loss of material and more than one hundred dead NVA troops and support personnel. In the area near the truck route more than a dozen trucks had been destroyed and a section of the roadway was obstructed by a rock slide dislodged by several rockets. Temporarily, at least, the cork was in the bottle at that border crossing.

The recon operations carried out around the trail rest areas inside Cambodia often lasted from a few days to two weeks. Even so, the SEALs preferred to avoid bulky and cumbersome rucksacks for carrying gear, electing to stay with their tac-vests and LBEs. Some missions, however, called for equipment or munitions that could not be carried in their vests or LBEs. In such instances, team members elected to stow extra gear in a small NVA-model backpack, or in an oversized version of what today is called a fanny pack. Whatever type of pack was selected, the main concerns were mobility, speed, and effectiveness.

Camouflage used in cross-border operations was no different from that used by SEAL personnel in other operational areas. The recon teams wore leaf-patterned or tiger-striped uniforms; they muted exposed skin with green, black, or tan greasepaint. Occasionally, some teams wore oversized versions of the VC black pajama uniform, so that they might be taken for VC. For similar reasons, some men carried AK-47s. If they used their weapons to take out an enemy, the familiar sound of the AK-47s might not arouse as much interest from VC or NVA as a shotgun blast or M16 discharge. Usually, however, SEAL camouflage and weapons used during cross-border operations were no different from those used by SEALs elsewhere.

Silenced weapons and quick kill techniques that proved effective in

SEAL operations in other AOs were used more extensively in SOG operations. SEALs working deep inside communist territory knew that quietly neutralizing an adversary was of critical importance. Hush Puppies and other silenced firearms, crossbows, knives, wrist rockets, and other exotic types of quiet-kill items were used extensively. More rudimentary techniques, such as choke holds, saps, or a tree limb used as a club, often proved useful. SEALs made use of whatever was available to get the job done. For example, I knew one SEAL, on a team that operated in the Laotian panhandle, who took down lone NVA soldiers with rocks. Some who operated with him claimed that he was as deadly accurate at throwing rocks at a distance of thirty feet as anyone else was with a Hush Puppy, and that his kills were quieter.

Because most of the communications between trail rest areas was by phone lines, wiretapping kits were carried by the teams. Acoustically enhanced surveillance gear was also used to eavesdrop on tactical sessions or random conversations. Team members would maneuver themselves close enough to camp structures to observe activities taking place within and listen in on what the occupants were discussing.

Some observations made by surveillance teams were mundane; others were important. For example, one SEAL, working with a team in northern Cambodia in December 1968, told of snaking his way into a rest camp one night and easing under a hootch near the camp's perimeter. As he lay there peering up through a tiny crack between the bamboo flooring, he could see and hear two NVA junior officers being entertained by a camp "hostess." The two men seemed to be drunk. The SEAL knew enough Vietnamese to understand that the two NVA were trying to impress each other and their female companion with boastful tales of their sexual prowess. The woman pretended to be entranced by their posturing, acting coy and refilling their cups with brandy. With each drink the two men spoke louder, though less coherently, while gesturing toward her and describing how completely they would satisfy her. Finally, one of them lurched toward her, but he lost his balance, falling against a chair and then the table. The woman helped him back onto a chair and then sat on his lap.

As the first officer made a few pawing moves at her breasts, the other knelt beside them on one knee, also attempting to fondle her. All the while, however, she stared into space, a bored expression on her face. She must have known that the two men were beyond being able to function much longer. Within minutes, both men were asleep on the floor, their arms draped over each other as the woman slipped out the door. The SEAL felt a sense of temporary solidarity with the two officers. Like any other two military guys on leave or a pass, the men got too drunk to function but would be mercifully unable to remember what happened when morning came.

The same SEAL also described something a little out of the ordinary while monitoring the camp later that same month. Half an hour after dark he worked his way into position amidst a small but dense patch of chest-high brush, within six feet of the rear window of one of the camp's larger structures. He chose that particular structure because he had watched fifteen to twenty NVA enter it, noting that a few of them were carrying notebooks. He watched and listened for nearly an hour as two political cadre officers used a tag team approach to address their audience. The SEAL learned that they were exhorting their listeners to stay firm in their convictions. They referred frequently to ample evidence in the international media that the tide of public opinion in the United States had shifted in their favor.

Finally, the speakers and their enthusiastic audience filed out of the building and headed toward the camp's sleeping quarters. The SEAL waited several minutes longer before easing out from his hiding place and moving quickly to the structure's rear window. He pulled himself through the window, moved briskly across the room, and quickly grabbed a fistful of documents from a pile of papers strewn across a table. Without examining what he had picked up, he backed out through the window and into the darkness, then made his way back to where the Boss and the RTO had set up their listening post.

They examined the papers under the dim light of a red-lens flashlight. Among them were political caricatures, revolution-inspired poems, and several wallet-sized, laminated photos. All the photos were identical and appeared to have been photocopied from a single newspaper photograph. They depicted a police officer wearing a hat with the distinctive checkered band of the Chicago police force; the man was wading into a crowd of long-haired, young civilians, his billy club raised high above his head ready to strike. The SEALs later learned that the photo had been taken during the rioting in Chicago in August 1968 at the Democratic National Convention. They assumed that the pictures were to be distributed to NVA troops for propaganda purposes.

Recon operations on the trail also involved prisoner acquisitions (snatches). A team would be directed to snatch some specified individual ("mark") or anyone who seemed to be of tactical value, such as NVA operations or intelligence officers, VC paymasters/couriers, or members of the Binh Tram. If intelligence supplied by MACV or ARVN sources identified a prominent mark in the area, a recon team would be deployed to set up an ambush and wait, sometimes for days, to make the snatch.

Snatches proved to be effective tactics because they not only enhanced the intelligence database but also had a tremendous psychological impact on the enemy. Snatch operations, therefore, increased in frequency as the SOG's activities continued. The tricky part, of course, was getting the mark out of the area without being intercepted. SEAL recon teams became widely used for such operations, due to their demonstrated expertise in conducting such operations elsewhere. Their overall effectiveness made the communist supply cadre and Binh Tram decidedly uneasy, even in what they had assumed was secure territory. Having comrades disappear suddenly without a sound or trace gave the impression that the trailside jungle had swallowed them up.

A snatch operation in the fall of 1968 was a good illustration of how effective a SEAL operation could be. A team had been working the area around a trailside rest area about forty miles southwest of Snoul in the Fishhook. One night they decided to snatch two NVA manning an ambush position about eight hundred meters east of the rest area. The snatch was carried out without any difficulty. After interrogating the prisoners for a short time, it became clear that they were elated at having been captured; they had learned recently that they were about to be sent across the border to join a local VC battalion near An Loc. They had heard stories about how bad things had gotten for the VC since the Tet Offensive, and did not want to leave the relative comfort and security of the rest area.

Since the Fishhook AO was thought to be the most likely site for the COSVN headquarters, all SOG units in that sector were trying constantly to develop information on its precise location. The prisoners, therefore, were interrogated on what they knew about the location of COSVN or the identity of its command personnel. Early intelligence had it that Gen. Nguyen Chi Thanh had been the original commander of all communist forces in South Vietnam but that he had died by late 1967. Not much more than this was known about COSVN or its chain of command. Both men said that COSVN camps were not permanent emplacements. Instead, they were highly mobile camps that were moved often to prevent detection.

One prisoner had heard of a temporary POW camp in the immediate vicinity, one of many transit camps used to hold both ARVN officers and U.S. personnel in preparation for transporting them northward along the trail to a large permanent camp near Hanoi. He believed that the camp was less than two miles southeast of the rest area the team had been monitoring. Since the prisoners seemed so cooperative and eager to help, the team asked them to lead the way to the transit camp.

They found the camp deserted, although a brief inspection showed that it had been inhabited within the previous twenty-four hours. There was a recently filled-in latrine trench and piles of bones from fish and chickens under some young sugar palms a short distance away.

One prisoner pointed out a set of large boot prints in the dirt near a bamboo cage used as a cell. The tread was typical of the standard U.S. jungle boot. The boot prints made it clear that one American had been held prisoner recently in the camp. He noted that the boot prints led away from the cage. American prisoners were given their boots to wear only when they were to be moved. Otherwise, they were kept barefoot, since their bare feet were far too sensitive to tolerate tramping around in the jungle. If a barefoot American prisoner tried to escape, he could be easily recaptured.

The VC prisoner explained that the fish and chicken bones were indicators that an American had been present. If just ARVN prisoners and NVA guards were in the camp, only a small amount of meat or fish would be needed for meals. But when Americans were being held, the amount of meat and fish was more than twice as much. It was nothing to see one American eat half a chicken or a whole fish at one sitting, not to mention rice and vegetables. Their appetite was catered to in the transit camps because they were less rugged than their NVA guards on long, arduous marches along the trail. Keeping them alive until they reached North Vietnam was critically important.

The team RTO immediately transmitted the coordinates of the camp and the assumed line of march taken by the camp inhabitants. Although they might have left the area hours before, there was still a chance that a team could be inserted farther north ahead of the line of march to intercept them. In the meantime, the team set a heading to follow their trail, although it was unlikely that they would be able to overtake them, since they had two prisoners of their own in tow. There was the small chance that their quarry might choose to hole up for the night after traveling a short distance. Knowing that an American was being taken north made the choice an easy one. Fortunately, after only an hour the RTO got word that the American POW had been recovered by a mixed team of Green Berets and Luc Luong Dac Biet ARVN Special Forces (LLDBs) who had ambushed the guards, killing six and capturing two.

Adding to the enemy's anxieties were the recon teams' frequent ambush operations against the convoys and rest area security patrols. The frequency of these operations increased greatly following the Tet-68 offensive, resulting in many more NVA and VC casualties. Although the ambushes did not cause a significant reduction in the flow of troops and material down the trail, they made the communists more cautious in the southward trek. Harassing fire against the rest areas deprived the weary travelers of an opportunity to relax or sleep, further keeping them on edge.

Adding to the communists' problems was the use of dirty tricks (booby traps) by GSG units. SEAL recon teams used them extensively in Cambodia, especially in and around the Parrot's Beak, Dog's Face, and Fishhook areas. Some booby traps were quite simple, such as the grenade and trip wire. Others were more sophisticated, designed to cause as much trauma to the enemy's psyche as to his body. A Claymore mine booby trap would be set in a rest area near the entrance to a bunker or in the low branches of a tree above a truck park. Those in the kill zone would be killed or severely wounded. Those surviving the blast had to ready themselves quickly to get back to the relative safety of the trail.

During their operations in the Delta and RSSZ, SEAL detachments experienced much success in using M14 antipersonnel mines. Sometimes called toe poppers or shoe mines, the M14 was the same size and shape as a can of tuna. They were dark in color with a matte finish, so when they were placed along well-used trails and covered with loose soil or a few leaves, they would usually go undetected. That the mine did not require trip wires to detonate made it highly adaptable to a wide variety of situations and terrain. When detonated, the resulting explosion did not kill but might blow off a victim's foot. The injury made the victim's comrades afraid and also forced them to carry him, slowing their rate of march.

The nature of GSG activities made it necessary for the GSG to work in close coordination with the ASG. When ASG surveillance aircraft received signals from their detection devices, and analysis made further investigation necessary, a GSG unit would be dispatched to the area of concern. When practical, members of the team would be flown over the area to conduct reconnaissance of the proposed area, taking note of terrain features while identifying potential landing zones for insertion and extraction by helicopter. Decisions would be made regarding the best insertion or extraction technique to use at each LZ.

The mode of helicopter insertion a SEAL recon team would use depended on weather conditions, the type of chopper, the condition of the LZ and surrounding terrain, the number of team members, and the type of equipment used. The most frequent was the touchdown, in which the chopper landed just long enough for the team to exit the bird with their gear. A slight variation had the helicopter hovering about seven to ten feet above the LZ as the team jumped out. Ground conditions dictated whether the hover technique was appropriate. An insertion might be impractical over LZs having grossly obscured or hazardous surface conditions. Fractured ankles could result in the operation being scrubbed.

Other hover insertion techniques were rappelling, rope ladder, or rapid rope descent (a variation of what is now known as fast roping). Rappelling from a chopper is similar to descending the sheer face of a cliff except that it involves only controlled descent as opposed to the more routine push, drop, and recover technique. The rapid rope descent was more simple but also more adventurous. It involved each team member, in turn, grabbing the rope in gloved hands and sliding down, controlling the rate of fall by increasing or decreasing the grip. Some SEALs elected to wrap one leg around the rope and slide down it like a firehouse pole. The simplest hover insertion method was the rope ladder.

The security of the insertion was a prime consideration because a team's best weapon was to keep their presence hidden from the enemy and draw as little attention to themselves as possible. Insertions were made during periods of darkness, half-light, rain, or heavy overcast. Even so, chopper engines made too much noise to go unnoticed, so the pilots would put their choppers through several false maneuvers both before and after the actual insertion, to prevent the enemy from getting a fix on the true LZ.

Immediately following the insertion, the team would depart the LZ at a forty-five- to ninety-degree angle to the proposed line of march. After following that temporary heading for several minutes, they would halt and listen for any evidence of detection. In some instances, the point man and/or the rear security (sometimes called the sweep, because his job was to erase any sign of the team's passage) would make a brief recon of the immediate vicinity, to ensure that no enemy were following or paralleling the team's line of march. If all seemed secure, the heading was changed and a crescent-shaped path was taken to put them on a heading toward the objective.

After completing the requirements of the operation, the team would move toward the extraction LZ. If at all possible, the line of march and the LZ would not be the same as those used in making the insertion and reaching the objective. To return along the same route to the insertion LZ was to tempt fate by walking into an ambush. SEALs had to remember that the primary objective of recon work was to make observations and then depart the area without being detected.

Despite doing everything correctly, teams occasionally found themselves in chance encounters with enemy patrols. If the point man thought that the enemy would pass without noticing the team, he would hold his fire. If detection was inevitable, he would open fire to give other team members the opportunity to take cover or move up on line to assault the enemy. Frequently, this tactic took the enemy so much by surprise that even with numerical and fire superiority, they might break and run. Once contact was broken, the team would move as quickly as possible toward the LZ for extraction.

These insertion/extraction and reaction techniques usually applied to all recon and ambush operations and aircrew recovery operations conducted by the SEALs and other GSG units. Locating and recovering downed aircrews was a vital function of both ASG and GSG units, especially in northern Laos and parts of North Vietnam. In northern Laos, many of the planes shot down were either U.S. Air Force prop-driven A-1 Skyraiders, AC-47 gunships, or OV-10 Broncos. All such aircraft were used heavily for low-level bombing and strafing runs against trail truck convoys, as well as for low level reconnaissance operations. Because they operated at such low altitudes, they were vulnerable to antiaircraft artillery fire, which was extremely heavy along the northern Laotian sections of the trail.

Downed aircrews would radio in their position, and in a short time a team consisting of a chopper (usually an HH-53 Jolly Green Giant) and several Skyraiders as escorts would move in to make the recovery, suppressing enemy activity in the area with covering fire from the Skyraiders.

In dense jungle canopies, the HH-53 recovery chopper would lower a hoist line to which a forest penetrator was attached to break through the trees and descend to the crew member below. When the penetrator reached the ground, one or two men at a time could mount it and be hoisted up to the hovering HH-53. This retrieval method was quite effective but only when a sizable enemy force was not at hand to take the chopper under fire. The dense canopy and close proximity of an enemy force to the aircrew would also hamper the Skyraiders in laying down suppressing fire. In such instances, SEALs or other GSG units might be deployed to locate the crew and move them to a more advantageous position for recovery by chopper.

Many aircraft used over the trail, as well as other parts of Cambodia, Laos, and North Vietnam, were engaged in highly classified intelligence-gathering operations. Each aircraft carried various types of sophisticated monitoring or tactical gear, such as laser sights, navigational/attack guidance systems, communications interception equipment, and thermal sensors. All of these were far in advance of anything then being employed by the armed forces of any other country. If the planes were shot down or crashed, special efforts were made to recover their downed crews and either retrieve or destroy any of the sophisticated gear that had survived the impact.

Both the Soviet Union and the People's Republic of China had been providing the communists with weapons, trucks, and advisers (both technical and tactical) throughout most of the war. Many of their advisers were also intelligence operatives who were to develop as much information as possible about U.S. tactics and equipment. Their overt activities were pursued not only inside North Vietnam but wherever NVA or VC forces operated. Equipment harvested from U.S. aircraft crashes would be brought to them by their NVA counterparts, a horror story in the minds of MACV and the CIA.

Some aircraft used openly in operations in Southeast Asia contained extremely sensitive intelligence gear, such as the Martin B-57 Night Intruder (laser targeting equipment), F-111A bombers (navigational/attack guidance systems), and NC-123 Providers (infrared and other more sophisticated low-/no-light sensors). Although most U.S. surveillance aircraft were known quantities to much of the military world, others were not thought to be in use over Southeast Asia. All operations dealing with the recovery of the downed flight crews or equipment from those planes are officially considered to have never occurred.

Aircraft that were "never there," such as the well-known U-2 and the

SR-71 (the equipment contained in both planes remains classified)—
were alleged to be based either in Thailand or Okinawa. When these
planes were performing their operations, specific units from the ASG,
MSG, and GSG were put on alert status. Should an aircraft go down,
recovery and sterilizing units were on top of the crash site within minutes.
Surviving crew members were whisked away; demolition/retrieval teams
either removed the sensitive equipment or usually destroyed it and the
planes in place.

In a typical area of operation, an ambush team was frequently left
behind to observe the crash site. If an NVA or a VC recon patrol showed
up to investigate the site, the team would only watch and wait for them
to leave. But if a Chinese or western adviser were present, they would try
to snatch the adviser and neutralize the patrol. If the enemy unit was too
large, they would be allowed to pass unmolested, but as soon as the RTO
could safely use the radio, an air strike would be called in. In keeping
with their firm preference and unwavering habit, SEAL ambush teams
tried to take advisers alive. Since SOG ops were clandestine and unre-
ported, there are no records of Soviet advisers being captured by U.S.
units in Southeast Asia.

During a late-afternoon crash site monitoring operation in August 1969,
just inside Laos not far from the Tchepone River, a well-hidden team
watched a nine-man NVA patrol tentatively approach. The light was fad-
ing fast, but they noticed that as the patrol came nearer in single-file formation, the third man in line was much taller and bulkier than the others.
When the patrol reached the downed aircraft they began to crawl over it
like flies on rotting meat. The team tossed two concussion grenades into
their midst, stunning most of them but not the big one and two others who
had been standing near him. As the team moved in, the big man and his
two companions fired on them. The team's return fire was brief but
intense, and in less than fifteen seconds all was quiet again. All of the
enemy force was either put down or disoriented from the effects of the
concussion grenade.

Unfortunately, only the big man and one other survived the brief firefight; both were seriously wounded. They were tended to rapidly, but it
was evident that the big one would eventually succumb to his multiple
wounds. The RTO called for a rapid extraction, and within less than ten
minutes a Huey touched down and the team scrambled aboard with the
two wounded prisoners. The big prisoner's size (six feet three and 200 to

210 pounds), the way he carried himself, and the fact that the other members of his patrol seemed to be following his lead made the Boss assume that he was probably an adviser from the People's Republic of China. Interrogation of the other prisoner confirmed that assumption, so they decided to go directly to Danang so that the CIA could question him.

By the time the prisoner was turned over to the CIA in the triage area of the naval hospital at Danang, he was extremely weak from loss of blood. He was said to have toyed with his interrogators by answering their questions in different languages: a question asked of him in English would be answered in French, one in French answered in German, and one in German answered in English. The interrogators planned to question the man again after he was operated on, but he did not survive the procedure.

A team operating in Cambodia in February 1969 also had an experience involving non-Vietnamese personnel. The team had been keeping tabs on a rest area and a nearby supply depot west of a village called Sok Nok in the Parrot's Beak. During four days they observed many different types of enemy personnel pass through the rest area, including NVA grunts, officers, political cadre, and even news reporters working for various news agencies in North Vietnam. One day, they were surprised to see a group of travelers who included decidedly different reporters.

The group totaled nine in all, including four armed NVA as security for the others. Of the remaining five members, one appeared to be a cameraman, another a sound technician, and a third the gofer, humping a rucksack bursting with 35mm cameras, lenses, and a tripod. The gofer looked like either a Khmer or a Vietnamese; the cameraman and sound technician looked more like Filipinos or Japanese. The remaining two men must have been reporters because they were giving the orders and carried very little gear. They both appeared to be westerners, although they spoke to their companions in French and with each other in what sounded like a mixture of French and German.

The group remained in the area for only a day, taking still and motion pictures of the camp and its occupants, permanent and transient alike. The group actually abetted the team's surveillance efforts. The team had already located a supply dump, but by noting areas that the Binh Tram went out of their way to prevent the reporters from entering, the team was able to identify other features of great interest, such as a well-hidden emergency rice cache, two phone lines (one leading to a staging area to the east, near the border; the other leading southwest toward the next rest area), and what later proved to be a temporary way station POW camp. By the time the reporters and their companions headed back north along the trail, the team was able to locate every important logistical feature within a square mile of the camp.

Rumors, of course, were rampant throughout the course of the Vietnam conflict regarding men with obvious western features operating with or leading NVA and VC units. That the rumors were probably true was not surprising because the USSR and other communist bloc countries actively supplied and supported the NVA's efforts at overthrowing the South Viet-namese government. The following are but two examples of encounters that SEALs and other SOG units are said to have had with non-Asian combatants.

The first occurred during the late spring of 1969 in Cambodia about ten miles northwest of Loc Ninh. A seven-man team, five SEALs and two LDNNs, had been working the area for several days, monitoring a nearby trailside rest area and heavily used infiltration route. At 0700 the team was making its way back toward the border, paralleling one of the infil-tration trails. It was raining heavily and the wind was blowing lustily. The team had been on the move for two hours already and the weather com-bined with the thick brush and thorny underbrush made the going so rugged that the men were on the verge of exhaustion. The Boss had them halt for a ten-minute rest in a stand of sugar palms, on the edge of a vast expanse of eight-foot elephant grass.

As they started to hunker down and relax, several figures suddenly emerged from the tall grass, laughing as they ran toward the team's posi-tion. Because of the heavy downpour and the wind, the team was unaware of their approach, but fortunately the oncoming NVA patrol was too intent on getting under the palms and out of the rain to be prepared for this chance encounter. Both units spotted each other simultaneously, hastily taking skirmish positions and opening fire. The firefight was intense, last-ing less than thirty seconds, with the SEALs and LDNNs dropping all six of their adversaries.

As the Boss, both LDNNs, and the corpsman checked out the fallen enemy, the point and the two others watched and listened for signs of other NVA who might be in the vicinity. As the corpsman reached the nearest body he noticed that it was much larger and stockier than the oth-ers. He snapped his fingers twice to direct the Boss's attention toward the dead man and used his foot to turn him over. He was obviously Caucasian. His uniform bore no insignia or flashes that might have identified his rank, unit, or nationality. The Boss knelt beside the body and searched the pockets for clues to the man's identity.

But before he went through the contents of the first pocket, two frags came thudding to the ground where he was kneeling. He yelled "Cover!" and then dove away from the body and the frags as they erupted, their fragments wounding the corpsman and an LDNN. The blasts were followed by automatic weapons fire from the elephant grass. The rest of the team returned the fire, and the Boss and the RTO grabbed the wounded men and began to drag them away. The other team members were able to follow a few seconds later without taking more casualties. Either the NVA decided to hold position and lick their wounds, or perhaps they were more interested in driving the team away from their fallen comrades.

The team escaped to an emergency extraction point a half mile to the west without further contact. Twenty minutes later, they were on a chopper headed for Tay Ninh, where the two wounded team members received treatment. The team was debriefed by four CIA people regarding the Caucasian member of the NVA patrol, but there was no way to determine who he was or why he was in the area. If they had not been hit by the second NVA unit, they would have been able to return with the body of the Caucasian.

A less dramatic encounter with non-Asian combatants occurred in the summer of 1968. A team had been doing bomb damage assessments southeast of Tchepone along a major tributary of the Bang Hieng River where the NVA had placed one of the most ingeniously camouflaged bridges ever constructed along the trail. It was made from local timber, generously painted with creosote to make the already dark wood as black as coal. The wood was then placed over a "roadway" of boulders and large rocks laid just below the surface of a shallow but wide section of the waterway. Because the dark-colored bridge lay a foot below the surface of the muddy dark brown water, it was almost impossible to spot, especially from the air.

The team was the first Allied force to locate the bridge, pinpointing its position for a subsequent air strike that was completely effective. A huge section of the bridge, as well as more than one hundred meters of road surface on either side of the crossing, was destroyed. After the strike, the team spent two days watching as more than fifty Binh Tram cleared debris and repaired the damage literally before the dust had settled. The NVA were obviously interested in keeping the bridge open because truck traffic could move south much quicker than when taking one of the side trails.

While keeping a close watch on the Binh Tram's repair efforts from a small hill south of the bridge, one man used his binoculars to check out the slope of a larger nearby hill on the other side of the crossing. His attention was drawn by some brief glints of light, but he could not make out the source of the reflections. The Boss tried to get a clear look at what was going on by moving up the hill, but he was able to see only some movements.

The team headed for the hill, which was about a mile away. To reach it they had to move through sparse cover teeming with Binh Tram and other enemy personnel. It took them about an hour to reach the base of the other hill. A third of the way up they located a well-traveled path that originated by the riverbank. As they began to parallel its course, they heard voices and the sound of movement approaching from above. They moved into ambush positions on either side of the path, setting up just in time to see five figures. Three of them were NVA enlisted men, one was an NVA officer, and the last was a Caucasian, only slightly taller than the others and dressed in a dark brown and green camouflage uniform and black beret.

The Boss motioned the capture team to take the NVA officer and the Caucasian; the rest would eliminate the other three men silently. When the group moved into the kill zone, the capture team tackled them, gagging and securing the two prisoners in a matter of seconds. At the same instant, the other three NVA were also tackled and neutralized with knife work. While the Boss and the capture team tended to the prisoners and watched for signs of approaching NVA, the others dragged the dead NVA well off the path and covered their bodies with leaves and dead branches. The gear belonging to the two prisoners and the three dead men was quickly searched and found to consist mostly of surveying equipment and maps. Only the maps were kept. The team then set out for their nearest extraction point, a quarter mile away.

The team was picked up within minutes of reaching the LZ and transported directly to Danang, where they were met by CIA personnel who took immediate charge of the prisoners. En route, the team already had determined that the Caucasian prisoner was a major and a member of the Cuban army. He and the NVA officer, also a major, were engineers who had accompanied a survey team to the top of the hill to get a better look at a section of the river just west of the bridge, where a second subsurface bridge was to be placed.

There were literally hundreds of stories and rumors about Allied units encountering non-Vietnamese personnel operating with communist forces during the war. Many of the stories were completely false. The person relating a tale may have taken a true event and added a little yeast to the batter. But a number of stories were completely accurate. After all, why should one find it strange that communist Chinese, North Koreans, Caucasians, and even Blacks would be with NVA and VC personnel? It was logical for communist bloc countries to send advisers and observers into the Southeast Asian turmoil because it provided them with a sterling opportunity to assess the effectiveness of the various branches of the U.S. armed forces and to be present during the interrogation of captured U.S. troops. This would have enhanced their intelligence base on the capabilities of U.S. soldiers in the field, especially when faced with guerrilla-type actions.

There was another reason for expecting to find nonindigenous combatants or mercenaries fighting alongside the NVA and VC, especially in Cambodia and Laos. Mercenaries have participated in wars through the centuries. Some mercenaries provide their services for economic gain; others fight for political and/or social ideologies. Others participate for the pure joy of the adventure. Although I never heard a truly credible tale of a mercenary having been killed or captured in the theater, I have no reason to doubt that they were there.

SEAL recon teams and other SOG units searched for Allied POWs particularly inside South Vietnam, Cambodia, and Laos. Most of the time, only recently vacated camps were found, but occasionally small camps containing a few prisoners and a handful of guards were located and liberated. The camps usually contained ARVN or civilian prisoners. Infrequently U.S. personnel were located. Interrogation of prisoners taken by Phoenix Program personnel revealed that U.S. prisoners from the III CTZ and IV CTZ usually were moved from camp to camp and taken quickly into Cambodia (often via the tunnel networks) for the long trek north along the trail.

Prisoner search operations were also conducted deep inside North Vietnam. A few small camps were situated on the North Vietnamese side of the Laotian border, fewer than twenty kilometers north of the DMZ. As in South Vietnam, few U.S. personnel were located in such camps. Even inside North Vietnam, U.S. prisoners were moved at frequent intervals. In many cases, if the NVA thought that an attempt to free their prisoners would be made, they killed the prisoners. Several camps were found containing the bodies of recently killed prisoners.

Some of the most ambitious search operations were carried out around Hanoi and Haiphong. In November 1970, a specially trained group of Green Berets and Air Force personnel raided a POW camp located at Son Tay, just northwest of Hanoi. Although no prisoners were recovered (they had all been moved to another site in the preceding weeks), the raid was remarkably daring and resulted in no U.S. casualties. Yet the raid was rumored to not have been the first incursion made inside North Vietnam's borders by U.S. units. Many months earlier, small recon units are alleged to have performed extensive nighttime recon operations to the south of Hanoi, locating a medium-sized camp, later code-named Skidrow.

Another rumored activity of the GSG was the training and supplying of indigenous espionage agents inside North Vietnam. The agents, known as Gray Ghosts, were trained in surveillance, infiltration, and ambush tactics, as well as the basic operation and maintenance of various types of long-range radio equipment. Their objective was to report on NVA troop deployments, SAM-2 radar sites, supply staging areas, and the location of U.S. prisoners. Such intelligence data was ordinarily transmitted by radio, the signals monitored by surveillance aircraft and relayed to the communications center in Danang. At frequent intervals, SOG units rendezvoused with the Gray Ghosts to resupply them with radio batteries, new radios, and replacement antennas and to debrief them in person. Personal debriefings were used to assess the agents' physical and emotional condition and to let them know that they were not really alone on their dangerous missions.

Although the SOG was an extremely diversified entity, its main goal remained the eradication of communist infiltrators and the interdiction of the Ho Chi Minh Trail. Over the years, SOG units, together with various mercenaries (such as the Abo, Nung, Hmong, Meo, Khmer, and Montagnard), inflicted heavy casualties on those making the long, arduous trip south. Thousands of communist trucks and tons of material were destroyed or captured. Sections of the trail and its bridges, rest areas, and pipelines were demolished. Yet, despite these efforts and the enemy's losses of personnel and equipment, the trail not only persisted, it expanded. Like the story of the little Dutch boy, the finger in the dike was a valiant but doomed endeavor.

12 PHOENIX

The SOG was but one of the organizations charged with providing the expertise and manpower for projects during the war that required special handling. The other major such organization, the Phoenix Program, was perhaps the most romanticized, vilified, and misunderstood of the Allied war efforts to break the backs of the VC, probably because, like the SOG, its operations were highly classified. Unlike the SOG, however, the Phoenix Program recorded and published certain aspects of its operations. It provided the press with frequent updates on the current numbers of repatriated, captured, or neutralized VC. But the exact nature of its day-to-day operations was kept secret.

The fact that its operations were conducted on the periphery of the general war's spotlight drew much attention from the world media. And media correspondents employed a tried and proven journalistic tactic. They gathered as many facts as they could; when they ran out, they ad-libbed. Assumption and innuendo were perceived too often as valid substitutes when answers could not be found. Sometimes they became valid substitutes even when answers and tangible evidence to the contrary existed.

The Phoenix Program was a joint effort of the CIA, MACV, and the Government of South Vietnam (GVN). Although it formally began in

1968, its roots derived from the Civil Operations and Revolutionary Development Support (CORDS) agency. CORDS was created in May 1967 to coordinate all pacification efforts in South Vietnam under the control of MACV. Its first director, Robert Komer, was convinced that the best way to eradicate the VC and their influence on the rural populace was to enlist the support of the populace. To that end, special teams of civilian and military personnel were formed and deployed in each of South Vietnam's forty-four provinces.

The Phoenix Program was placed under the direction of William Colby (previously the CIA station chief in Saigon and later the director of the CIA in Washington, D.C.). Because it was spawned by CORDS, one primary objective remained, at all times, the unifying of the populace against the VC. Its other objectives were to root out the Vietcong and their infrastructure and neutralize them. Military units supporting Phoenix Program operations came from ARVN and U.S. forces. The primary ARVN organization participating in the Phoenix Program (called Phuong Huong by the GVN) was the Luc Luong Dac Biet (special forces). It later was called the Special Mission Service (SMS). Also participating in the project were the Quan Cahn (QC) and the ARVN military police.

U.S. military personnel operating in support of the Phoenix Program were the Army Special Forces (Green Berets) and the SEALs. Both groups were already famous as experts in waging clandestine special warfare operations. Both groups had proven their remarkable ability to operate well inside enemy territory and develop great quantities of high-quality intelligence data. The Green Berets and SEALs had extensive experience as tactical advisers which made them ideal for instructing and advising the Provincial Recon Unit (PRU), the action arm of Phoenix.

Often, SEAL advisers would operate with individual PRUs and live with them in their fortified villages. Some operations were conducted on the squad level, but frequently operations were conducted on the platoon level as well. Platoon-level operations were usually reserved for instances in which the potential for making contact with large numbers of VC was great. Operating in support of SEAL ambush teams or with SEAL advisers while conducting snatch operations in the dead of night, the PRUs proved to be extremely effective.

At MACV, most people felt that the SEALs and PRUs were simply meant for each other, and in many ways they were. Both groups were highly motivated and intent on significantly reducing the numbers of active VC and VCI operating in all areas of the Delta and RSSZ. They were also comfortable with the physical environment and were willing to deal with the harshest elements of those places to get the job done. Both groups understood how important patience, emotional flexibility, and perseverance were to the success of their operations. Waiting for a mark to show up sometimes took hours or days because the VC, aware that security leaks could occur, changed routes and transit times abruptly to avoid capture.

Some people who felt that SEALs and PRUs were well matched thought so for decidedly negative reasons. They saw them as undisciplined assassins and pirates, sadists who enjoyed bringing a reign of terror to where they operated and did not care who got hurt in the process. Such generalizations may have satisfied certain individuals who, for whatever reason, wished to attribute all of the natural barbarism of warfare to a small number of combatants. Such generalizations were grossly inaccurate to both the PRUs and the SEALs.

PRUs were not regular military forces. Although some wore an ARVN-type field uniform (it included a shoulder flash depicting the fabled phoenix bird rising up out of the ashes), many others did not. That caused some regular army types to view them as mercenaries, undisciplined and with decidedly felonious intentions. Because the PRUs were dedicated and energetic in their efforts to locate and eradicate both VC and VCI alike, perhaps such erroneous notions seemed plausible to the casual observer. Although a few PRUs may have taken liberties in pursuing their mission, these instances were not indicative of all PRUs' actions.

Basically, the PRUs were organized to operate within their own provinces and districts. It was assumed that their familiarity with their home turf would make them more effective. This proved to be correct; the PRUs and their SEAL advisers quickly began to produce large numbers of VC prisoners, KIAs, and *chieu hoi* defectors. Because the PRUs were operating in their own backyards, their ability to act on information dealing with the identity and location of VC or VCI suspects was immediate. Suspects were pounced upon before they could flee the area.

By the end of 1968, the SEALs and the PRUs were neutralizing seven hundred to eight hundred VC and VCI per month in the Delta and RSSZ. This was a disastrous turn of events for the VC because they had already lost approximately 80 percent of their tactical forces as a result of the Tet-68 offensive. VC agents who had infiltrated many province, district, city, and village government organizations were being identified by defectors or recently captured prisoners, causing their removal from the game. Within the first year of their existence, Phoenix Program units had neutralized several thousand VC and facilitated the defection of another several thousand.

To understand the problem of locating and neutralizing the VC and their infrastructure, one would have to define why the problem even existed. That the VC were waging a guerrilla war on behalf of a shadow government meant that identifying them was not simple. They and their government were considered outlaws throughout the land, so they could not maintain a permanent, centrally located capital, and their officials could not openly identify themselves. The same was true for their tax collectors, supply and transportation cadres, couriers, intelligence officers, medical personnel, and troops.

But the VC had a decided advantage of literally being no different in appearance than every other man or woman. (Women made up a significant percentage of the VC's total troop strength.) They did not wear uniforms (the VC garb, black pajamalike shirt and pants, was the standard day-to-day wear of the peasantry), live in prescribed areas, or typically go around shouting, "Hey! We're over here!" During the day, they were the local fishermen, farmers, ferrymen, bus drivers, or doctors; at night they were members of VC ambush or sapper units. In some areas of the country, almost every family had a relative or friend who was a soldier with the local VC battalion or otherwise supported its activities, so civilians were reluctant to identify those VC with whom they had longstanding social or familial ties.

It was also difficult to identify the VC because their forces, even on the divisional level, were not large units. Companies, battalions, and divisions did not usually operate as such. Each division was usually divided into three regiments, broken down into a number of battalions. The battalions were, in turn, divided into several companies, consisting of several three-man squads. The squads were the basic building block of all other VC units and were the routine operational arms of the VC army. Although squads were parts of companies, they neither billeted nor operated together.

Further confusing the issue was the fact that the VC command structure was not an easily defined or identified entity, because the VC knew that loyalty is an all too frequently fluid state. Sometimes, loyalty to a belief or a cause is passionate and unflagging. At other times (for example, when under intensive interrogation), loyalty can be bought or bartered with money, privilege, freedom, or cessation of torture. To offset the obvious drawbacks to waging a civil war, from the insurgent's viewpoint, the VC used its three-person cells for its command structure. This meant that only a small number of VC in an area ever knew who all three members of its command staff were. This decreased the potential for one VC grunt to compromise the integrity of district leadership.

The best method of identifying and neutralizing the VC and their supporters was to capture and interrogate other VC willing to cooperate in the effort. That, of course, became the main emphasis of the Phoenix Program. Prisoners and other detainees, interrogated by U.S., ARVN, or police units, provided the names of most of the VC who were subsequently taken into custody by the SEALs, Green Berets, and PRUs. Thorough, effective interrogation resulted in the identification and arrest of other VC and VCI. That process, which began as a trickle, gradually grew into a torrent, sweeping up hundreds of suspects a month.

The rule of thumb among Phoenix Program units was that snatching a suspect would be considered only if he had been identified by a minimum of three reliable sources, many times by other suspects. But just as many tips came from local civilians, tired of being kept in the middle of a tedious, ongoing confrontation that injured more innocent bystanders than actual combatants. Critics of the program suggest that many suspects were the victims of enemies who saw an opportunity to remove a business/romantic rival. This may have been true in isolated cases, but interrogation of such suspects most often revealed them to be true VC or VCI.

Once information regarding the identity of a suspect was turned over to the Phoenix Program, an order for the snatch was passed down to the PRUs and their advisers. The information consisted of the mark's identity, position within the VC organization, most probable present location, and (if possible) a listing of known associates. Information regarding the location of any suspected safe houses or rural sanctuaries was also provided, in case the mark escaped from the snatch team or left the area before the snatch could be initiated. If the mark did escape capture, PRUs and SEALs would descend on these safe houses and sanctuaries and search them thoroughly, sometimes resulting in the capture of more suspects than had been anticipated originally.

The snatch team interrogated suspects to determine if they could provide information on other VC. The suspects were then turned over to the National Police, the QC, or the SMS for further interrogation and handling. Suspects judged to be VC were transported to Con Son Island for incarceration. Located about seventy miles southeast of the Ca Mau Peninsula, the island was used as a penal colony for VC prisoners and was frequently referred to as Phoenix Island.

The SEALs and the PRUs with whom they operated pursued VC suspects throughout much of South Vietnam. But most of their activities were carried out in the Mekong Delta and the Rung Sat. Their tactics were essentially the same as those used by the SEALs in these areas since 1966; that is, speed and mobility were often considered more important than firepower, because their primary objective was to take suspects into custody. Killing was to occur only if there was no way to subdue the mark, or if taking him into custody entailed too great a risk to members of the snatch team. Since the SEAL detachments had engaged in snatch operations routinely long before the Phoenix Program began, their tactics were pretty much SOP. Because few snatch operations were ever memorialized in after-action reports, the following examples are composites.

The first example took place a few months after the Tet Offensive in May 1968. The AO was a village just south of Ben Tre, the capital city of Kien Hoa Province.

Four *hoi chanh* (VC deserters taking advantage of the GVN's Chieu Hoi amnesty program) turned themselves in to three QC sitting in a jeep on a street in Ben Tre just after midnight. One man said that he was the aide to the S-2 officer of the local VC battalion. All four indicated that the battalion's morale had been destroyed by the huge VC losses from the Tet Offensive. Interrogation of the four *hoi chanh* provided the name of a VC intelligence officer who lived south of Ben Tre near the Ham Luong River.

The name was not new to the Phoenix network, and coming from men with assured amnesty made it reliable enough to use. Consequently, three SEAL advisers from Detachment BRAVO and six PRUs were briefed on the location and identity of the mark. Because he was on a list of suspects, his pictures were given to the team. They were advised that the mark was always accompanied by bodyguards who would be nearby when the snatch took place and would, in all likelihood, have to be neutralized.

The three SEAL advisers went over the operation's requirements with their PRUs, including a layout of the village, hastily drawn by one of the *hoi chanh*. The mark's hootch was on the edge of the village near the river. The location was typical because it offered a means of rapid escape if the village came under attack. That was of little consequence to the team, since they conducted snatch operations during the night or early morning hours, when the mark would be less alert.

Shortly past midnight, a PBR approached the village from upstream. When it came to within two hundred meters of the village's northern edge, it swung to port near the riverbank. The SEAL team leader and three of the PRUs jumped ashore. As the PBR backed into the river's main channel, the four men moved quickly toward the village perimeter. Several minutes later, the PBR again swung toward the riverbank to port, approximately fifty meters south of the village, and the remaining two SEALs and three PRUs slid into the shallow water, waded ashore, and moved toward the southern edge of the village, staying close to the river.

Thirty minutes later, the first group, which was to make the actual snatch, was in place along the northern wall of the mark's hootch. At the same moment, the second group took up positions fifteen meters south of the hootch. The second group was to provide security by laying down covering fire for the snatch team should any of the mark's associates be residing in the neighboring structures. If any villagers were to emerge from their hooches while the operation was in progress, the security team would either encourage them to duck back inside or take them down. The desired outcome would be for the team to snatch the mark and then depart the area without anybody else's sleep being disturbed.

Both groups held their positions until 0100, when the Boss and two PRUs moved into the hootch. They were armed with shotguns. One PRU played the beam from his flashlight around the structure's interior. Asleep on three cots, across from the doorway where the capture team stood, were the intelligence officer and his two bodyguards. All three men were roused, tied, blindfolded, and gagged. The PRU with the flashlight was an RTO. He signaled the security team that the mark was under control and that the team was ready to move out. As the capture team exited the hootch and started moving north, the security team's RTO signaled a Seawolf helicopter that had left Ben Tre at about 0105 to move in for extraction. The security team then quickly caught up with the snatch team.

Three minutes later, all nine men and their captives heard the chopper's rotors. A strobe signal was set out and the Seawolf touched down just long enough for the team and the suspects to scramble aboard. Interrogation was begun during the short flight into Ben Tre. Two AK-47s and an SKS were seen in the hootch, confirming the men's status as

VC. Although the VC protested that they had found the weapons and were planning to give them to the local ARVN company up the road, the men were turned over to the SMS for further interrogation and final disposition.

Some snatch operations involved more than merely deploying to a village in the dead of night, quietly entering a hootch, securing the intended mark, and spiriting him away. Often, a team had to stake out a village, hootch, trail, or waterway because the best available intelligence detailed only a suspect's last known location or most probable route of travel. Patience and stealth again would be among the snatch team's most useful and potent weapons. Sometimes snatches happened after a team had staked out a location for hours or days before the mark came into view.

As the Phoenix operations became more successful, the VC and VCI got more skittish. It was more usual than not that a planned arrival, departure, or rendezvous was changed suddenly in case a recently captured VC decided to give up his comrades. One such example took place during June 1969, starting in Sa Dec with the arrest of a local prostitute who had been offering "comfort" to the local ARVN officers. She had also been developing intelligence data on the comings and goings of MRF units as they conducted operations in nearby sections of the Plain of Reeds. This came to light when she was stopped by two QCs conducting a random identity card check. While going through her handbag, a QC came across some scraps of paper containing her scrawled notes. During an extended interrogation session, she supplied the name of the local intelligence officer to whom she reported. Coincidentally, the same name had been supplied to the SMS by several recent *hoi chanh*s.

The *hoi chanh*s also stated that the intelligence officer had a printing press, used to turn out a newspaper and a variety of propaganda tracts, located in a small hamlet a short distance northwest of Sa Dec, near the village of Tan Khanh. All *hoi chanh* agreed that the suspect usually came to the hamlet twice a week to debrief his operatives and oversee the printing operation. Unfortunately, his schedule was thoroughly unpredictable because he did not want to establish a pattern that might lead to capture.

The name supplied was not his real name, but based on his physical description the SMS was able to provide pictures of four men with similar physical characteristics. One was of a man who worked as a cook in a large restaurant in Cao Lanh. He was identified immediately as being the intelligence officer. Several copies of his picture were given to an SMS unit, which headed immediately for the restaurant. Others went to a snatch team that set out for the hamlet near Tan Khanh.

The snatch team, made up of four SEALs, two LDNNs, and eight PRUs set out for the hamlet a little after midnight during a steady, heavy rain. Two SEALs, one LDNN, and two PRUs embarked aboard a STAB, with the rest transported to the AO by PBR. When both vessels were a few hundred meters east of the AO, the STAB slipped into an irrigation canal that swung around south of the hamlet. As it came within fifty meters of the hamlet, it cut its engines and drifted amidst a dense stand of tall reeds that swept out from the left shoreline and into the center of the waterway. The PBR simultaneously moved farther up the river until it was within about fifteen meters north of the hamlet. It too swung into an area of thick cover and cut its engines.

Three team members slipped into the hamlet to check out the hootch where the printing press was supposed to be, and three others began to check out the other hootches. The rest of the team spread out to provide security, watching the river, canal, and trail approaches to the hamlet as well as staying alert for any signs of movement coming from any other hootch. If they were lucky, the suspect would be in the hootch with the printing press and vulnerable to a snatch. As it turned out, however, he was nowhere in sight. Assuming that he was en route, everyone pulled back to areas of dense ground cover to keep the hootches under surveillance.

An hour before dawn, the PBR moved about one hundred meters farther upstream and slipped into another area of thick cover along the riverbank. The STAB presented a low enough profile to risk letting it remain in position among the reeds near the hamlet.

The morning started with a heavy downpour, gradually giving way to a lighter but steady drizzle throughout most of the afternoon. By early evening, the sky grew darker and the rain picked up again. There was still no sign of the VC, but the rain kept the civilians indoors, which allowed a few team members to get close enough to the hootches to hear and see what was going on inside. They learned that the printing press was in the target hootch and two VC were busily using it to turn out a rudimentary newspaper. In a second hootch one occupant was repairing an NVA field radio.

Two hours after nightfall, the low growl of an outboard engine was heard coming from the river west of the hamlet. As it got louder, the dim light from a carbide lantern grew brighter, until it was evident in the bow of a slowly approaching sampan. The craft was beached near where the PBR had been positioned originally and three men stepped ashore, each carrying an AK-47 and a bundle or pack slung over his shoulder. The team held their positions, waiting until the VC got inside the hootch before making their move. They would have to ease up to the dwelling and peek inside to identify the suspect. His capture was too important to risk blowing it to merely take down three VC grunts.

The capture team, consisting of three SEALs, one LDNN, and two PRUs, moved to the rear of the target hootch. The Boss looked through a side window, and saw five people, three of whom were the new arrivals. One of them was the VC intelligence officer. The five VC suspects (four men and one woman) were quite relaxed, all talking at once and laughing loudly. While the three new arrivals were changing out of their wet clothes, the woman ladled soup into some bowls.

After watching briefly, the Boss signaled the capture team to bag the suspect and his four companions. The remaining members of the team moved into position to observe the other hootches and provide security for the capture team. As soon as they were all in position, the capture team swarmed into the target hootch just as the newly arrived VC had sat down to eat their soup. At first it seemed that all five VC had been taken so offguard that there would be no trouble in securing them. But the woman suddenly grabbed a homemade stick-handled grenade, pulled the pin, and let it drop to the floor.

Two SEALs grabbed the intelligence officer, shoved him behind the printing press, and piled on top of him. The rest of the team also dove for cover, one behind the stove, two behind an overturned table, and one across the bed. Fortunately, the grenade was not very potent. Although the concussion and shrapnel killed the woman and two of her comrades, the blast only slightly wounded the LDNN and the two SEALs who had used their bodies to shield their suspect. With everyone's heads still reeling, the capture team secured the three remaining suspects and scanned the room for anything of intelligence value. Their search was aborted, however, by the sounds of a rapidly building firefight outside.

Within seconds of the grenade blast, the security team began to take incoming fire from two of the other hootches. Although they suppressed that initial burst, less than a minute later a heavy concentration of automatic weapons fire erupted from an area of dense cover south of the hamlet. The security team quickly suppressed that fire as well and took two prisoners in the process. As it turned out, a five-man VC patrol had been en route to the hamlet for shelter. Also captured were three AK-47s, one SKS carbine, an RPG launcher, and four rockets. Three VC in the patrol were killed. Also dead were the four VC who had fired from the two hootches.

The PBR sped to the scene at the first sounds of automatic weapons fire. The RTO called for Seawolf gunship support. The VC intelligence officer and the other prisoners were loaded onto the chopper and whisked off to Saigon for questioning. A complete search of the hamlet turned up the printing press, several maps, ten pounds of documents (some of which listed the names of local VC operatives and the locations of two safe houses in Long Xuyen), and a half dozen automatic weapons. The items, except for the printing press, were loaded onto the PBR and the STAB for transport back to Sa Dec. The press was blown in place, being too bulky to transport. The operation was highly successful, not only resulting in snatching an important VC officer, but also locating a previously unknown VC hamlet.

All snatch operations did not unfold as uneventfully. Many times the mark resisted and in the ensuing struggle was wounded or killed. If a capture team felt that there was a substantial risk of resistance from the marks, they would toss concussion grenades into the room first. Their deafening roar almost always caused considerable disorientation of the victims, making them incapable of resistance for several minutes afterward. If a mark resisted to a degree that the security of the snatch team was endangered, he would be neutralized.

Not all snatch operations were used to grab VC or VCI. A team might snatch a local temporarily to obtain intelligence on the identity of suspects, the location of safe houses and meeting areas, or information about new faces in the vicinity. On rare occasions, intelligence agencies were lucky enough to have a recently captured suspect or new *hoi chanh* warn that the VC had become suspicious about an Allied operative. In this case, a team would quickly deploy to the area in question to snatch the operative before he could be captured by an assassination squad.

A situation like this occurred in late 1968 in Ca Mau. A young Vietnamese woman had been providing the local VC intelligence network with information on QC activities. She was the mistress of a QC lieutenant who had let his gonads control his better judgment. She decided to turn herself in to the local ARVNs as a *chieu hoi,* stating that she could provide them with a huge amount of information on the local VC tax agents working in Ca Mau, Hong My, Dam Doi, and other nearby cities and villages. She also knew the name of a pharmacist in Bac Lieu, the S-2 officer for the local VC battalion, and the locations of several safe houses between Ca Mau and Vinh Chau. But there was a small price for her assistance.

She asked that her family, living in a village near Kien Long, be re-located. This was important because when the VC learned of her defection, an assassination squad would kill her family as an example to discourage others. In most such cases, the VC even killed a targeted family's livestock and pets for emphasis. In anticipation of her future assistance, a snatch team was dispatched to her home village, and her family was taken to a safe area near Can Tho.

More than twenty thousand VC along with their infrastructure were neutralized as a result of Phoenix. More than that number were captured, and an equally large number elected to take advantage of the Chieu Hoi Program. Those actively opposed to U.S. involvement in the war have alleged that these statistics were manipulated intentionally to conceal that three to five times as many suspects had actually been killed during Phoenix operations. They also alleged that torture was a main interrogation tool. In general, they painted a picture of the Phoenix Program as nothing more than a sadistic killing machine, without adequate leadership, totally out of control.

Some of these allegations are, unfortunately, true. In some areas of South Vietnam, indefensible excesses did occur, with certain district and province officials using the cover of the operation to eradicate present or future political or personal foes. In such cases the victim's fate was sealed if the power of the unscrupulous perpetrators was sufficient for them to manipulate the local PRUs or ARVN officials. In many ways the atmosphere of Phoenix operations in isolated areas was similar to that of Salem, Massachusetts, during the despicable period of its witch hunts.

But excesses were not the norm and did not define the leadership and usual activities of the Phoenix Program. The purpose was not merely to eliminate the VC, their infrastructure, and their ability to operate effectively. It was also to release the general populace from the cycle of terror to which they had been subjected for years at the hands of the communists. A wholesale, unbridled orgy of indiscriminate arrest on the part of the Allies and murder of innocent civilians was no way to win the hearts and minds of the citizenry. If such excesses had, in fact, been routine practices, the program would have had a reverse effect. It would almost certainly have served to swell the ranks of the VC and hasten the eventual overthrow of the government by several years.

The truth of the matter obviously differed from the allegations. Because the program's effectiveness hinged on the participation of the populace in identifying the VC, maintaining the goodwill of common citizens was essential. These peasants were firmly behind the anti-VCI efforts, and their active participation increased with each succeeding week. Each identified and arrested VC coming from civilian cooperation opened doors to areas of the VC's household previously hidden to the Allies. By the end of 1969, the VC had almost literally ceased to exist as a viable political or tactical entity in the Mekong Delta and the Rung Sat.

Phoenix Program operations continued until 1972, although, as with all other wartime activities, active participation by U.S. forces had been significantly scaled back after 1969 to bring about Vietnamization. This pertained to all U.S. personnel including those in the various SEAL detachments. Those working with MRF, SEALORDS, the SOG, and the Phoenix Program were to work actively in training their South Vietnamese counterparts in the skills necessary for them to assume full control of the war effort. Although the SEALs followed orders, their approach to the vietnamization process was to continue going into the field with the LDNN and PRUs as advisers. Even though the numbers of SEAL personnel and detachments were gradually scaled down until the final withdrawal of all tactical U.S. forces in 1972, SEALs remained in the field to the very end. I assume that SEALs remained in parts of South Vietnam, Laos, and Cambodia continually until the final fall of South Vietnam in 1975.

CONCLUSION

The effectiveness of SEAL detachments during their participation in the Southeast Asian conflict is indisputable. Their ability and considerable expertise in waging their own unique approach to guerrilla/counter-guerrilla tactics frustrated the VC and NVA units against whom they operated. The SEALs brought that expertise to all levels of their activities while engaging in routine operations in support of Market Time or Game Warden operations and supporting the SOG and the Phoenix Program. Perhaps the best measure of their effectiveness is the fact that, even though they inflicted tremendous personnel losses upon the communists, SEAL detachments lost fewer than forty killed in action and less than two hundred wounded during the entire course of the conflict. Most conservative estimates indicate that for every SEAL killed in action, the VC lost fifty to sixty.

Even more remarkable was the fact that the SEALs were still a relatively new organization when they arrived in country in 1966, in existence only since 1962. What they had not already learned about guerrilla tactics they quickly picked up and mastered from their experiences against VC and NVA units in the field. It did not take them long to out guerrilla the VC, causing them to rapidly leave and stay away from those areas where SEALs typically operated.

As with all successful guerrilla groups, the VC had learned the role of predator, employing stealth and camouflage in stalking their prey and then subduing it via ambush. SEAL ambush teams were given the mission of countering and neutralizing the VC with similar tactics. They were also assigned the task of turning the tables on the VC by bringing the action to them in their safe areas, showing them that they were as vulnerable as the rural villagers on whom they had preyed for so long.

It cannot be denied that the SEALs thoroughly performed the mission for which they had been sent to South Vietnam. When the last SEALs were finally withdrawn, the communists were relieved to know that there were no longer any men with painted faces lurking in the shadows, no more demons to rise out of the mud, no more swimmers among the trees.

EPILOGUE

It's just about 9:30 P.M. on one of those hot, humid nights so typical of the Delaware Valley section of southeastern Pennsylvania during late August. Two men—one in his late forties, the other in his twenties—sit on a front porch, talking softly amidst the sounds of crickets chirping and an occasional car passing along the road at the end of the driveway.

"So, now that we've talked about baseball and the weather, is there anything else you want to chat about before you finally get at what's on your mind?" the older man asked the younger one.

The younger man took a sip of his beer and then slowly smiled.

"Uncle Artie, you amaze me," he said. "How did you know that I wanted to talk to you about something?"

Artie got up from his chair, walked across the porch, and then turned to face the younger man.

"Matt, I could bullshit you about being able to read you like a book, or some other trash like that, but the fact is your mom called me this afternoon and said you had a problem. Something about going to Ranger school next week."

"Yeah, she told me that maybe I should talk to you 'cause you'd have the answer."

"Well, let's get at it then! No need to waste time out here when you could be with your girlfriend."

Matt got up, took another swig of beer, and then slowly walked to the porch railing and stood beside his uncle.

"Don't get me wrong, Uncle Artie, I still want to be a Ranger, but lately I've been thinking a lot about what it might be like if we get into another war. What's gonna happen if I actually have to kill somebody?"

Artie turned around, placed both hands on the porch railing, and stared out toward the dim silhouette of the pine trees.

"Go on," Artie said, quietly but firmly.

"Well, when I was younger, back before Dad died, he used to tell me loads of stories about when you were a SEAL. He sure was proud of you. Mom said he always idolized you and couldn't have loved you more if you two had been brothers."

"Yeah, Vern was a great friend," Artie answered softly.

"Well, my dad said that in the three tours of duty you did in Vietnam, you wound up taking out a lot of VC. He said you didn't like to talk about it much, but he'd met some guys you'd served with and they said your numbers were really up there."

Matt stared at Artie as though he expected a response of some kind. But Artie never moved. He just kept staring out toward the pines. Finally, Matt took another, longer hit of beer and then moved back to reclaim his seat.

"Uncle Artie, you killed a lot of men. Now, I'm pretty sure it must have been a hard thing to do, at first. But at some point . . ."

He cut himself short, searching his mind for the right words.

"It got easier?" Artie asked, turning to face Matt.

"Well, yeah! I mean, no, not exactly that," Matt answered. "I guess what I really want to ask is, at some point you got used to it, right?"

The question hung in the humid air between the two men as they stared at each other, silently, for what seemed like several minutes. Then, Artie slowly eased himself down to sit on the porch floor, his back leaning against the railing, his face tilted upward toward the dim yellow lightbulb.

"There's one story your dad didn't tell you about my time in 'Nam because I never even told it to him," Artie said, sounding suddenly very tired and more than just a little sad. "It was right at the beginning of my first tour. I'd been assigned to Nha Be, in the Rung Sat. On my second day in country a bunch of us new guys were taken out on a 'cherry popper.' That's what we called going out in the field for the first time. Three of the guys who were about to rotate back to "The World" took us out to a place about two klicks south of Nhan Trach, where they'd ambushed a VC squad about two weeks before.

"We'd only been working the area for a little more than an hour when the point man heard some voices up ahead. Since it was not quite dark, he was able to make out three figures moving in the shadows, and he opened up on 'em with his shotgun. As soon as he cut loose we started taking rounds from both flanks. Nothing big, just small arms, but really intense.

"Anyway, I was about to crouch down when I picked up a flash of movement out of the corner of my eye on our left flank. As I turned to face it, here comes a VC right at me, screaming his head off and firing his SKS. How he missed me I'll never know, because he was no more than ten feet from me when I hit him with three quick blasts from my 870. And just as you'd expect with shotgun blasts at that range, I near about cut that sucker in half.

"For a second the sight of the chewed-up VC made me feel sick to my stomach, but I didn't have time to think about it because we were still in the midst of a firefight. So, I kept pumpin' and firin' until the ambushers were all down. When the firing stopped, I suddenly had this strange tingling feeling all over my body and I felt great. But I noticed that everybody was staring at me kinda funny. So, I looked down to give myself a once-over and that's when I saw what they'd been staring at. I'd puked all over my piece, the forearm on my pump hand, my left pant leg, and even my boots. Without even realizing it, I had puked all over myself when I'd seen my rounds tear apart that first VC."

Artie and Matt sat quietly again for a while, staring at each other.

"Matt, I always remembered that first time whenever I had to kill another VC," Artie finally said, the words coming slowly, his voice a husky-sounding whisper.

"But it must have gotten better . . . easier, after that first time," Matt blurted.

"Well, even though I never had to puke again after that time, each kill made me feel like I would," Artie said matter-of-factly. "So, I guess you could say it did get easier."

"But how could you put yourself through that, time after time, Uncle Artie? It must have driven you crazy!"

"Matt, war is crazy and so is everybody in it. It's a nightmare, it's brutal. But you do what you have to do and, when it's over, you come home."

"But what do you do with the feelings, Uncle Artie?"

"Matt, you do the only thing you can do with any feelings. You learn to deal with them as best you can."

GLOSSARY

AAA: Antiaircraft Artillery, also referred to as triple A.

ACOUBUOY: Acoustical Buoy. This sound-sensitive electronic intrusion detector (rocket shaped, approximately two to three feet in length, weighing about twenty-five pounds) was dropped from Air Studies Group (ASG) aircraft, via parachute, over areas of dense forest canopy. The parachutes would snag in the treetops, suspending the detectors above suspected enemy infiltration routes. Data generated by the ACOUBUOYs was transmitted to patrolling surveillance aircraft overhead for evaluation.

ACOUSID: Acoustical/Seismic Intrusion Detector. Similar to the ACOUBUOYs in size, shape, and mode of delivery, ACOUSIDs were not only sound sensitive but seismic sensitive as well.

ADSID: Air Delivered Seismic Intrusion Detector. Although this seismic detector was the same shape and size as the ACOUBUOY and ACOUSID, it was designed to be dropped without a parachute, causing it to embed itself in the ground on impact, leaving its small transmission antenna visible above ground.

Air America: A "civilian" airline operating throughout all of Southeast Asia during the Vietnam conflict, engaging primarily in routine commercial activities, Air America was actually controlled and funded by the CIA and supported a wide variety of CIA operations.

Air Studies Group (ASG): Air arm of the Studies and Observations Group (SOG). Most of ASG's activities were devoted to deploying ADSIDs, ACOUBUOYs, and ACOUSIDs, as well as monitoring and evaluating data generated by those electronic surveillance devices.

AK-47: The Avtomat Kalashnikovas assault rifle was the preferred automatic weapon used by the NVA and VC. Although initially produced and supplied to the communist forces in Southeast Asia by the Russians, the Chinese eventually turned out larger numbers of the AK-47, along with the Type 56 and the Type 56-1, their versions of the same weapon. The AK-47 and its variants all fired a 7.62mm round at a cyclic rate of six hundred rounds per minute. It was considered by knowledgeable people to be one of the most dependable basic infantry weapons ever made.

AO: Area of Operations, or operational area.

APB: This self-propelled barracks/supply ship, usually a modified World War II–era LCU (Landing Craft, Utility), functioned as a floating base for the Mobile Riverine Force (MRF). More than one hundred feet in length, the APB had a docking platform alongside that could accommodate several ATCs at once. The APB was also fitted with a steel platform, allowing the vessel to serve as a mobile helipad.

ARVN: Army of the Republic of Vietnam.

ASG: Air Studies Group.

ASPB: Assault Support Patrol Boat, sometimes called ASP Boat. The only vessel designed specifically to conduct riverine operations, the ASPB was approximately fifty feet in length, could sustain speeds in the fifteen-knot range, and was manned by a crew of six. Armament usually consisted of one or two 20mm cannons, two 40mm grenade launchers, two .30-caliber machine guns, and, occasionally, one or more .50-caliber machine guns. A few ASPBs were fitted with 81mm direct-fire mortars, each with a .50-caliber machine gun piggybacked on top. ASPBs were quite versatile as insertion/extraction vehicles for SEAL ambush teams, as escorts for other MRF vessels, and for interdiction of VC river traffic.

ATC: Armored Troop Carrier. This mechanized landing craft provided the MRF with its main means of riverine troop deployment. A typical ATC was from fifty to more than sixty-five feet long. Some were capable of speeds approaching fifteen knots. Armament of some ATCs might consist of only two twin .50-caliber machine guns and one or two 40mm grenade launchers. Larger ATCs might also be armed with two 20mm cannons and two to six .30-caliber machine guns. A few ATCs were also fitted with raised steel helipads to accommodate medevac missions. ATCs had a six-man crew and were capable of carrying forty fully equipped troops.

B-40 Rocket: The basic round fired by the communist-made RPG-7 portable rocket launcher, it could penetrate ten to twelve inches of armor plate, so the VC and NVA units used it extensively as a basic antipersonnel weapon against Allied tanks, personnel carriers, and all varieties of riverine craft.

BAS: Battalion Aid Station.

Binh Tram: This NVA unit was responsible for maintaining the integrity of the Ho Chi Minh Trail, constructing and defending the trail rest camps, and providing them with a broad spectrum of logistical support.

Bloop, Blooper: M-79 grenade launcher, also referred to as a thump gun or thumper.

BSU: Boat Support Unit. Another important part of the U.S. Navy's Special Warfare Group, BSU crews and their vessels provided SEAL detachments with transport and fire support.

CAWS: Close Assault Weapon System. This fully automatic shotgun, developed by the U.S. Naval Weapons Support Center and the Limited Warfare Laboratory, was similar to the Stoner and the M16 in appearance. The CAWS had a cyclic rate of four hundred to four hundred fifty rounds per minute from a ten to twelve-round magazine. The weapon's recoil was similar to that of an M16, and it fired a wide assortment of ammunition (00 buckshot, flechettes, flares, and even HE). The weapon was favored by many SEALs due to its punch and ability to be held on target with a minimum of recoil when being fired on full auto.

CCB: Command and Control Boat. These converted LCMs served as floating headquarters for MRF naval and ground forces. CCBs were heavily armored, could reach speeds of eight to nine knots, and carried armament consisting of three 20mm cannons, at least two 40mm grenade launchers, and varying numbers of .30-caliber and/or .50-caliber machine guns.

CH-53: Sikorsky's heavy assault helicopter was used primarily by U.S. Navy and Marine units for troop and cargo transport. A variant of the same basic chopper was the HH-53, used by the Air Force for rescuing downed pilots. Both aircraft were affectionately referred to as Jolly Green Giants.

Charlie: This common reference for Vietcong was derived from basic phonetic abbreviation for Vietcong—Victor Charlie—used by Allied forces during routine radio chatter.

Chieu Hoi Program: This special amnesty program was initiated by the South Vietnamese government (GVN). The phrase literally translated as "open arms." The program offered VC defectors an opportunity to return to the fold without fear of retribution. Those who came in under the program were called *hoi chanh,* or rallier, many of whom then acted as scouts for U.S. units. Unfortunately, although many of these Kit Carson scouts, as they were called, did provide honorable service, most were regarded with suspicion, since many scouts were actually acting as spies for the VC.

Claymore: An antipersonnel mine. This extremely important part of the arsenal of Allied forces was often used as part of perimeter defenses.

CORDS: Civil Operations and Revolutionary Development Support. Jointly controlled by MACV and the CIA, this was the main group to oversee and administer the many pacification programs designed to keep the rural peasants loyal to the GVN.

COSVN: Central Office for South Vietnam. The main NVA headquarters was established for maintaining control over VC activities in the South. Its exact location was never determined but was assumed to be somewhere near an area known as the Fishhook, a little more than seventy-five miles northwest of Saigon on the Cambodian border.

CTZ: Corps Tactical Zone. Major military regions established by U.S. forces in South Vietnam, these designations divided the country into four basic zones: I Corps (the five northernmost provinces), II Corps (the twelve provinces making up most of the country's Central Highlands section), III Corps (extending from the southern part of the Central Highlands to the northern part of the Mekong Delta), and IV Corps (the southernmost region comprising most of the Mekong Delta).

Dac Cong: Vietcong special forces personnel. These demolition experts, extremely adept at compromising Allied perimeter defenses, were often used as sappers.

DMZ: Demilitarized Zone. This five-mile-wide buffer zone along the seventeenth parallel was established by the 1954 Geneva Accords to divide Vietnam into the separate entities of North Vietnam and South Vietnam.

DPM: This communist-made 12.7mm belt-fed heavy machine gun was used by NVA and VC troops throughout the entire Southeast Asian theater of operations. It was the communist version of the Browning .50-caliber heavy machine gun, which was used by U.S. and other Allied forces.

Dust-off: Slang term for medical evacuation (medevac) of wounded personnel via helicopter.

81mm Mortar: This U.S. intermediate mortar had a maximum effective range of 3,650 meters.

82mm Mortar: This communist intermediate mortar had a maximum effective range of 3,000 meters.

FN (L1A1): This Belgian-made 7.62mm semiautomatic weapon was favored by Australian and New Zealand military forces.

Grunt: This slang term for the basic U.S. infantryman, derived from his laboring under the burden of a heavy rucksack and flak jacket, the combined weight often in excess of eighty pounds.

GVN: Government of South Vietnam.

HE: High Explosive.

HEAT: High Explosive Antitank round.

Hootch: A hut, this was the basic dwelling found in most of Vietnam's rural villages and hamlets.

HSSC: Heavy SEAL Support Craft. A specially modified LCM, this heavily armored craft was capable of sustained speeds of fifteen knots or more. Armament consisted of two or three .50-caliber machine guns, a like number of 40mm grenade launchers, and often a 106mm recoilless rifle. A few HSSCs were later fitted with six-barreled 7.62mm miniguns capable of firing six thousand rounds per minute.

Huey: UH-1 helicopter. The nickname probably derived from the fact that the helicopter had originally been designated as the HU-1. The Huey was the workhorse of the Vietnam conflict, serving reliably in a wide variety of missions, including resupply, troop deployment, fire missions, and medevacs. Armament could include nose-mounted 40mm grenade launchers, door-mounted M60 machine guns, .30-caliber machine guns, and even 20mm cannons, depending on the chopper's intended mission.

Hush Puppy: Originally a generic term used for any silenced firearm, Hush Puppy later became the nickname of one specific weapon, the Smith & Wesson Model 39 automatic pistol. The Hush Puppy had a highly specialized silencer incorporated into its barrel, making its discharge almost inaudible. Developed especially for the SEALs, the weapon was used extensively in a wide variety of situations.

K-50: This was the VC version of the Russian PPSH-41 and the Chinese Type 50 7.62mm submachine gun.

KPV: This communist-made 14.5mm belt-fed heavy machine gun was used extensively by communist forces against Allied armored elements, MRF craft, and aircraft.

LSSC: Light SEAL Support Craft. This modified twenty-four-foot utility boat was equipped with inboard water jet propulsion engines similar to those used in the PBR, giving the LSSC the capability of reaching speeds in excess of twenty-five knots. Typical armament consisted of one 40mm grenade launcher and two M60 machine guns. (A few LSSCs substituted a .30-caliber machine gun in place of one of the M60s.) The LSSC was also equipped with radar designed to track riverine traffic and the movement of trucks and pedestrians ashore.

M1A1: The Thompson submachine gun, made famous during World

War II and by Hollywood in dozens of movies about the Prohibition era, was a highly dependable .45-caliber automatic weapon occasionally used by some SEALs who wanted a gun that could hit with authority.

M3A1: More commonly known as the Hyde-manufactured Grease Gun, this stubby-barreled World War II–era .45-caliber automatic weapon was favored by some SEALs due to its ability to take abuse and hit with authority.

M14 Rifle: This 7.62mm rifle was the basic infantry weapon of U.S. units at the start of the Vietnam conflict. It was later replaced by the 5.56mm M16 rifle. However, the M14 continued to be used widely and was actually preferred by some units as a sniper rifle.

M16 Rifle: The basic infantry weapon of U.S. forces, the rifle eventually was used by most other Allied units in Vietnam. Although it fired only a 5.56mm round, it did so with a muzzle velocity of 3,250 feet per second, giving the round great stopping power at distances of four hundred yards or less. Initial difficulties with jams and an effective range of only four hundred yards gave the weapon a reputation of being less than adequate.

M18A1: 57mm recoilless rifle. Used by SEAL detachments and other U.S. units during the Vietnam conflict, this weapon was about five feet in length and weighed just under fifty pounds. Its maximum range was 4,000 meters, but its effective range was only about 450 meters. SEAL ambush teams employed this rifle as a light artillery piece, often using it to blow up VC bunkers or other fortified structures. Ammunition for the piece included HE, HEAT, and WP. Because the weapon had a rifled barrel (one turn per thirty calibers), it was deadly accurate, allowing the gunner to take out on the first try almost any target he could clearly see. The weapon's weight, however, prevented it from being used by SEAL field elements on a day-in, day-out basis.

M46 Field Gun: This communist-made 130mm artillery piece was used by the NVA against U.S. fire support bases. It was capable of firing a seventy-four-pound HE round to a distance of at least thirty-one thousand meters with good accuracy.

M79 Grenade Launcher: This single-shot 40mm grenade launcher weighed just over six pounds and was capable of firing seven to ten rounds per minute with great accuracy. The maximum effective range was 400 to 450 meters; the ammunition was HE, HE airburst, WP, illumination flares, CS gas, colored flares, buckshot, or flechette-type antipersonnel rounds. It was the most widely used grenade launcher among U.S. forces.

Mark 3 Grenade: A concussion grenade (also called stun or flash-bang grenade) especially useful in snatch operations, this armament was designed to disorient the intended detainee and anyone in close proximity to him/her.

Mark 19: This 40mm belt-fed automatic grenade launcher weighed about seventy-five pounds and was capable of firing 325 to 375 rounds per minute with a maximum effective range of one mile. The available ammunition consisted of antipersonnel HE, armor-piercing HE, WP, and flares.

MAT-49 Mod SMG: This communist version of the French 9mm weapon converted the weapon to 7.62mm.

MON: Monitor Boat. A heavily armored MRF LCM that resembled the Civil War vessel *Monitor,* the MON was usually fitted with either one 105mm howitzer or one 40mm Bofors gun mounted in a forward turret, one 20mm cannon in an aft turret, and .30-caliber and/or .50-caliber machine guns mounted on the bridge alongside one or more 40mm grenade launchers. A few MONs were even fitted with M10-8 flamethrowers, located port and starboard just aft of the Bofors gun. Such MONs were nicknamed Zippos.

Mu Gia Pass: The start of the Ho Chi Minh Trail, this pass cut through the Truong Son Mountains on the western border between North Vietnam and Laos. The pass was located about seventy to seventy-five miles north of the DMZ.

PBR: River Patrol Boat. These fiberglass-hulled (later versions were aluminum hulled) boats were thirty-two feet long and were powered by twin diesel water jet engines capable of generating speeds of twenty-five knots. Typical armament aboard a PBR consisted of one twin .50-caliber machine gun mounted forward and a single .50-caliber machine gun mounted aft. Also available to the PBR crew was at least one 40mm grenade launcher and occasionally one 60mm mortar.

PCF: Inshore Fast Patrol Craft. More commonly known as a Swift boat, this fifty-foot long, all-metal vessel was capable of sustaining speeds of twenty-five to twenty-eight knots. Armament consisted of two .50-caliber machine guns in a twin mount atop the pilothouse, plus one other .50-caliber machine gun mounted piggyback style atop an 81mm direct-fire mortar. The mortar was meant to be fired horizontally, utilizing such ammunition as HE, WP, or antipersonnel rounds called flechettes, or "beehive" rounds.

Phoenix Program: A joint effort by the GVN, MACV, and CIA to eliminate the VC by neutralizing their infrastructure personnel, the Phoenix Program included the ARVN's Luc Luong Dac Biet (special forces, later known as the Special Mission Service), the Quan Cahn (or merely QC, the ARVN military police), the U.S. Navy SEALs, and theU.S. Army Green Berets.

PRU: Provincial Reconnaissance Unit. The action arm of the Phoenix Program, the units consisted of indigenous personnel and operated only in and around the provinces where the personnel typically resided. The units were usually taken into the field by SEAL or Green Beret advisers, although, occasionally, some were led by CIA personnel.

PTRD: Communist-made antitank rifle. This single-shot 14.5mm weapon fired a tungsten-core round capable of piercing 25mm of heavy armor at a distance of five hundred meters. Because of this, it was popular among communist forces as an antitank/antiaircraft weapon.

QC: Quan Cahn, ARVN military police. See Phoenix Program.

RPD: Communist-made 7.62mm light machine gun.

RSSZ: Rung Sat Special Zone. Topographically dense area just south of Saigon that was used as an encampment for NLF forces.

Seawolves: U.S. Navy light helicopter attack squadrons. The squadrons were usually split up into detachments of two or three UH-1Bs each and operated from fixed bases scattered about the Mekong Delta. Seawolf choppers and crews were valuable adjuncts to MRF operations throughout the war. However, much of the Seawolves' time was spent in support of SEAL operations, providing ambush/recon teams with rapid insertion/extraction capability, fire support, and resupply missions. Their UH-1B choppers were armed with two door-mounted M60 machine guns, handled by the crew chief and the door gunner, as well as four fixed M60s mounted outboard, two per side piggyback fashion, on special weapon pylons. A pod of FFAR 2.75-inch rockets was also mounted on each pylon.

Shotgun: Favored by SEALs and many other U.S. personnel, the weapons performed well in the close-range engagements (usually five to fifteen meters) typical of firefights during the Vietnam conflict. The most common models available at that time were the Remington 870 Express, the Ithaca Model 37 Stakeout, and the Winchester Defender. All had pump action and fired twelve-gauge rounds (either 00 buckshot, consisting of nine .30-caliber-plus pellets, or a special antipersonnel load consisting of eight flechettes weighing more than a gram apiece). Shotguns were highly respected for their ability to break up ambushes.

60mm Mortar: Smallest of the mortars. Capable of firing at a rate of thirty rounds per minute, this mortar had a maximum effective range of one mile.

SKS: The Soviet-manufactured Simonov 46 was a highly reliable 7.62mm carbine/rifle used by communist forces and often favored by VC snipers.

Smith & Wesson Model 76: 9mm submachine gun. Potent, highly reliable, and easily maintained in the field, this weapon was ideal for SEAL ambush operations.

STAB: Strike Assault Boat, also known as a SEAL Tactical Assault Boat. This open-deck speedboat, approximately the same size as the LSSC, was powered by inboard water jet engines and was capable of reaching speeds of twenty-six to twenty-eight knots. The four-man crew had a potent arsenal aboard consisting of four M60 machine guns and one 40mm Mark 19 automatic grenade launcher. The vessel's shallow draft (about eighteen inches) made it ideal for use in areas such as the Plain of Reeds, where the water level could fluctuate drastically over short distances. The boat was also equipped with a radar system capable of tracking riverine traffic, pedestrians, and surface vehicles ashore.

Starlight Scope: The AN/PVS-2 was mounted on a rifle and allowed the user to see with extreme clarity at night to a distance of four hundred meters.

Stoner M63A1 Weapon System: This multipurpose weapon included a component kit containing belt and magazine feed system variations, butts, pistol grips, and several different barrel lengths. The kit's varied components enabled the system to be transformed from a rifle to a carbine to a light machine gun (belt or magazine fed), flexible medium machine gun, or fixed heavy machine gun. It fired 5.56mm ammunition at a sustained cyclic rate of 650 to 850 rounds per minute. The weights of the different configurations ran from eight pounds in the assault rifle mode to eleven pounds in the heavy machine gun mode. The weapon's light weight, easy field maintenance, and rapid fire made it ideal for SEAL ambush teams and their guerrilla/counterguerrilla tactics.

Swedish K-40: This 9mm submachine gun was favored by SEALs interested in a personal automatic weapon that packed a big punch.

Truong Son Corridor: Utilized by communist forces, this secondary supply route was located inside the South Vietnamese border parallel to the Ho Chi Minh Trail.

Type 24 Heavy Machine Gun: Chinese-made 7.92mm heavy machine gun. This belt-fed weapon fired at a cyclic rate of about four hundred rounds per minute. It was often employed as an antiaircraft weapon.

Type 52 75mm Recoilless Rifle: This Chinese-made weapon was capable of firing HE at a maximum effective range of 6,675 meters. A HEAT round was also available for the Type 52, but the maximum effective range for that round was only about eight hundred meters.

WP: White Phosphorus. Also called Willie Peter, WP was delivered by artillery/mortar rounds or grenades.

XM148: This 40mm grenade launcher, mounted on the underside of an M16's barrel, provided the many benefits of an M79 but had the M16's rapid fire capability. It did not add significantly to the M16's weight, so several members of a squad could carry it, adding significant punch to the unit's firepower.